TEACHING

POETRY

PROPHECY

GW00541614

Editor: Rick Joyner
Contributing Editors: Jack Deere, Francis Frangipane, Dudley Hall
Managing Editor: Deborah Joyner Johnson
Project Manager: Dana Zondory
Layout and Design: Dana Zondory
Copy Editors: Suzanne Hirt, Tracey Selvey, and Deborah Williams

The Morning Star Journal® USPS012-903 is published quarterly, 4 issues per year, by MorningStar Publications, Inc. A division of MorningStar Fellowship Church, P.O. Box 440, Wilkesboro, NC 28697. Fall 2005 issue. Periodicals postage rates paid at North Wilkesboro, NC and additional mailing offices. CPC Agreement #1472593. ISSN# 10832122

POSTMASTER: Send address corrections to *The Morning Star Journal*®, P.O. Box 440, Wilkesboro, NC 28697

Subscription rates: One year $16.95; Outside U.S. $24.95 USD.

MorningStar Publications is a non-profit organization dedicated to the promulgation of important teachings and timely prophetic messages to the church. We also attempt to promote interchange between the different streams and denominations in the body of Christ.

To receive a subscription to *The Morning Star Journal*®, send payment along with your name and address to *MorningStar Publications*, P.O. Box 440, Wilkesboro, NC 28697, (336) 651-2400 (1-800-542-0278—Credit Card Orders Only); fax (336) 651-2430. One year (4 quarterly issues) U.S. $16.95; Outside U.S. $24.95 USD. Prices are subject to change without notice.

Reprints—Photocopies of any part of the contents of this publication may be made freely. However, to re-typeset information, permission must be requested in writing from *MorningStar Publications Department*, P.O. Box 440, Wilkesboro, NC 28697

BIOS

Francis Frangipane is the senior pastor of River of Life Ministries in Cedar Rapids, Iowa, and the president of Advancing Church Ministries. The Lord has used Francis to unite thousands of pastors in prayer in hundreds of cities. With more than a million copies of his best-selling books in print, and with an expanding radio and television ministry called "In Christ's Image," Francis is in much demand worldwide. His newest book is entitled, *This Day We Fight!*

Mike Roberts is originally from the Charlotte, North Carolina area and has been involved at MorningStar for about ten years. He is a graduate of the MorningStar School of Ministry, and has a heart for the prophetic ministry and teaching. Mike is currently on staff at MorningStar Publications and Ministries and lives in Moravian Falls, North Carolina.

Hombre Liggett is ordained through MorningStar Fellowship of Ministries and is the founding pastor of Church of the Harvest, located in Dover, Ohio. Hombre's heart is to lead the members of the body of Christ into prophetic worship, equipped to fulfill their purpose, and provide a platform for them to function. The foundation of his twelve-year ministry is the love of God and the unity of the Spirit.

Dan Duke has thirty-four years of ministry experience in approximately fifty nations. He and his wife of thirty-five years, Marti, currently reside in Belo Horizonte, Brazil from where they travel extensively throughout the nation. Dan graduated with a Doctor of Theology degree from the Jacksonville Theological Seminary and is the author of several books including: *Apostolic Ministry, The Impartation, Messages for the Revival Generation,* and *The Encyclopedia of Proper Names and Numbers of the Bible.* Dan and Marti have four children and seven grandchildren.

Deborah Joyner Johnson is the managing editor for MorningStar Publications and Ministries. She shares with her brother, Rick Joyner, a desire to see the body of Christ provided with the highest quality spiritual food that is relevant for our times. Deborah's second book, *Pathway to Purpose,* was recently released through MorningStar. She has a gifted teaching ministry and shares at conferences and women's groups. Deborah lives in North Carolina and has three children: Matthew, Meredith, and Abby.

Steve Thompson is the associate director of MorningStar Fellowship Church, and he oversees the prophetic ministries for all of the MorningStar Fellowships. A gifted teacher and prophetic minister, Steve travels extensively throughout the United States and abroad as a conference speaker. Steve's newest book, *A 20th Century Apostle, The Life of Alfred Garr,* was released through MorningStar. Steve and his wife, Angie, reside in North Carolina with their five children: Jon, Josh, Madison, Moriah, and Olivia.

Trevor Tiessen is originally from Saskatchewan, Canada. In the fall of 1996 Trevor came to Charlotte, North Carolina to attend the MorningStar School of Ministry and graduated in the spring of 1999. Since that time Trevor has been serving MorningStar Fellowship Church in the areas of church and conference administration as well as in the ministry of helps.

Robin McMillan is currently the pastor of MorningStar Fellowship Church at our H.I.M. facilities near Charlotte, North Carolina. With a unique preaching style, prophetic giftings, and a desire for the release of God's power, many are impacted by Robin's ministry. Robin and his wife, Donna, live in North Carolina and have four children: John Mark, Christopher, Andy, and Katy.

Paul Goulet is the senior pastor of the International Church of Las Vegas. Since he came to Las Vegas in 1992, the church has grown from 270 attendants to over four thousand. He has a vision to start two thousand churches by the year 2020. Pastor Goulet travels extensively sharing his life-transforming messages at conferences, crusades and churches all over the world. He has written many books, including *The Breakthrough Series, Jesus I want to know Him, The Power of Impartation, The Power of Impartation in the Home, The Five Powers, and The Threshold.*

John Paul Jackson is the founder and chairman of Streams Ministries International located in North Sutton, New Hampshire. A popular teacher and conference speaker, John Paul travels around the world teaching on prophetic gifts, dreams, visions, and the realm of the supernatural. His newest publication, *Moments With God Dream Journal,* offers a unique approach to dream recording. To order his books and tapes, please call 1-888-441-8080, or visit his website at www.streamsministries.com.

BIOS

Rick Joyner is the founder, executive director, and senior pastor of MorningStar Fellowship Church. Rick is a well-known author of more than thirty books, including, *The Torch and the Sword*, the long awaited sequel to *The Final Quest* and *The Call*, and his latest, *Delivered From Evil*. He also oversees MorningStar's School of Ministry, Fellowship of Ministries, and Fellowship of Churches. Rick and his wife, Julie, live in North Carolina with their five children: Anna, Aaryn, Amber, Ben, and Sam.

Sally Boenau is an MFM and MST member who is actively involved in the prayer ministries of her church and community. Sally has recently founded "Spirit and Life Lighters" which distributes marketplace friendly products such as seed packets, magnets, and soaps with messages based on the words of Jesus. To learn more about Sally's products, email her at: bripatch@brinet.com. Sally and her husband, Doug, have been married for forty-two years and have one daughter and two grandchildren. They live in Hendersonville, North Carolina.

Paul Keith Davis and his wife, Wanda, are founders of WhiteDove Ministries. They travel extensively imparting the end-time mandate of preparation for the glory and manifest presence of Christ. He and Bob Jones write *The Shepherd's Rod*, yearly. Paul Keith has also written the book, *The Thrones of Our Soul*. He and his wife reside in Alabama. Together they have five children and three grandchildren.

Colin Brown oversees Shiloh Fellowship, a ministry and church in Australia, based in Ulverstone on Tasmania's northwest coast. With his wife Tina, and two of his four children, they spent eighteen months with DaySpring Christian Fellowship in Sydney through the end of 2004. An important aspect of the ministry of Shiloh Fellowship is Colin's writing, in order to bring timely encouragement and insight, especially in the face of these exciting yet sobering times. You may email him at: www.shilohfellowship.org.au.

The MEASURE of MATURITY

by Francis Frangipane

It has been my experience that too many of us, as Christians, have been confused about love. We have assumed that attaining the look of love is the same reality as actually being transformed into a loving person. I am not saying that we have consciously planned on being shallow or noncommittal, but that somehow we have settled on the cosmetic instead of the real.

We have developed an "altar" ego, a look for church that lasts at best just a few minutes longer than the church service itself. All we have really accomplished is to perfect the art of acting like Christians. I think we have yet to learn to consistently walk according to the standards of Christ's love. I hear how quick some are to speak about the flaws of those they supposedly love, and I wonder what kind of love demeans individuals behind their backs? When I witness unloving words from a Christian's mouth, I am reminded that we have much to learn about Jesus and what it means to follow Him.

David prayed, **"Let the words of my mouth and the meditation of my heart be acceptable in Thy sight, O LORD, my rock and my Redeemer" (Psalm 19:14).**

Our words are the by-product of our meditations. Whatever is brooding in our hearts will eventually ascend to our lips. If we have unforgiveness prowling within, our conversations will be barbed with negative comments—even in moments of lighthearted banter. If we are harboring bitterness, it will slice through our speech. Jesus taught that **"the mouth speaks out of that which fills the heart" (Matthew 12:34).** We cannot fix our words without first fixing our hearts.

When the Lord judges us for our words, it is because He is seeking to purify our hearts. True, the heart is deceitful above all things and it is difficult to know our own iniquity. Yet if we simply pause and listen to how many of our words are without love, we can track them back to the real problem: loveless hearts.

A New Anointing

Christians are in the fire of God. The Holy Spirit is purging the church from negative chatter. A fresh anointing is at hand where God's people shall speak with the character necessary to represent Him. What the Lord told the prophet Jeremiah, He is speaking also to us:

> Therefore, thus says the LORD, "If you return, then I will restore you—before Me you will stand; and if you extract the precious from the worthless, you will become My spokesman" (Jeremiah 15:19).

Let us pray that as God exposes our lack of love that a time will soon come when we will pray with credibility: "You have tried my heart; You have visited me by night; You have tested me and You find nothing; I have purposed that my mouth will not transgress" (Psalm 17:3).

Do we see this? God judges the quality of our entire lives by the soundness and substance of our words. Thus Jesus warned, "But I tell you that every careless word that people speak, they shall give an accounting for it in the day of judgment" (Matthew 12:36). Let us consider Christ's warning soberly. He

continued, "For by your words you will be justified, and by your words you will be condemned" (Matthew 12:37 NKJV). James adds, "judgment will be merciless to one who has shown no mercy; mercy triumphs over judgment" (James 2:13). I have a holy fear in my heart concerning these warnings. I know if I am merciless toward others, God will be merciless toward me.

Character Counts

Sometimes I think we try to mask our critical attitude by calling it "discernment." The fact is, most of what manifests in our discussions about others is simply judging after the flesh. If we truly love individuals, we will be as loving in their absence as we are in their presence.

Jesus said His disciples would be known by their love (see John 13:35). Paul said that the love of Christ is supposed to control us (see II Corinthians 5:14), which means it is the nature and discipline of love that keeps us from joining in verbal attacks or even subtle criticisms. You see, it takes character to avoid being sucked into gossip and criticisms. There is a high road we can take. It starts with prayer; it extends to grace; it is slow to speak; it approaches an individual with a meek heart; it talks privately with the person; it is forgiving when wronged and patient with the spiritually immature.

Of course, if someone is involved with criminal activity or seriously endangering others through his sin, we must love the greater community and take steps to protect the innocent. There is a time to discipline or even publicly expose sin (see Matthew 18:15-17), but it is after we exhaust other means of correction—and even then, our motive should communicate our hope of redemption and not allow our disclosure to become a smokescreen for revenge. In all things, love must guide our words.

> "WHEN SOMEONE LOVES YOU, THE WAY THEY SAY YOUR NAME IS DIFFERENT. YOU JUST KNOW THAT YOUR NAME IS SAFE IN THEIR MOUTH."

Child's Eye View of Love

Recently my youngest daughter, Eden, sent me a list of quotes that came from little children. Each child was asked to describe what love meant to them. Their answers were, at times, quite intriguing. One in particular, from a four year old boy named Billy, has stuck with me. He said, "When someone loves you, the way they say your name is different. You just know that your name is safe in their mouth."

That thought seems to say it all: "When someone loves you…your name is safe in their mouth." Behold this clarity of vision as love is defined by a little child. When we truly walk in Christ's love, those around us will be safe, and others will see the love of Christ that controls us.

Beloved, to walk in covering love is to show ourselves truly acquainted with Christ. Let us ask God, "Father, show me my heart. Is Your love ruling, even in the unseen areas of my life? Are the names of others safe in my mouth?" ■

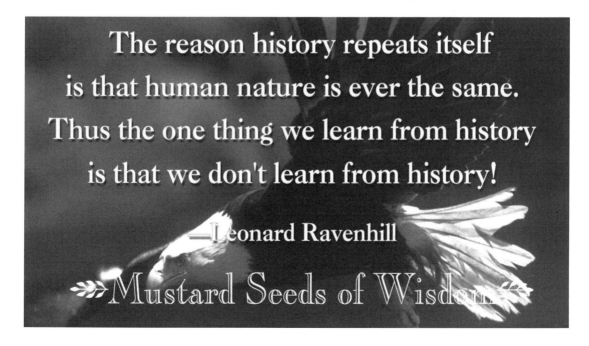

The reason history repeats itself is that human nature is ever the same. Thus the one thing we learn from history is that we don't learn from history!

—Leonard Ravenhill

Mustard Seeds of Wisdom

TO BE OR NOT TO BE

by Mike Roberts

Have you ever considered what makes a person great? If you were asked to make a list of people who achieved greatness, who would come to mind? Most people would probably think of Winston Churchill, Abraham Lincoln, Mother Teresa, Michael Jordan, or some other monumental figure. Businessmen would probably make mention of Warren Buffet, Bill Gates, or Jack Welch, and as Christians, we would certainly add Billy Graham, Queen Esther, the apostle Paul, and Corrie Ten Boom to the list.

Let us briefly consider some of these remarkable people. Winston Churchill has been nearly immortalized in the pages of history because he helped lead one of the greatest marches in the preservation of freedom the world has ever known. Michael Jordan is known all over the world for his accomplishments as an athlete; Mother Teresa will forever be remembered for her life of sacrifice and genuine compassion for the poor and needy; Billy Graham is perhaps the most respected man in recent history, and he is especially endeared in the hearts of Christians for uncompromising integrity in his life and ministry as he has shared the gospel of our Lord to literally millions of people.

As we consider these extraordinary people, what did they do that made them great? What ingredients did they have in their lives that others seemed to be missing? How did they rise to the top of their generations?

What are the Key Ingredients?

All of these people, and others like them, probably have several things in common. However, being from a privileged background, having wealth, or getting all the good breaks and opportunities is not a common thread. So what brought them the success they experienced?

Although an extensive study of several remarkable people might produce a long list of common characteristics, the purpose of this article is to examine two of the most important: personal habits and close relationships. A person's habits and the people with whom he associates the most closely will be major determining factors in the quality of his life and accomplishments.

A Matter of Habit

There are few components in a person's daily life that are as instrumental in determining his level of accomplishment as his personal habits. Whether a person accomplishes great things or lives his life at a level far below his potential, his habits will be largely responsible.

Our habits will either work for us or they will work against us. They are completely within our ability to control, and if we control them, they will be some of our greatest assets. However, if we allow them to control us, they will prove to be some of our greatest liabilities.

At first thought, this subject may not seem very spiritual, but the Bible has a great deal to say about our personal habits. They affect nearly every area of our lives: our jobs, our personal relationships, and even the way we think. Our habits are very important to the Lord and our walk with Him will be enhanced or hindered by our habits. Let us examine just a few of the practical ways our habits affect our lives.

Whatever Works

Most of us spend a great deal of time working at our jobs, and work is a part of God's purpose for us. Even before the Fall, God instructed Adam to cultivate and keep the Garden (see Genesis 2:15). Work is fundamentally a part of our calling and purpose, but occasionally a "new idea" surfaces that guarantees quick success without hard work. These ideas have robbed many people, including Christians, of lasting fruit in their lives. The Bible says that:

> **The plans of the diligent lead surely to advantage, but everyone who is hasty comes surely to poverty (Proverbs 21:5).**

> **He who tills his land will have plenty of food, but he who follows empty pursuits will have poverty in plenty (Proverbs 28:19).**

We can be sure that any method which claims to lead to instant success, but does not involve diligence and hard work, will lead only to shallow, short-lived achievements. If we are going to be successful and produce results that are truly lasting, it will be because we have been diligent in cultivating good work habits.

Reach Out and Touch Someone

God has made us relational creatures. We will never be the people God has purposed us to be without each other, and our habits can have a direct effect on the quality of our relationships. For example, let us consider how habits of communication can affect a married couple.

> **...every relationship we have will be helped or hurt by our habits, and we can decide which it will be.**

At the beginning of a marriage, probably few things consume the heart of each partner as much as thoughts of the other person. They can sit and talk for hours at a time, staring deeply into one another's eyes, and it only seems to be a few minutes. However, less than a year later, they rarely resemble the same couple they were just a short time ago. Now they are impatient with each other; the husband may not call home to let his wife know that he will be missing dinner, and they often do not take the time to talk and make decisions together.

Although there are many factors that can cause this digression in a relationship, one common reason is that bad habits have developed over time and gone unchecked. The opposite is also true.

When a couple has been together for a long time, and they still glow with the same love and respect for each other, it is largely because they have taken the time to cultivate good habits of communication, forgiveness, and understanding.

It is the same with all relationships. Whether it is parents and children, teachers and students, brothers and sisters, or pastors and church members, every relationship we have will be helped or hurt by our habits, and we can decide which it will be.

You Are What You Think

One of the most common, but over-looked, areas where our habits have a major effect in our lives is in our thoughts. The Bible teaches that the thoughts we consistently think will help determine who we are (see Proverbs 23:7). We have the ability to decide what our thoughts will be. The apostle Paul understood this, as he said in Philippians 4:8:

> **Finally, brethren, whatever is true, whatever is honorable, whatever is right, whatever is pure, whatever is lovely, whatever is of good repute, if there is any excellence and if anything worthy of praise, let your mind dwell on these things.**

If our thoughts are mostly negative, we will be negative people much of the time. If we tend to focus on the problems we face instead of trusting the Lord for the solutions, we will tend to constantly move from one defeat to another. In this life we can be assured that we are going to have to deal with difficult situations, and at times, difficult people. We cannot always control what happens to us, but we are responsible for the way we respond. Defeat in any situation in life often begins with a defeat in our mentality.

However, if our thoughts are positive, this will also be reflected in our lives. If we develop a mentality of being solution oriented, obstacles and unfortunate situations will never be able to stop us, but we will come through them victorious. We will become more than conquerors who are constantly experiencing victory (see II Corinthians 2:14 and Romans 8:37).

The Importance of Relationships

Like our habits, our personal relationships really can "make us or break us." Just like our thoughts, our relationships will play a huge role in determining who we are and what we do. Have you ever heard any of these adages: "You are known by the company you keep," "Lie down with dogs and you will wake up with fleas," or "Birds of a feather flock together?" These are just a few of the many witty, but true, observations that most likely originated with someone who learned this principle the hard way.

The Bible also has much to say about this subject. In I Corinthians 15:33 the apostle Paul said:

Do not be deceived: "Bad company corrupts good morals."

King Solomon also understood this, as he said:

The righteous should choose his friends carefully, for the way of the wicked leads them astray (Proverbs 12:26 NKJV).

He who walks with wise men will be wise, but the companion of fools will be destroyed (Proverbs 13:20 NKJV).

If an aspiring athlete spends time around other athletes who are committed to excelling in their sport, he or she will go much further than they ever would by spending most of their time with people who are content to be mediocre. A young businessman who is mentored by positive, hard-working influences, is more likely to experience long-term success in his career. If our closest relationships are with people who are godly and who have our best interests at heart, they will constantly call us higher and closer to the Lord.

> **Just like our thoughts, our relationships will play a huge role in determining who we are and what we do.**

However, this same principle works the other way. Many a fine young lady has been persuaded to compromise her convictions by giving in to the pressures of friends who did not share her standards. A young man can grow up in a Christian home and then fall into the wrong company in college and, consequently, find himself on a track that will lead to regret ten years later. Whether our closest associates are positive or negative, we will become like these people. This is obviously pertinent for young people, but our friends' ability to influence us never ends with age—that's why it is so important for our close relationships to be good ones.

> **Let us determine to never settle for being less than the very best God has purposed for us to be.**

Just like our habits, our relationships will have a direct effect on our level of achievement. Anyone who has ever achieved greatness and true success surrounded themselves with people who were good influences. Let us determine to do the same.

Conclusion

This article obviously only begins to scratch the surface of these important subjects, but it is helpful to understand the value of our habits and relationships. It is also important to understand that we can determine how they affect our lives, whether negatively or positively. In Matthew 22:14, Jesus made this observation: **"For many are called, but few are chosen."**

He was not saying that it had to be that way, but He said that it commonly was that way. Everyone has potential, but few ever pay the price to walk in the fullness of it. Jesus also talked about a master who gave three of his servants a certain number of talents. The first two people used their talents and actually doubled what their master initially gave them. The third person buried his talents in the ground and never used them (see Matthew 25:14-30).

God has given everyone talents and abilities, and like the first two people in Jesus' parable, some people put their talents to good use. They experience life at a level the ones who bury their talents will never know. Which do we want to be? Do we want to bury our potential in the ground of bad habits and negative relationships or do we want to cultivate these fertile fields to help us produce a bountiful crop with the seeds God has given us? Let us determine to never settle for being less than the very best God has purposed for us to be. Let us consistently surround ourselves with positive influences and discipline our habits so that they work for us, not against us. Taking these two steps can help propel us into a life of greatness and **"an abundance for every good deed" (II Corinthians 9:8).** ∎

NO MAN CAN SEE ME AND LIVE

by Hombre Liggett

"**B**ut He said, 'You cannot see My face, for no man can see Me and live!'" (Exodus 33:20). Throughout Old Testament history it was understood that if a person encountered the manifest presence of God and saw His face, then he would die. The Lord wants us to clearly know the consequences of getting close to Him and seeing His face, which is death. With that knowledge, He then wants us to choose to pursue a close relationship with Him and see His face!

Seeing God's face is like looking into a spiritual mirror. To see God is to clearly see oneself. Many feel this experience would be an easy one, but in the light of God's perfect holiness, righteousness, and power, our own imperfections are magnified. The state of our hearts and lives become clear in His presence.

In the year of King Uzziah's death, I saw the Lord sitting on a throne, lofty and exalted, with the train of His robe filling the temple.

Then I said, "Woe is me, for I am ruined! Because I am a man of unclean lips, and I live among a people of unclean lips; for my eyes have seen the King, the LORD of hosts." (Isaiah 6:1,5).

Even though Isaiah was a seasoned prophet, when he came face to face with God he said, **"Woe is me, for I am ruined!"** God's presence displays an awesome power, which is the most extreme threat to our natural way of living. The day the Lord appears to us is a great and terrible moment for our flesh and carnal lifestyles. His presence leaves no hope for carnality and brings certain doom to remaining as we were before the experience.

When Moses got a glimpse of the Living God, the Bible says **"so terrible was the sight, that Moses said, 'I am full of fear and trembling'" (Hebrews 12:21).**

God first made it clear that if anyone sees His face they will die, but as stated, He also intentionally encourages us to seek after His face.

EVERY TIME I GET A GLIMPSE OF HIM, A LITTLE MORE OF MY LIFE DIES, AND MORE OF HIS LIFE COMES ALIVE IN ME.

And (*if*) My people who are called by My name humble themselves and pray, and *seek My face* and turn from their wicked ways, then I will hear from heaven, will forgive their sin, and will heal their land (II Chronicles 7:14, emphasis mine).

Seek the Lord and His strength; seek His face continually (I Chronicles 16:11).

If we seek and see His face, then won't we die? Yes! That is the point. Death is the goal. God desires to bring death to

our old nature, or more specifically, God desires to kill the natural in us that we might live in the supernatural.

For God to intimately hear us, forgive us, and bring healing to that depth in our lives, we must humbly seek His face...and die. This reality is continued in the New Testament.

And He was saying to them all, "If anyone wishes to come after Me, he must deny himself, and take up his cross daily, and follow Me.

For whoever wishes to save his life will lose it, but whoever loses his life for My sake, he is the one who will save it" (Luke 9:23-24).

I have had experiences where I have found myself in the unique manifest presence of God, and on each occasion I knew that I would never be the same. It is a result of seeking God's face that the most profound heart level changes have been made in my life. Every time I get a glimpse of Him, a little more of my life dies, and more of His life comes alive in me.

When we see God, we then also see ourselves for who we are. We see our hearts compared to Him, and in that moment we know that things about us must die. In this experience it becomes clear that the level of changes needed to be made in our lives could never be done on our own. It appears that Isaiah may have been thinking something like this when he saw the Lord, "How can I continue? I am unclean to the point to which I could never remedy! Who am I compared to such awesome holiness and power? There is no way to go on! I am ruined!"

Yet, it was also in that moment that God prepared Isaiah for the greater part of his ministry on the earth. It is an oxymoron to say we want to experience God's presence, but at the same time not be willing to be personally changed. It is a dilemma for many Christians. Some say they want to change, and yet they do not seek God's face. Others say they want to see God's face, but fight any real change in their lives.

We can only truly be changed in God's presence. We must not make the mistake of trying to develop our lives into a condition that we feel is worthy of approaching God. There is no such condition. He is God, and there is none like Him who could ever compare. We are not to try to change ourselves in order to come into God's presence, but by the blood of Christ we should come into God's presence in order to be changed.

One of the things that made King David so unique and useable by God is that he did not resist the operable hand of the Lord in his life. David knew God's love, and therefore he did not fear the Lord's face. He understood that seeing God meant difficult changes in his life, yet his passion for God caused him to pursue the Lord and allow those changes to be made at any cost.

David was not a perfect man when God called him, nor was David worthy of God's calling. God did not find David the way He needed him. He found him

teachable, breakable, and reformable. David was willing to die and be recreated according to God's design. Listen to what he wrote concerning seeking God's face.

> **When You said, "Seek My face," my heart said to You, "Your face, O LORD, I shall seek" (Psalm 27:8).**

> **Seek the LORD and His strength; seek His face continually (Psalm 105:4).**

> **And He was saying to them all, "If anyone wishes to come after Me, he must deny himself, and take up his cross daily and follow Me" (Luke 9:23).**

WE MUST NOT MAKE THE MISTAKE OF TRYING TO DEVELOP OUR LIVES INTO A CONDITION THAT WE FEEL IS WORTHY OF APPROACHING GOD.

People often try to figure out how to take up the cross of Christ, and like Paul, to die daily. Every day there are practical opportunities to take up our crosses and live for God. Coming to the cross of Christ daily is built upon the foundation of seeking God's face daily. This is by the design of God, and it has always existed for man. By doing this we will both die to things in our lives that are offensive to the Lord and make higher level sacrifices in our service to Him.

Before the Fall, Adam was accustomed to walking with and seeing God every morning in the Garden. Isaiah also developed a comparable relationship with the Lord. He became accustomed to being with God every morning and allowing the Lord to teach and instruct him. Isaiah wrote:

The Lord God has given me the tongue of disciples, that I may know how to sustain the weary one with a word. He awakens me morning by morning, He awakens my ear to listen as a disciple (Isaiah 50:4).

ENTER GOD'S PRESENCE WITH A WILLINGNESS TO EARNESTLY EXPOSE THE IMPURITIES IN YOUR HEART...

Those daily opportunities become aggressively easier to embark upon as a result of spending time seeking the Lord's face. They are less of a burden when we are more dead to self, living in a greater revelation of God and in a closer fellowship with Him.

If we would begin to pursue God in this nature, then the results of such a pursuit would develop in our lives quickly. God draws near to those who draw near to Him, and He rewards those who are seeking after His face.

And without faith it is impossible to please God, because anyone who comes to him must believe that he exists and that he rewards those who earnestly seek him (Hebrew 11:6 NIV).

There are practical ways to seek after the face of God, which speaks of evolving an intimate relationship with Him. We need to meditate upon God's Word (see Psalm 1), be devoted to prayer (see Luke 18:1), and maintain a strong relationship with a fellowship of the body of Christ (see Hebrews 10:24-26). Additionally, God desires to bring extra-biblical like experiences to your relationship with Him. This would include, but not be limited to: angelic visitations, visions, dreams, and most importantly, His manifest presence.

As you seek Him, do not fight the things you begin to see in yourself. Do as King David did. Enter God's presence with a willingness to earnestly expose the impurities in your heart, and then allow God to forgive, change, and heal you. This is a large part of the process of dying daily, and it will help your decisions throughout the day. Your service to God will come easier and with greater anointing.

God is clearly calling us to come seek His face and die to our self-life (the natural life), so that we might grow in the supernatural life of Christ Jesus our Lord. Seek the Lord's face and live! ∎

The Manna Ceased

by Dan Duke

"The manna ceased..."
(Joshua 5:12)

That is such a simple statement of fact isn't it? The manna ceased...end of subject.

Well not exactly. The day after they crossed over the Jordan into their Promised Land they ate the old corn of the land. After forty years of doing things in a particular and dependable way, the manna ceased. For the generation born in the wilderness it was all they had ever known and all they had ever eaten or tasted (though they did get quail in response to the whining of their fathers). When they entered their Promised Land, the sweet manna of the wilderness was to be no more.

Without any previous warning, God was now going to do something new and provide for them in a different way. No longer could they wake up a little early before the sun became hot and go outside and gather a basket of manna so breakfast could be prepared.

I suppose those entering the much acclaimed Promised Land were a bit surprised and even a little disappointed. The old corn did not come close to the taste of the sweet manna from heaven that fell fresh every day.

Change and promotion can be, and most of the time is, disguised. For example, when the children of Israel were "delivered" from the bondage of Egypt and journeyed into the wilderness (which incidentally was to be a brief journey), they immediately discovered this "deliverance" was not at all what they thought it was going to be. After all, they carried with them their 430 years of back wages. They were all wealthy and healthy but, alas, there was no water to be found at any price. There was, in fact, nothing to buy at all. The only place to spend their money was on the tabernacle in the

Dan Duke 17

wilderness. They were to finance a house for God and a place of worship.

From that moment, the complaining set in. The murmurings in the wilderness replaced the sound of the crack of the Egyptian's whip. "At least we had onions in Egypt," was their pitiful cry.

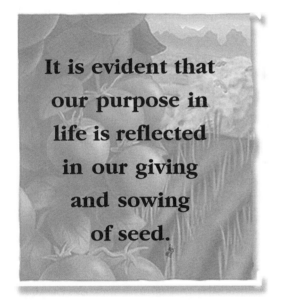

It is evident that our purpose in life is reflected in our giving and sowing of seed.

God's ways are not our ways. The sooner we discover this, the better. The Promised Land was indeed a land of milk and honey. However, God's plan for their provision had changed. Those who resist God's change remain in the wilderness regardless of where they are.

The wilderness generation only knew daily provision. They never had a new pair of shoes in all their life. I suppose those little sandals they had as babies grew as their feet grew. Can you imagine wearing the same pair of shoes for forty years?

God's loving desire was to bring His people from a daily provision of just enough to a much greater measure. In the Promised Land, it was to be from harvest to harvest. The small basket used to gather a day's allotment of manna was to be replaced by barns and threshing floors. The daily limitation was to be thrown out and replaced by a limitless supply of harvest depending on the seed that was sown. In the Promised Land they could determine their own harvest, both in size and description.

Before there was an Israelite nation there was the Word of God recorded in Genesis 8:22, **"While the earth remains, seedtime and harvest, and cold and heat, and summer and winter, and day and night shall not cease."** The plan and purpose of God was to bring the people of Israel into the supernatural provision and kingdom prosperity that sowing and reaping alone can produce. No longer were they to live by a day-to-day existence. It was no longer to be just enough for today and no more, they could determine their harvest by the seed they would sow.

We see this principle carried over into the New Testament with the words of the apostle Paul: **"he who sows sparingly shall also reap sparingly; and he who sows bountifully shall reap bountifully. Let each one do just as he has purposed in his heart, not grudgingly or under compulsion, for God loves a cheerful giver (II Corinthians 9:6-7).**

It is evident that our purpose in life is reflected in our giving and sowing of seed. Those of small purpose, which is an "I, me, mine, enough for today mentality" are, and always will be, small givers. Their harvest will be small because their seed is given sparingly. They, therefore, limit themselves to a small harvest. Religion has so shaped their mentality so to have enough to pay their bills and meet the basic needs of their family and is interpreted as the blessing of God and life in the Promised Land. I remind you that it was in the wilderness they met the basic needs of their family by gathering manna each day.

God had something better for them in the land of promise—if they could only see it. But it came to them in the form of old corn—hardly what they expected. It will profit you greatly to remember that the seed never looks like the fruit. An apple seed looks nothing like an apple. You have to recognize it for what it is—a seed.

I have made the decision as to where I choose to live—the wilderness or the Promised Land. That decision determines how I live and how my provision comes. I have chosen to cross the Jordan and live in my Promised Land so I must accept the way it is...seedtime and harvest is to be my provision. To coin an old phrase, "it comes with the territory." My opinion, likes or dislikes, do not matter. I live by the law of the land or I do without. The law of Genesis says...my harvest comes from my seed. *No seed, no harvest.*

If I want to determine my own level of living, which I do, then I must accept the reality that "with the same measure that I measure [my giving] it shall be measured to me again." My purpose which

is to be a blessing must be reflected, not in word alone, but in action. That is why I have the goal to give something to someone every day of my life. I passed a woman, someone's mother, sitting barefooted in the street today. I gave her some money. She wept. "Now I can have food," she cried. The few bucks I gave her meant nothing to me, but it meant everything to her. We must learn to weep with those who weep.

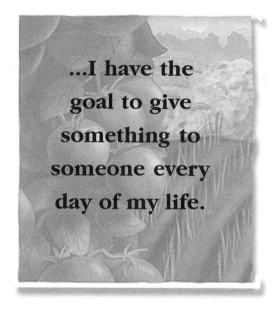

...I have the goal to give something to someone every day of my life.

There are at least four things that I aspire to do every day. I worship, pray, read my Bible, and give an offering to someone as a seed sown. There are days I fall short of one or more of those things but those days are few. It is my goal to accomplish those four things every day. My life, then, does not reflect my value as a preacher or my value as an employee of an organization. My lifestyle reflects my giving. Literally, I live by giving. In the Promised Land, one moves from a day-to-day living into a harvest-to-harvest living. If you desire a harvest, sow a seed. If you desire a harvest as a lifestyle then giving must become your lifestyle. What could be simpler?

The wisest and the wealthiest man in the Bible, Solomon, gives us this free advice, "Cast your bread on the waters, for you shall find it after many days. Give a portion to seven or eight, for you do not know what evil shall come on the earth...In the morning sow your seed, and in the evening withhold not your hand, for you don't know which shall prosper, either this or that, or whether they both shall be good" (see Ecclesiastes 11:1-6).

> Do not make the mistake Israel made by becoming, in their own eyes, the object of God's blessing.

Again, Solomon, our financial counselor and wise mentor says, **"The liberal soul shall be made fat; and he that watereth** [others] **shall be watered also himself."** The Portuguese Bible translates the verse this way: **"The generous soul shall become prosperous" (Proverbs 11:25 KJV).** Do you believe it?

When I die I want to leave behind the legacy of being a generous man. I would like for my friends and family to say of me, "Dan was the most generous person I have ever known." In order for that to be a reality I must live in the Promised Land. I must always have a harvest sufficient for what I need for my immediate family and for my greater spiritual family. To give is my life and my joy. I pray it can be yours as well.

"Be a giver. Be a generous person. Look for people and projects to give to and seek to be a channel of provision to as many people as possible." God made a promise to Abraham that in his seed all the nations of the world would be blessed (see Genesis 22:18). That promise was directly fulfilled in Jesus, the Promised Deed. However, you who are of faith are also the seed of Abraham our father in the faith.

Do not make the mistake Israel made by becoming, in their own eyes, the object of God's blessing. They were to be the channel of God's blessing, not the object. When you become the object, the blessing stops. When you are only the channel of God's blessing flowing out to others, the well will never dry up, the meal barrel will never become empty, and the oil will never stop flowing. ■

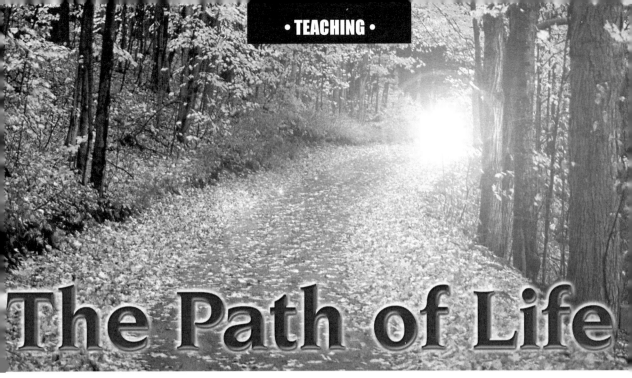

The Path of Life

by Deborah Joyner Johnson

Following the path of life will lead us to an extraordinary life filled with purpose. More importantly, this path will lead us to a closer walk with the Lord.

At times, however, the path may seem very narrow and hard to see. Our vision may become clouded as discouragement or even the temptation of sin seeks to sway us off the path of life. All around us the enemy is looking for ways to entice us to walk onto his path—an imitation of what God intends for our lives, a path of destruction. Many have fallen prey to the enemy's traps, but with wisdom and the Lord's guidance we can walk past his snares, never suffering from the consequences to which he would have us fall. And then, we can savor the sweetest kind of victory, knowing we have pleased the Lord by being true to Him.

Jesus, Our Guide

When Jesus called Peter and Andrew to be His disciples, He said: **"Follow Me"** (see Matthew 4:19). From that day of decision to follow Him, they began an empowering relationship with Jesus that changed their lives forever. Jesus taught, guided, rebuked, healed, nourished them, and became their Friend. Peter, Andrew, and the rest of His disciples led tremendously rewarding lives, developing a close relationship with Jesus because they chose to follow and spend time with Him.

Jesus is simply saying to us: **"Follow Me,"** so we can do the same. As we follow the Lord and learn of His ways and wisdom, He will become the perfect Guide, steering us away from the enemy's trap, and onto the path He desires for us to follow. We will then experience the most rewarding life ever imaginable as we become closer to Him.

Soon after Jesus died and rose again, He commissioned His disciples to teach others about Him. As He was departing to be with His Father, He gave this promise: **"Lo, I am with you always, even to the end of the age" (Matthew 28:20).** The disciples did what Jesus asked and taught others about Him. In so doing, their relationships with Him continued to deepen even down a most difficult path upon which they were asked to walk. They held onto His promise that He would always be with them. Their love for Him became so great that it did not matter what others thought, that they were persecuted, and even that they died horrible deaths. To proclaim that Jesus was Lord was worth it all! Nothing stopped them from following Him.

Similarly, we are to teach others about Him, that they may come to know the Lord. We must be sure to inform them when they begin their walks with Him that the path ahead will not be easy. But if they will be faithful to follow the Lord wherever He leads, clinging to the promise that He will always be with them, they will live the most amazing and rewarding lives possible.

The Shepherd's Voice

In John 10:27-28, Jesus said: **"My sheep hear My voice, and I know them, and they follow Me; and I give eternal life to them, and they shall never perish; and no one shall snatch them out of My hand."** We all know the voice of our closest friends. Likewise, the secret to following Jesus is to know His voice—that we might hear His counsel.

We have the opportunity to set our vision toward Him and follow Him, knowing that He will not lead us astray. The only time we can be led astray is when we take our vision off of Him so that we no longer hear His voice. We have an enemy who is trying to stop us at every turn. Do not give him a chance. With the Lord's guidance, we can thwart the enemy's plans and finish the courses the Lord has set before us.

The Greatest Pleasure of All

We would never intentionally hurt those we love. Sometimes I think about how much it must hurt the Lord to see His children going astray. If you have ever experienced your own child or a close friend falling into sin, then you have just an indication of what the Lord must feel when we sin. He wants to bless us, but sinning saps the blessings He wants to so freely give. He has given us the choice to follow Him or follow the ways of the world. The latter is far easier to succumb to in a world where sin is constantly all around us. Therefore, we must know Jesus as our Guide, Friend, and even Rescuer. If we truly love Him, then no sin is worth the cost of displeasing Him.

Jesus knows our hearts; He knows everything we are going through. He implores us to look at Him and away from sin, so we can rise above in victory. Sins are just fleeting pleasures, and even if they bring some form of temporary happiness, that is all they are—temporary. Brief pleasures will cause us to lose ground in our walk with Jesus. Jesus offers us the most gratifying pleasure possible—to know Him, the Son of God. No passing sin could ever compare to knowing the Son of God!

We have all sinned and displeased God, so we should not let our pasts keep us from walking forward into a life of freedom and joy in Him. We can ask forgiveness and our sins will be no more, just as we read in Psalm 103:12: **"As far as the east is from the west, so far has He removed our transgressions from us."** With forgiveness, we can begin again on the path He has chosen for us, but we must also recognize that we will have to gain back the ground we have lost. We will have to take the time to make right whatever we did wrong. Thankfully, the Lord's help is only a prayer away and He will show us how to make things right again.

The Lord's love is infinite. **"Greater love has no one than this, that one lay down his life for his friends" (John 15:13).** A true shepherd will lay down his life for his sheep. Jesus, our Shepherd and Guide, did this for us. Because of His love for us, He died so that we might live. He is the truest Friend of all.

Remain faithful to Jesus. The reward of not sinning is that we will be become more like Him with every victory. If we remain faithful to Him, we will find true communion and a new depth of love for Him, making us more determined to stay on the path of life.

The Choice Is Ours

How can we repay the One who paid the ultimate price of dying for our sins? We can touch His heart and live for Him. We have the opportunity to bring Jesus joy by living our lives to please Him. Being pure is a choice. Being righteous is a choice. Living for Him is a choice. It may be hard at times to live such a life, but what greater gift could we give Him?

> WE HAVE ALL SINNED AND DISPLEASED GOD, SO WE SHOULD NOT LET OUR PASTS KEEP US FROM WALKING FORWARD INTO A LIFE OF FREEDOM AND JOY IN HIM.

Jesus has a purpose for all of us. We can never fulfill the totality of what we have been called to do if we are not following the Lord. While spending time with Him, He will reveal details of our purposes and what He wants us to do. The time He has given us is precious, and every breath we breathe is a gift. We must use our time wisely and to the fullest, walking steadily forward upon the path He has chosen for us to follow.

The late Erma Bombeck once said, "When I stand before God at the end of my life, I would hope that I would not have a single bit of talent left and I could say, 'I used everything you gave me.' Then the Lord would say, **'Well done, good and faithful servant'** (Matthew 25:21 NIV).

We all want to hear those words. We will if we follow the Lord daily on the path of life. When we overcome and are true to Jesus, even when temptations and battles are raging all around us, we will achieve the greatest victory of all in this life: We will bring pleasure to the Lord because we have wholeheartedly followed Him and have accomplished His will for our lives. Additionally, we will receive the highest reward when we at last see Him— we will live forever in constant happiness with Him. There is nothing on this earth that can ever compare to what He is offering us. We simply have to follow Him.

"Let not your heart be troubled; believe in God, believe also in Me.

"In My Father's house are many dwelling places; if it were not so, I would have told you; for I go to prepare a place for you.

"And if I go and prepare a place for you, I will come again, and receive you to Myself; that where I am, there you may be also" (John 14:1-3). ∎

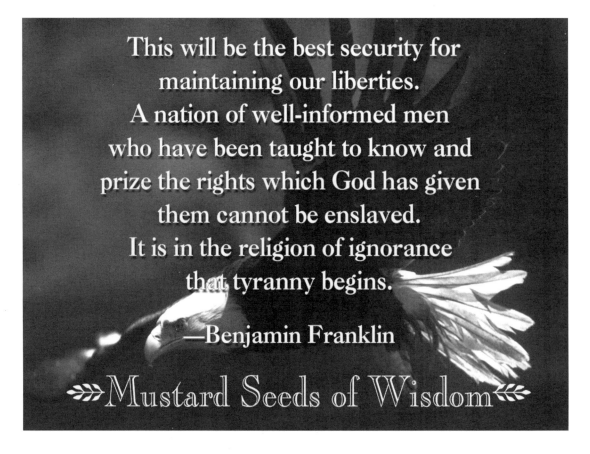

This will be the best security for maintaining our liberties.
A nation of well-informed men who have been taught to know and prize the rights which God has given them cannot be enslaved.
It is in the religion of ignorance that tyranny begins.

—Benjamin Franklin

Mustard Seeds of Wisdom

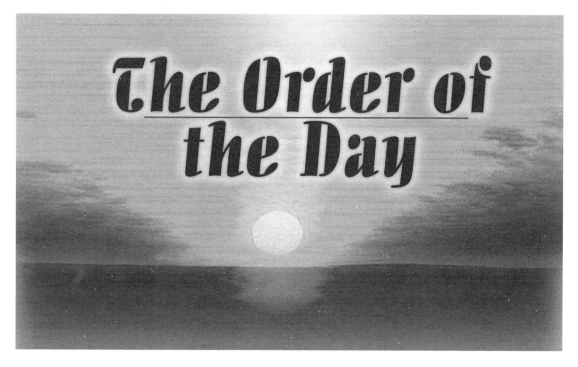

The Order of the Day

All Scriptures are King James Version.

by Steve Thompson

In spite of our modern emphasis on comfort, convenience, and ease, people today are frazzled. Not only unbelievers, but many dedicated believers are just plain weary. This state of weariness is not confined to the elderly or the overworked. It seems almost everyone today talks of being worn-out. Tiredness seems to be the order of the day.

Recently, the Lord showed me that tiredness was the order of the day for many because our day was ordered wrongly. My first thought went to misplaced priorities, and that is partially true. However, the Lord showed me something more foundational about how we live our lives. We have literally reversed the order of the day that God created, and we are experiencing the exact opposite of God's intention for our lives.

God's Order

God never ordained that we would be perpetually wearied and worn-out. His intention is the exact opposite. God wants us to thrive in life, not just survive it. He wants us to be increasingly invigorated through our lives and even through our labor. God has provided for us to have life and to have it abundantly (see John 10:10), not just the things of life, but life itself.

Let's be honest though. Most people, young and old, begin and end their day tired. They wake each morning to enter the workday not refreshed, but looking forward to being done so they can catch some rest. By the time their workday is done, they "crash" or "vegetate," but they do not really find rest. The cycle continues the next day from being less rested than the day before.

In reality, this is the exact opposite of God's plan for our lives. God wants us to thrive, not just survive. So great is His intention that He ordained from the beginning that the structure of the day itself would promote well-being, not tiredness.

In the fifth verse of the Bible there is a small, almost hidden key to experiencing God's intention for our well-being. While keys are small and look insignificant, they make the way for us to enter new realms and realities. Genesis 1:5 provides us with a key to reordering our day and entering the reality of rest and refreshing that God has for us.

And God called the light Day, and the darkness he called Night. And the evening and the morning were the first day.

This verse says that **"the evening and the morning were the first day."** The day that God created starts with the evening and finishes with the morning and daytime. This Scripture provides the foundation for the Jewish day which begins at sundown.

While this may appear to be a seemingly insignificant mention in Scripture, it is really an earth-shattering revelation, which will bring a revolutionary change in our lives. If we adopt God's order of the day, which is opposite of our thinking, consider how profoundly our experience would change.

Reorder Your Day

Our day would begin in the evening, by fellowshipping with those we love. The first thing on God's heart for us is to have communion with our family and to share a meal together. Then after a time of food and fellowship, we rise up, not to work, but to rest and sleep. Then after a full night of rest, we arise not to work, but to another time of fellowship and food with those we love.

> **LET YOUR SOUL FIND DEEP REST IN GOD AND HIS CARE OVER YOUR LIFE.**

Then, after eating twice and fellowshipping with those we love, at the end of our day, we work. We work from being fully rested and refreshed, and are able to give ourselves completely to our work. Now instead of our labor being tainted with the weariness of our souls, it will be impregnated with the joy of life and the presence of God that He intends.

We are encouraged by Paul in Galatians 6:9 to **"not be weary in well doing."** We are called to give ourselves, even more than we are currently, to doing well. But if we will focus first on *being* in Christ, not *doing* for Him, we will end up doing significantly more than if our focus was first set on doing.

Reorder your day, both naturally and spiritually. God's order for you is this: Fellowship with Him and those you love. Have a nice meal—**"taste and see that the Lord is good" (Psalm 34:8).** Rest in God and His mercy toward you—let your soul find deep rest in God and His care over your life. Rise up and have another meal, spiritual and natural, and fellowship again with those you love. Then it's time to work. ■

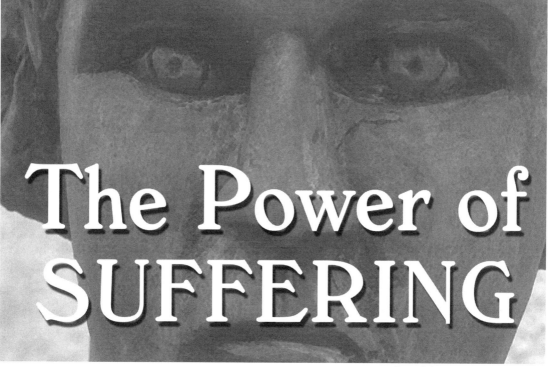

The Power of SUFFERING

All Scriptures are Amplified Version.

by Trevor Tiessen

In western society suffering is not something that is promoted or desired. On the contrary, we do everything we can to avoid it. Even in the church, suffering is not something we usually embrace willingly. While many of us enjoy religious freedom, Jesus reminds us that if they persecuted Him, they will persecute us also (see John 15:20). It is important for us as believers to see the value and power of suffering for the gospel from a biblical standpoint.

Paul and Silas

When we suffer for the sake of the kingdom, the power of the Holy Spirit is released into the earth. Just as worship, prayer, and fasting release the Lord's power, so does suffering for righteousness sake.

In Acts 16 Paul and Silas came to Philippi, a Roman colony in the region of Macedonia. While ministering in this city, they were approached by a slave girl who had a spirit of divination. For several days she had followed Paul and Silas around, shouting out that these men were servants of the Most High God. Finally, Paul commanded the spirit to come out of her.

When the slave girl's owners realized that they had lost their means of income from this girl, they had Paul and Silas stripped, beaten, and thrown in jail. Paul and Silas had done a righteous thing by casting the demon out of this slave girl and they suffered unjustly for it. They were Roman citizens, yet they did not receive a fair trial. Sitting in a jail cell late at night, bloody and beaten with their feet in stocks, they began to do the unthinkable—they began to praise God!

But about midnight, as Paul and Silas were praying and singing hymns of praise to God, and the [other] prisoners were listening to them,

Suddenly there was a great earthquake, so that the very foundations of the prison were shaken; and at once all the doors were opened and everyone's shackles were unfastened.

When the jailer, startled out of his sleep, saw that the prison doors were open, he drew his sword and was on the point of killing himself, because he supposed that the prisoners had escaped.

But Paul shouted, Do not harm yourself, for we are all here!

Then [the jailer] called for lights and rushed in, and trembling and terrified he fell down before Paul and Silas.

And he brought them out of [the dungeon] and said, Men, what is it necessary for me to do that I may be saved? (Acts 16:25-30)

Under the circumstances, it would have seemed like an opportune time for Paul and Silas to be upset at their injustice, curse the jailer, and feel sorry for themselves. Instead, they not only suffered for righteousness sake, they responded to their suffering in a righteous manor—they praised God. They suffered for doing right and were truly honored and overjoyed to do so.

God's heart was so moved by their willingness to suffer with honor that there was a great earthquake and the jail cells were opened. The shackles not only fell off Paul and Silas, they fell off all the prisoners in the jail! The jailer, who had put them in stocks, knelt at their feet and asked to be saved. Later, not only the jailer was saved, but his whole household as well. Who would have imagined that all this would happen as a result of two men willing to suffer for the gospel? Had Paul and Silas not seen past their own suffering and demanded justice for themselves, it is unlikely that this miracle would have taken place. It is an amazing reality that the salvation of our enemies may depend on our willingness to suffer at their hands.

> God's heart was so moved by their willingness to suffer with honor that there was a great earthquake and the jail cells were opened.

God is not blind to the injustice suffered by His saints. He will move in amazing ways if we choose to lay our lives down for the gospel. Our suffering will not only bring about our deliverance, but the deliverance of others. There are times when it is appropriate to seek justice, but for us as believers, there is a higher way—

the way of righteous suffering that releases the power of God.

Saul's Conversion

Saul of Tarsus, who would later become the Apostle Paul, was a Pharisee zealous for the Law. He relentlessly persecuted the church with violence, throwing both men and women in jail (see Acts 8:3). On his way to Damascus to persecute the church there, Saul had a supernatural encounter with God:

> He relentlessly persecuted the church with violence, throwing both men and women in jail.

Now as he traveled on, he came near to Damascus, and suddenly a light from heaven flashed around him,

and he fell to the ground. Then he heard a voice saying to him, Saul, Saul, why are you persecuting Me [harassing, troubling, and molesting Me]?

And Saul said, Who are You, Lord? And He said, I am Jesus, Whom you are persecuting. It is dangerous and it will turn out badly for you to keep kicking against the goad—[to offer vain and perilous resistance].

Trembling and astonished he asked, Lord, what do You desire me to do? The Lord said to him, But arise and go into the city, and you will be told what you must do (Acts 9:3-6).

This supernatural encounter with the Lord led to Saul's conversion. We know that he was called to be an apostle and a preacher of the gospel (see II Timothy 1:11), but what released this power into his life? He was certainly not seeking this experience himself. Why Saul and not one of the other Pharisees? There are many Christians who have not had an encounter of this magnitude, much less someone who hated the church. The answer is found in Acts 6 and 7.

Stephen, a deacon in the church, was moving in great power and miracles. This provoked an attack by the Jews, who could not refute the miracles or his teaching. As a result, they brought false accusations against him and had him brought before the Sanhedrin (see Acts 6:8-15).

After a discourse on God's history with Israel, Stephen rebuked the Sanhedrin for their resistance to the Holy Spirit, which caused further attack.

Then they dragged him out of the city and began to stone him, and the witnesses placed their garments at the feet of a young man named Saul.

And while they were stoning Stephen, he prayed, Lord Jesus, receive and accept and welcome my spirit!

And falling on his knees, he cried out loudly, Lord, fix not this sin upon them [lay it not to their charge!] And when he had said this, he fell asleep in death.

AND SAUL was not only consenting to Stephen's death he was pleased and entirely approving..." (Acts 7:58-60, 8:1).

Stephen not only suffered and died unjustly, he cried out for the Lord to forgive those who were killing him. Stephen's suffering and forgiveness released power from heaven into Saul's life, who was presiding over Stephen's death.

> **Could it be that some of the greatest enemies of the church today are called to be our greatest prophets and apostles?**

Stephen did not live to see the fruit of his suffering, but his suffering and forgiveness resulted in the salvation of one of the greatest Christian leaders of all time. Who would have predicted this prior to Saul's conversion? Could it be that some of the greatest enemies of the church today are called to be our greatest prophets and apostles? Rather than responding with anger and criticism of those who treat us unfairly, should we not love and forgive them and pray that they too are transformed from enemies to allies? Our greatest victory is not to see the wicked punished, but to rescue them

from the camp of the enemy and help them become a trophy of God's grace.

Choosing to Suffer

Most of us hate to see injustice. If we had the power to prevent it from happening, we would. It is no wonder that superhero movies are so popular. It is inspiring to see a hero use his supernatural powers to thwart evil and bring about justice. But what if we had the supernatural power to prevent our suffering and refrained from using it? That seems preposterous, but that is exactly what Jesus did.

> And behold, one of those who were with Jesus reached out his hand and drew his sword and, striking the body servant of the high priest, cut off his ear.
>
> Then Jesus said to him, Put your sword back into its place, for all who draw the sword will die by the sword.
>
> Do you suppose that I cannot appeal to My Father, and He will immediately provide Me with more than twelve legions [more than 80,000] of angels?
>
> But how then would the Scriptures be fulfilled, that it must come about this way? (Matthew 26:51-54)

Jesus was not a victim. He had very real power to save His own life. Legions of angels were at His disposal. He had the power at any given moment, right up until His crucifixion, to deliver Himself, but He chose not to. How many of us, with that kind of power, would freely choose to suffer? For the joy set before

Him, He endured the cross, knowing that multitudes would be saved as a result of His obedience to the Father. He could see past His suffering and know that it was worth it. Jesus had an eternal perspective, not a temporal one.

It is interesting to note that He also refused Peter's help, when he drew his sword to defend Jesus. Peter's intent to protect Jesus could certainly be understood. Most of us would have been inclined to act in a similar fashion, yet when Peter drew his sword to fight, the Lord told him to put it down. Jesus did not need Peter's help. Furthermore, Peter's actions were in direct conflict with God's plan. How many of us could have understood this at the time it was happening? God's ways are certainly above our ways. It actually would have been a disaster if Peter had "successfully" defended Jesus.

Not only do we need to be careful about taking up justice for ourselves, we need to be careful about letting other people come to our defense. It is not usually in the best interest of the kingdom for someone to take up our offenses. If we are permitting people to take up our offenses, it shows that we are still trying to hold on to our rights. To endure suffering, we must be prepared to lay down our rights.

In John 19:10-11, Jesus affirms that He is not simply a victim of circumstance.

So Pilate said to Him, Will You not speak [even] to me? Do You not know that I have power (authority) to release You and I have power to crucify You?

Jesus answered, You would not have any power or authority whatsoever against (over) Me if it were not given you from above. For this reason the sin and guilt of the one who delivered Me over to you is greater.

Jesus understood that He was not a victim of the authorities, but that His Father was really in control. Jesus still had the power to deliver Himself, but chose to remain in submission to the Father's will. He did not blame Pilate or the Jews for His situation, but recognized that He was called to suffer at their hands.

> **Not only do we need to be careful about taking up justice for ourselves, we need to be careful about letting other people come to our defense.**

Without the understanding that Jesus had, most us would be doing everything we could to get out of a situation like this. We would be appealing to the Lord to deliver us. There may be times when the Lord delivers us from trouble, but at other times it may actually be the Father's will for us to suffer at the hands of others to bring about a victory for the kingdom. As believers we need to recognize that the Father cares about our welfare and is in control. If we are either protected from or delivered into suffering, it is not at random. Jesus trusted the Father with His life and so can we.

> **The power released through His suffering resulted not only in the supernatural occurrences at His crucifixion, but in salvation and healing for the whole world.**

The Ultimate Injustice

Jesus was completely innocent, yet suffered terribly at the hands of wicked men. He had broken no laws, but He suffered as a criminal. He was arrested, beaten, cursed, spat on, had His beard ripped out, and was forced to wear a crown of thorns. He was then taken outside Jerusalem where He was crucified. Although Jesus had the power to deliver Himself, He not only allowed this to take place, He forgave those who stood by and sneered as He died on the cross.

Power is released when we suffer for righteousness sake. When Jesus died on the cross, there was an immediate release of power.

> **And Jesus cried again with a loud voice and gave up His spirit.**
>
> **And at once the curtain of the sanctuary of the temple was torn in two from top to bottom; the earth shook and the rocks were split.**
>
> **The tombs were opened and many bodies of the saints who had fallen asleep in death were raised [to life];**
>
> **And coming out of the tombs after His resurrection, they went into the holy city and appeared to many people.**
>
> **When the centurion and those who were with him keeping watch over Jesus observed the earthquake and all that was happening, they were terribly frightened and filled with awe, and said, Truly this was God's Son! (Matthew 27:50-54)**

The suffering of Jesus caused an earthquake, raised people from the dead, and the veil of the temple was torn in two. The greater the suffering, the greater the release of power. What looked like a defeat for the kingdom was actually the greatest victory of all time.

The ultimate injustice was the persecution and crucifixion of the Lord Jesus. He was the spotless Lamb of God, without sin or blemish. He was the perfect representation of the Father to a fallen world that hated and rejected Him. The power released through His suffering resulted not only in the supernatural occurrences at His crucifixion, but in salvation and healing for the whole world, for everyone who calls upon His name. The words of Isaiah were most certainly fulfilled by our Messiah:

> **Surely He has borne our griefs (sicknesses, weaknesses, and distresses) and carried our**

sorrows and pains [of punishment], yet we [ignorantly] considered Him stricken, smitten, and afflicted by God [as if with leprosy].

But He was wounded for our transgressions, He was bruised for our guilt and iniquities; the chastisement [needful to obtain] peace and well-being for us was upon Him, and with the stripes [that wounded] Him we are healed and made whole.

All we like sheep have gone astray, we have turned every one to his own way; and the Lord has made to light upon Him the guilt and iniquity of us all (Isaiah 53:4-6).

> Rather than see our enemies punished, let us forgive and see them touched by the power of God.

Summary

As we endure suffering as Christians, whether it is false accusations, injustice, or any other kind of offense, let us not forget the greater good that is at stake. Jesus laid His life down for those who hated Him, and so must we. Rather than see our enemies punished, let us forgive

and see them touched by the power of God.

The enemy cannot win. If we receive justice, we can be thankful. If we suffer injustice, power from heaven will be released and his plan will backfire. Let us take joy in persecution and consider ourselves honored to suffer for the sake of the gospel. Whether we live to see the fruit of our suffering or not, let us not forget the eternal perspective that the Lord has given us.

Blessed and happy and enviably fortunate and spiritually prosperous (in the state in which the born-again child of God enjoys and finds satisfaction in God's favor and salvation, regardless of his outward conditions) are those who are persecuted for righteousness' sake (for being and doing right), for theirs is the kingdom of heaven!

Blessed (happy, to be envied, and spiritually prosperous—with life-joy and satisfaction in God's favor and salvation, regardless of your outward conditions) are you when people revile you and persecute you and say all kinds of evil things against you falsely on My account.

Be glad and supremely joyful, for your reward in heaven is great (strong and intense), for in this same way people persecuted the prophets who before you (Matthew 5:10-12).

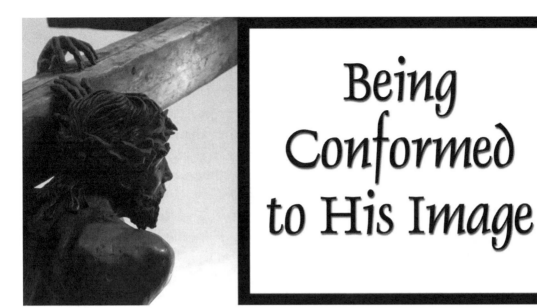

Being Conformed to His Image

All Scriptures are New King James Version.

by Robin McMillan

Paul the apostle had an amazing revelation of the eternal purpose of God.

> **For whom He foreknew, He also predestined to be conformed to the image of His Son, that He might be the firstborn among many brethren (Romans 8:29).**

God wants many other children who are like His Son Jesus in their very nature. It is not an outward conformity that God desires where two people look, act, or dress alike, but an inner one where our lives are empowered by the very life of the Son of God who dwells inside us. This is what it means for Christ *to be* our lives.

> **When Christ *who is our life* appears, then you also will appear with Him in glory (Colossians 3:4).**

Living this way is not automatic. While the salvation experience is instant and justification comes by faith, being conformed to the image of Christ is a process. It is achieved over time as we yield to God in the specific dealings He has designed for each of us.

One popular method of living like Christ involves asking in any given situation, "What would Jesus do?" and then behaving accordingly. This method gives us a practical guide on how to respond in certain situations. However, being conformed to the image of Jesus is something that must occur on a much deeper level. Our lives must embody Christ's life flowing through us. We should fit together like a hand fits inside a glove. This process of breaking and being molded to the "hand of God" is similar to the way a baseball glove is prepared to conform to the player's hand.

Noah Liberman's book, *Glove Affairs, The Romance, History, and Tradition of the Baseball Glove,* describes the process of how a baseball glove endures to conform to the hand of the player who owns it in order to fulfill the purpose for its creation. Particularly in the early days of baseball's history, gloves were stiff and stubborn and required an extensive process to change them into useable and reliable pieces of equipment. This process provides a prophetic picture of the things we go through to be conformed to the image of Christ.

The Process of Conforming

Will Wedge, a reporter for the *New York Sun,* wrote the following article in 1925 that described one process used by the New York Yankees professional baseball team to break in a glove:

The Yankees are fortunate in having one of the best glove doctors in the majors. He is [former major leaguer] Charley O'Leary...He can take a glove that is inclined to buck and shy at grounders and break it in like a Western cowboy and rodeo rider would break in a bad tempered bronco...It's said he whispers things into the fingers of stiff and unwieldy gloves that gives them the secret of snaring everything that comes their way...He takes gloves apart and rebuilds them nearer the heart's and fingers' desire. He unlaces the new glove and amputates excess padding...It is really the way Charley talks to a glove and discusses things with it that makes it the dapper and well-groomed object it becomes when he has finished with it...(Glove Affairs, page 35-37).

Yogi Berra

Yogi Berra, the enigmatic Hall of Fame catcher for the New York Yankees played from 1946 to 1965. He had his own patented method of breaking in a catcher's mitt before it was suitable for use:

Just put [the mitt] in the whirlpool, soak it, until it stops bubbling. Wrap balls in it with rubber bands. Then dry it out. We used to have a clothes dryer. It was like a heater. Put [the mitt] in there for two or three days (page 39).

Bill Davis

Bill Davis of Lorton, Virginia, a current glove collector, was once a bat-boy for the Philadelphia Phillies in the 1960s. Part of his duty was to assist the players, one of whom asked him to break in his new glove. Davis did not know exactly how to do it and "was working on it in the dugout when Jim Busby, then coach of the Astros, came up. He said, "Kid, let me show you how to break in a mitt." He then proceeded to pound the daylights out of the glove with a baseball bat" (page 40).

Ron Santo

Ron Santo, a five time Gold Glove award winning third baseman had his own method:

I would put two baseballs in it, wrap it real tight with string and then put it in water and let it sit all night, take it out the next day and let it dry out. Then I would go play catch with it. And I would keep spitting in it, and after the first day get it kind of soft in the pocket but leave it firm on the outside. Then I'd put oil on it in the pocket (page 40).

Ouch!

These unorthodox methods were typical ways both professional and amateur ballplayers prepared their gloves for playing the game. Unfortunately, people are a lot like new baseball gloves—stiff, stubborn, and un-pliable. We must often experience extreme circumstances before we effectively yield to the life God has already put within us.

Spiritual Parallels

This "breaking in" process of a baseball glove has amazing similarities to our spiritual development. Hebrews 12:5-6 contains a promise most of us are not anxious to claim:

> **"My son, do not despise the chastening of the LORD, nor be discouraged when you are rebuked by Him;**
>
> **for whom the LORD loves He chastens, and scourges every son whom He receives."**

Scourging is a painful process, one God promised that every son would experience. His chastening is not a sign of rejection but one of the surest signs of His love for us. His purpose is that we profit from His attention and are fully trained in the way of righteousness. The writer of Hebrews alerts us to this truth about God so that we will not **"become weary and discouraged in our souls" (see Hebrews 12:3)** and reminds us that even Jesus Himself endured great hardships and adversity yet was without sin.

Confinement

Most ballplayers break in their gloves using confinement and restriction. They tie the glove around several baseballs to forge a re-shaping that make it better suited to catch the ball. God often uses confining circumstances to help us conform to His purpose. Sometimes the confinement is disciplinary, because we do not want what the Lord wants for us, or we are not listening to Him. He uses the confinement to get our attention and speak to us. However in many cases there is no rebellion or sin involved; but, like a young sapling or tomato plant, we are tied and grounded to ensure our proper growth and development.

Charlie O'Leary's method involved speaking to the gloves as he took them apart and put them back together. This, too, describes how many people feel in the discipline of the Lord, as they are taken apart and put back together. Even then, the Lord is quick to speak and encourage us.

The prophet Hosea describes this process in chapter 2:14-15 of his book:

> **"Therefore, behold, I will allure her, will bring her into the wilderness, and speak comfort to her.**
>
> **I will give her her vineyards from there, and the Valley of**

Achor as a door of hope; she shall sing there...

God reveals His ultimate purpose of securing the hearts and love of His people, even if it means bringing them into a place of distress. In that needy place they discover God's abundant provision, even fruitful places like vineyards and places of renewed hope. The Valley of Achor means the valley of tribulation. When we discover that God can provide hope in times of the worst trouble, we are encouraged to know that He can do anything. Even there His people will learn to trust and depend upon Him alone. This, too, is part of the process of being conformed to the image of His Son.

Circumcision

O'Leary would also amputate part of the padding if it made the glove awkward or hindered its effectiveness. This speaks of the circumcision of the flesh, the cutting away of those attitudes and actions that every believer must experience.

In Him you were also circumcised with the circumcision made without hands, by putting off the body of the sins of the flesh, by the circumcision of Christ (Colossians 2:11).

That ongoing experience is part of our identification with Christ and His death, burial, and resurrection. Without the cutting away, the new growth will not bear its maximum fruit.

Soaking

Many ballplayers soaked their gloves in water to make them change their shape.

Soaking causes the fibers in the leather to separate, adapt to the change in form, then relink when they dry. This soaking process speaks of two things—applying the life-altering Word of God to our lives, and spending time in the presence of the Lord. Both are absolutely necessary.

The Water of the Word

We truly need to soak in the Word of God. We know from Ephesians 5:25-27 that the washing of the water of the Word is vital:

Husbands, love your wives, just as Christ also loved the church and gave Himself for her,

that He might sanctify and cleanse her with the washing of water by the word,

that He might present her to Himself a glorious church, not having spot or wrinkle or any such thing, but that she should be holy and without blemish.

The washing of the water of the Word sanctifies and cleanses the church of its spots and wrinkles, becoming functionally holy and flawless. That is the kind of bride the Father wants His Son to have.

Psalm 37: Soaking in His Presence

Psalm 37 describes the practical way to soak in the presence of the Lord.

Do not fret because of evildoers, nor be envious of the workers of iniquity.

For they shall soon be cut down like the grass, and wither as the green herb.

Trust in the LORD, and do good; dwell in the land, and feed on His faithfulness.

Delight yourself also in the LORD, and He shall give you the desires of your heart.

Commit your way to the LORD, trust also in Him, and He shall bring it to pass.

He shall bring forth your righteousness as the light, and your justice as the noonday.

Rest in the LORD, and wait patiently for Him; do not fret because of him who prospers in his way, because of the man who brings wicked schemes to pass.

Cease from anger, and forsake wrath; do not fret—it only causes harm" (Psalm 37:1-8).

First of all we must not fret, a word meaning "to worry continually about something." Instead, we should trust in the Lord, do good, and feed on the facts of His faithfulness. To be even more saturated by Him, we should delight ourselves in Him, commit our ways to Him, and rest in Him. The natural result of this process is that the Lord gives us the very desires of our hearts and brings out of us and through us both righteousness and justice, as bright as the noonday sun. We must soak in the Lord to be conformed to the image of His Son.

Constant Use

For a glove to be reliable in a game, it needs to be used consistently beforehand. We are the same way. Until we function consistently in our purpose, we never become fully proficient in it.

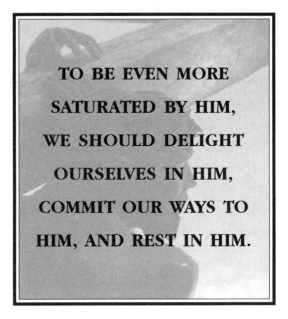

TO BE EVEN MORE SATURATED BY HIM, WE SHOULD DELIGHT OURSELVES IN HIM, COMMIT OUR WAYS TO HIM, AND REST IN HIM.

Jesus understood from a young age that He had a job to do and sought to accomplish it. At the age of twelve He went with His family to Jerusalem to celebrate the Feast of Passover. When the family party returned home, Jesus remained in the city. After three days His parents found Him in the temple asking questions and listening to the priests. When His parents questioned Him about His behavior, Jesus said:

"Why did you seek Me? Did you not know that I must be about My Father's business?" (Luke 2:49)

At the age of twelve Jesus was already engaged in His purpose. By the age of thirty-three He would conclude:

"I have glorified You on the earth. I have finished the work which You have given Me to do" (John 17:4).

We, too, should have the same perspective and live to finish the work the Father has given us to do.

Oiled

A significant part of the preparation of any baseball glove is the periodic application of oil. The oil softens the pores of the leather enabling the glove to maintain its shape and durability. We, too, must be "oiled," anointed with the Spirit of God to live as He has called us to live. Without that oil we become hard, then brittle, begin to lose our shape and, eventually the inward presence and power of the Lord.

Each Player's Loyalty to His Glove

Professional ballplayers have a peculiar possessiveness and loyalty about their gloves. They almost become an extension of their body and personality. One famous third basemen, Brooks Robinson of the Baltimore Orioles, refused to replace his worn-out model. Ira Beckow of the *New York Times* found it to be hideous. *"He described a cracked pocket, ripped insides, dark and shrunken wool padding, a small, dirty piece of tape along the heel and another on the web, the whole thing 'a tobacco-juice brown'"* (page 44).

Phil Rizzuto, an infielder with the Yankees, kept the same glove for fourteen years, but he sent it to the Rawlings

factory each off season for repairs. *"He probably played 14 years with the same glove. At least he looked on it as being the same glove,"* says Roger Lueckenhoff, a Rawlings glove executive for forty-two years, until 1933. *"[Glove designer] Harry Latine would refurbish it every year and replace parts, and he kept gradually replacing parts to where it was a new glove, but in Rizutto's mind it was the same glove"* (pages 46-47).

> WITHOUT THAT OIL WE BECOME HARD, THEN BRITTLE, BEGIN TO LOSE OUR SHAPE AND, EVENTUALLY THE INWARD PRESENCE AND POWER OF THE LORD.

I grew up playing sports in a highly competitive family where both parents coached and played sports on the college level. I began playing ball when I was nine years old and did not stop until after my freshman year in college. I, too, had a special glove. As a ten-year old sportsman, my parents gave me a Wilson catcher's mitt for Christmas. It was a Del Crandall turtle-back model. It was called a turtle-back because when turned upside down it looked like a turtle.

The glove instantly became my prized possession. I was mesmerized by the feel of it on my hand, the smell of the leather, and the sound of the baseball as it "thwacked" loudly into the pocket when I caught it. When I wore the glove, in my mind I was instantly in the World Series catching Whitey Ford's pitches for the New York Yankees as we beat the Cardinals or the Dodgers, or whoever else dared to challenge our supremacy.

> **GOD NUMBERS OUR WANDERINGS, PUTS OUR TEARS IN A SPECIAL BOTTLE, AND RECORDS ALL OUR ACTIVITIES IN ONE OF HIS BOOKS!**

I played with it day and night. It was rarely out of my sight. Even when at bat I was aware of where it sat by the bench near my other equipment. When it got dirty, I cleaned it with saddle soap and oiled it with either olive oil (smelled too bad!), or neat's foot oil to be sure it stayed in top shape. At night it did not stay in the closet or on a shelf somewhere. For the first year or so it stayed safely in bed with me right next to my pillow.

The love of a child for his first baseball glove, and the love of God for a specific person may be a weak analogy, but both are very personal and heartfelt. In each case, because of great affection and delight, the smallest peculiarities and nuances do not go unnoticed.

As I looked at my glove I could remember each scar on it and what event caused it. "Oh, that slash happened when Ben tried to steal home and I cut him down at the plate. Man was that a collision!" God knows much more about us and records all of it. Jesus said: **"the very hairs of your head are all numbered" (Matthew 10:30).** Furthermore, God numbers our wanderings, puts our tears in a special bottle, and records all our activities in one of His books! (see Psalm 56:8). What kind of God is He Who keeps up with such insignificant aspects of our being? The kind we have!

In Conclusion

Being conformed to the image of His Son is much more than getting saved; it is a lifelong pursuit. In Galatians 4:19, Paul expressed the deep desire of his heart for those he had introduced to the Lord:

> **My little children, for whom I labor in birth again until Christ is formed in you.**

He wanted them to be like Jesus. He also wanted the same thing for himself and pursued it with all his heart. He never claimed to have arrived, but he knew he was on his way and that he lived a life in hot pursuit of this goal. His own words confirm it:

> **Not that I have already attained, or am already perfected; but I press on, that I may lay hold of that for which Christ Jesus has also laid hold of me.**

> **Brethren, I do not count myself to have apprehended; but one thing I do, forgetting those things which are behind and reaching forward to those things which are ahead,**

> **I press toward the goal for the prize of the upward call of God in Christ Jesus (Philippians 3:12-14).**

Though we may be predestined to bear the image of His Son, if we do not yield ourselves to the process, it will never fully happen. If we understand the necessity of this process, we will more readily embrace the dealings of the Lord and progress in the Christian life. We must press on. ■

Quotations taken from *Glove Affairs, The Romance, History, and Tradition of the Baseball Glove*, Noah Liberman, Triumph Books, Chicago, IL, 2003.

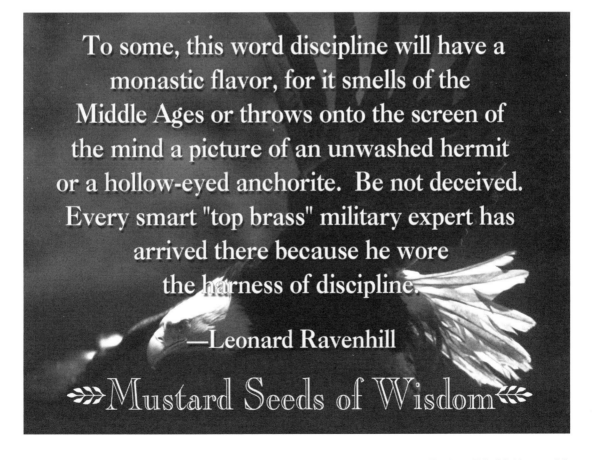

To some, this word discipline will have a monastic flavor, for it smells of the Middle Ages or throws onto the screen of the mind a picture of an unwashed hermit or a hollow-eyed anchorite. Be not deceived. Every smart "top brass" military expert has arrived there because he wore the harness of discipline.

—Leonard Ravenhill

⫸Mustard Seeds of Wisdom⫷

TURNING A VISITATION INTO A HABITATION

All Scriptures are New King James Version.

by Paul Goulet

Have you ever experienced a great move of God in your church, youth group, or during a retreat? If you are like the thousands of people that I have seen through the years, the pressing question that troubles all of us is: "Why did the move of God stop?" "Why was it so brief?"

So many wonder what they could have done to continue this visitation of the Holy Spirit. Others speak wistfully about these visitations, wrongfully concluding that their short-term nature is unavoidable. The purpose of this article is to discuss the incredible details of a sustained move of God in Las Vegas, Nevada. It is not my purpose to present our experiences as the norm. I encourage you to read our experience prayerfully. Ask the Holy Spirit to give you divine applications to your life and your ministry.

In 1992, my wife Denise and I assumed the leadership of a small church in Las Vegas, Nevada. All of my training was in psychology and pastoral counseling. Consequently, I felt woefully inadequate for the tasks of being a senior pastor. As a result of my feelings of insecurity, I started fasting one day a week, while I prayed on a mountain or in the desert.

In October of 1994, during one of these days on the mountain, the Lord touched me in ways my graduate degree could not explain. Urged by a member of our congregation, we attended a pastor's conference in Canada that opened our eyes to the explosive power of God. I like to identify this type of power as a *dynamite encounter*. In Acts 1:8, this power, *dunamis[1]* is promised to the believers. God introduced me to this type of power on the last night of this Canadian Leaders' Conference.

I will never forget how my life was dramatically altered when I asked God to bring revival to my city. Only God could bring revival to Las Vegas. Some might call it a modern-day Sodom. I would prefer to think of it as a Nineveh that is going to repent and change. That fateful night found me at the altar asking a leader to pray for my city. Instead of praying for Las Vegas, he insisted on praying for me. At first I refused, but then I opened myself to a powerful visitation from the Holy Spirit.

On my first Sunday back in Las Vegas, the power of God touched our church. This move of God lasted a few weeks. Not everyone in our church received the Holy Spirit with open arms. As the pastor, I also felt confused by the controversy and I was afraid of the fallout. Eventually, I asked the Holy Spirit to stop touching me with this great power because I felt so out of control. To my surprise, everything supernatural seemed to stop completely.

The Holy Spirit came because I asked for revival. But when He came He was not welcomed. After a few months of silence, I realized I had made a dreadful mistake. Motivated by my personal pride and a desire to please people, I had grieved the Holy Spirit. Instead of fighting me, the Holy Spirit backed off. I assume that He has done this in many churches. Perhaps the Holy Spirit has discovered that pastors

---

[1]Spirit Filled Bible, New King James Version © 2002
dunamis: **energy, power, might, great force, great ability, strength**

and leaders want Him to visit, but they are unwilling for Him to move in. The pain and the shame of my error caused me to review my mistakes, repent of my sins, and pray for a second chance.

ONLY GOD COULD BRING REVIVAL TO LAS VEGAS.

During the absence of visible power and miracles, the church started to grow again. We acquired fifteen acres on the highway and built our first series of buildings. It amazed me that God was so gracious. In spite of my rejection of His Spirit, He still blessed and added to the church. Eighteen months later, He also gave me a second chance. During a conference for pastors, Claudio Freidzon gave a word of knowledge that someone had been praying for a second chance. As I ran to the altar, my expectations were met by a merciful Holy Spirit who touched me with His dynamite again. I did not just want a touch, I wanted to be transformed and used. I will never forget the question God asked me as I lay on the ground: "Paul, do you really want My power?" "Yes Lord," was my answer. He then said, "Ok, but this time you must die."

The vision that transfixed me for the next few minutes is forever branded on my mind. I saw my left hand being pierced by a nail. I was being nailed to a sinner's cross. As the blood poured from my hand, God started to list my sins and ask me if I was willing to die to them. One by one I saw them written on a scroll that hung below my hand. I wept for almost two hours. I agreed to die to people-pleasing, pride, anger, lust, selfish ambitions, and other issues. Paul understands what I went through that night:

> **I have been crucified with Christ; it is no longer I who live, but Christ lives in me; and the life which I now live in the flesh I live by faith in the Son of God, who loved me and gave Himself for me (Galatians 2:20.)**

> **Likewise you also, reckon yourselves to be dead indeed to sin, but alive to God in Christ Jesus our Lord (Romans 6:11).**

Claudio frequently returned to my prostrate position with exhortations of "Reciblo" and "Mas, Senor, mas!" The power that touched me that night was unbelievable. I had committed to do whatever it took to keep this power and learn whatever I needed to learn.

The past eight years have been a journey that Paul described in Philippians 3:10: **"...that I may know Him and the power of His resurrection, and the fellowship of His sufferings, being conformed to His death..."**

The word **"know"** is a very specific Greek term that means an intimate knowledge. It is *ginosko*, which is how God deserves to be known. A life of discovery will never exhaust this desire.

I have been married for twenty-four years. Denise and I both testify that the journey of discovery continues even to this day. What a great journey! Through its ups and downs and successes and failures in this relationship, we have invested into weekly dates, counseling, marriage retreats, and heart-to-heart talks. Our intimate relationship with the Holy Spirit, with His power, and with His sufferings will never cease. I realized that not only did I need to repent for grieving Him, but I also had to confess my failures to the church.

> **OUR JOURNEY OF REDISCOVERY WITH THE HOLY SPIRIT HAS ENABLED US TO CONTINUE TO GROW BOTH IN NUMBERS AND MATURITY.**

On my first Sunday back from the conference, I asked for forgiveness and pledged to surrender every service to the Holy Spirit. I invited all of those that were interested to return that evening for a time of impartation.

Roman 1:11 provided me with a biblical framework to help me understand what I had experienced. Our journey of rediscovery with the Holy Spirit has enabled us to continue to grow both in numbers and maturity. The purpose of this article is to underline seven principles to which we attribute our ongoing revival at International Church of Las Vegas. We have discovered seven priorities that have kept us on course to a lifelong journey of the Holy Spirit. It is my prayer that these seven priorities will become a source of inspiration and guidance for turning a visitation into a habitation of the Holy Spirit.

It is our deepest desire to have the Holy Spirit turn your church or ministry in a habitation of the Lord. We do not want misplaced priorities to be an end to this move of God. I am sure that you feel the same way.

#1 Priority: Keep Soul Winning as Your Priority.

As the Holy Spirit filled our services with His power, we reminded the people of the purpose for this outpouring. Acts 1:8 is so very clear about this issue: **"But you shall receive power when the Holy Spirit has come upon you; and you shall be witnesses to Me in Jerusalem, and in all Judea and Samaria, and to the end of the earth."**

The ultimate purpose of the Holy Spirit is to fill us in power so that we can reach the lost for Christ. It is very easy to get caught up with the initial response to a visitation of God. The falling, crying, and other reactions to His presence are only temporary. We cannot pitch our tents around physical reactions to the supernatural presence. In I Corinthians 12:7, Paul explains that there is a difference between a reaction to the Holy Spirit and a manifestation of the Holy Spirit: **"But the manifestation of the Spirit is given to each one for the profit of all."**

The Greek word used for **"manifestation"** is *emphanidzo*, which means "to cause to shine, to appear, to reveal, to come to view, to exhibit or make known."

The manifestation of the Holy Spirit is the way He shines through people for the good of the body of Christ and the world. The initial physical reaction depends more upon each person's personality and needs.

When the wind of the Holy Spirit blows, we all respond differently. Some of us are oak trees, others are weeping willows, but all of us are called to reach the world. At ICLV we do not emphasize falling down or standing up; we emphasize the purpose of the infusion of the Spirit of God. We are not concerned about whether people feel the Holy Spirit, but whether they receive what He is depositing at the altar.

I have seen many Christians get stuck at one response to the power of God, instead of allowing His power to equip them to bear much fruit.

#2 Priority: Keep Intimacy With Christ and His Power as Your Focus.

As we have become intimate with His power, we have discovered that God fills us with different types of power for different purposes. Many of us are familiar with the four Greek words that are translated as love in our English version: agape, eros, phileo, and storgi. Each word has a distinctive meaning that is lost in English. In like manner, the word "power" is used for five different Greek words that are unique.

Let us take some time to study these words because they play a huge role in revivals worldwide.

A. Dunamis

In Acts 1:8, we were introduced to the Greek word *dunamis*, meaning "energy, power, might, great force, great ability, strength." This type of power filled the disciples on the Day of Pentecost.

That day was marked by an earthquake, tongues of fire, and a mighty wind. There was such a commotion that it drew a large crowd. Was it the one hundred twenty who were speaking in tongues and prophesying, or was it the way they walked that caused the people to think that they were drunk?

It seems clear that when God fills people with the *dunamis,* signs and wonders usually follow. In our services, we have seen the *dunamis* touch and deliver thousands.

In many Pentecostal circles, this expectation that *dunamis* will touch people is very common. In fact, if this does not occur, they believe that God has not moved.

B. Exousia

Mark 3:14-15: **"Then He appointed twelve, that they might be with Him and that He might send them out to preach, and to have power to heal sicknesses and to cast out demons."** A move of God is always marked by the power of God being deposited in the lives of His servants. In Mark 3:14-15, Jesus imparted a type of power that would enable them to use His *dunamis. Exousia* is the authority or right to act. It is the ability or capacity to do something. In this passage, Jesus imparted authority, described their mission, and received reports of their success.

For a revival to continue for years or generations, every believer needs to receive a divine impartation of authority.

We are talking about the priesthood of believers being empowered to change the world. We are talking about the key ingredient to Ephesians 4:11-12. If every believer in your church walks in diverse authority, God will heal the sick, save the lost, and deliver the oppressed.

C. Energes

Hebrews 4:12 says **"For the word of God is living and powerful, and sharper than any two-edged sword, piercing even to the division of soul and spirit, and of joints and marrow, and is a discerner of the thoughts and intents of the heart."** Have you ever been engaged by the Word of God or by a Spirit-led sermon? In Hebrews 4:12, the author uses the word *energes* to describe a unique type of power. It means that "something is at work." We get our word energetic from it. It is active and effective.

It is important to understand that when we ask God for power He may answer us with what we need most. If we need dynamite, He will explode into our lives. If we need authority, He will give us *exousia*. If we need more energy and inspiration, He will give us *energes*.

A church in revival will need different types of power at different times. The Spirit-filled walk should never be boring! Every day should be a day of discovery.

D. Kratos

which He will manifest in His own time, He who is the blessed and only Potentate, the King of kings and Lord of lords,

who alone has immortality, dwelling in unapproachable

light, whom no man has seen or can see, to whom be honor and everlasting power. Amen (I Timothy 6:15-16).

Kratos refers to the dominion strength and manifested power that the Lord exerts in this world. Could it be that He would also fill us with this dominion power? Isn't this the level of power that the disciples worked with as they turned the world upside down? Haven't we been called to rule and reign with Him?

A few years ago I chose over a dozen businessmen to mentor and train. I believe that everybody needs a prophet or priest or pastor to help them spiritually, emotionally, relationally, and practically. The prophet, Nathan, played this role in David's life in II Samuel 12. My primary objective was to help these businessmen take dominion, to rule and reign as kings and priests. In just a few years, I have seen this happen.

I am convinced that God wants to pour His *kratos* power into believers and the church as a whole. How else could we change cities and transform nations? How else can a man lead his family and business? How else can a mother receive the ability to lead her home?

E. Ischuros

II Corinthians 10:10: **"For his letters,"** they say, **"are weighty and powerful, but his bodily presence is weak, and his speech contemptible."** *Ischuros* means great strength. When was the last time that you needed a dose of great strength? Paul's letters to the Corinthian church were full of great strength. In our generation, we need great strength to confront problems in our families, cities, and around the world. We need great strength to face our challenges. We need great strength to confront corruption even in the church. We need great strength to start ministries, to confront wolves, and to keep the flames of revival burning.

#3 Priority: Keep the Vision Clear.

II Corinthians 3:18 says: **"But we all, with unveiled face, beholding as in a mirror the glory of the Lord, are being transformed into the same image from glory to glory, just as by the Spirit of the Lord."** Real revivals continue for generations when the vision is clear. The vision has to be other-people centered. The vision must include strong venues of discipleship such as home cells or small group Bible studies.

The vision must contain opportunities for service to God. Everyone can find their place of service in the body of Christ. What is the vision for your life, family, and church? Is it a God-breathed vision?

#4 Priority: Keep the Altars Safe.

The safety of your altars will be an important element in the ongoing outpouring of the Spirit. Having well-trained altar workers who are led by the Spirit is important. Here are a few guidelines that have helped keep our altars safe.

1. Men pray with men; women pray with women.
2. No pushing or shoving to cause people to fall.
3. Only trained leaders can minister at the altar.

#5 Priority: Keep the Word and Worship as Center.

Although we have had incredible times at the altar with people being healed, saved, and delivered, we always prioritize the need to worship God and the need to hear the Word of God.

Many churches have done away with true worship. We firmly believe that worship is the open door to His presence and His power. No matter what may happen in a service, we always include a time of preaching or teaching from the Word. People want to experience the power of God but they also need to experience the power of the Word.

#6 Keep the Leadership Pure.

Scripture warns us that there are three real dangers to our continued revival: **"the lust of the flesh, the lust of the eyes, and the pride of life,"** found in I John 2:16. The anointing and power of the Holy Spirit can be very exciting. He can open wonderful doors of blessing and influence. However, leaders can take advantage of this power. They can try to use it to manipulate people or take advantage of them. Strong accountability is required to keep our teams pure. We do not want to defile the holiness of a great move of God.

#7 Stay Flexible to the Holy Spirit.

Jesus taught His disciples to remain open and flexible to the Holy Spirit. In John 14:16, Jesus prophesied that the Holy Spirit would come in the form of a Comforter: **"And I will pray the Father, and he shall give you another Comforter, that he may abide with you for ever"** (KJV). In John 14:17, He would come as the Spirit of truth: **"Even the Spirit of truth; whom the world cannot receive, because it seeth him not, neither knoweth him: but ye know him; for he dwelleth with you, and shall be in you"** (KJV). In John 14:26 He reveals Himself as a teacher: **"But the Helper, the Holy Spirit, whom the Father will send in My name, He will teach you all things, and bring to your remembrance all things that I said to you."** In John 16:7, He proves to be a true helper: **"Nevertheless I tell you the truth. It is to your advantage that I go away; for if I do not go away, the Helper will not come to you; but if I depart, I will send Him to you."** As we remain submitted to the Holy Spirit, He will minister to every person in our services in a unique way: His way.

Conclusion

A Spirit-filled life is a life of revival. A Spirit-filled church is one of continued growth and maturity. An outpouring of the Holy Spirit does not have to be short-lived. It can surely lead us from glory to glory: **"But we all, with unveiled face, beholding as in a mirror the glory of the Lord, are being transformed into the same image from glory to glory, just as by the Spirit of the Lord"** (II Corinthians 3:18).

Ephesians 3:20-21 explains so clearly what our lives should look like: **"Now to Him who is able to do exceedingly abundantly above all that we ask or think, according to the power that works in us, to Him be glory in the church by Christ Jesus to all generations, forever and ever. Amen."** I challenge you to embrace nothing less and to expect so much more. ∎

Marked by the LORD

All Scriptures are New King James Version unless otherwise indicated.

by John Paul Jackson

God's name is our heritage, our authority, and our hope. It is our very life essence—a part of God's glory we need desperately. His name, and the fullness that comes with it, must be seared into our very being. To carry it properly, we must have character above reproach, standing pure and holy before Him.

God is calling us to be a people marked by His name, to become willing vessels who have removed any unconsecrated things from our lives and unholy affections from our hearts.

We will be stretched and will have to deal with new issues that He reveals to us as we grow daily in Him. While our friends may get away with certain behaviors, God will call us to a higher standard of holiness and morality. His name needs to become dearer to us than anything else.

The Mark of Consecration

In order for God to create the necessary consecration in our lives, He will have to help us in submitting different levels of our lives to Him. God wants to align our hearts more perfectly with His. He desires for us to shed any affection that might steal away our hearts' focus from Him. Our lives need to be consecrated at this level of thinking: A consecrated life has learned to focus its thoughts on whatever is pure, right, holy, and good (see Philippians 4:8) rather than on any worldly cares and concerns.

A consecrated people will experience a purging of activities in their lives; many things will be cut away—things that may have been good but not spiritually profitable or fruit-producing. God will free us from the distractions and entanglements that have kept us from fully pursuing Him.

We can no longer afford to waste our energy on pursuits that do not really matter and are not truly profitable.

How do we use our time? Do we lavish it on ourselves, or do we lavish it on others through the service of our lives and resources? Stewardship of time, too, has been consecrated to the Lord. The Sabbath, a period of rest, is observed in the life of such a believer because it is a weekly reminder that our lives are not our own and that all we have is truly His.

Our finances are an investment into our life passions. The life marked by the Lord's name is truly humble and servantlike—a life that does not spend money selfishly, but freely invests in others. This lifestyle understands **"it is more blessed to give than to receive" (Acts 20:35)** and depicts godly wisdom and understanding in which finances are used to advance God's kingdom. This is a life that implements the law of the harvest and is not bound by a spirit of poverty.

God is not merely looking for people who are obedient, but rather He is seeking people who are *submissive* to His will. God is looking for willing vessels He can trust to put His name upon.

The Mark of His Presence

But you shall seek the place where the LORD your God chooses, out of all your tribes, to put His name for His dwelling place…(Deuteronomy 12:5).

My friend Bob Jones once said, "Where God puts His name, His Presence abides." When God puts His name on us, His Presence will live with us continually.

We will not merely visit His Presence at certain moments in our week, but His Presence will remain in us. Where we go, He will go.

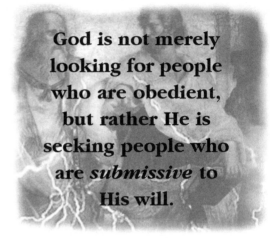

God is not merely looking for people who are obedient, but rather He is seeking people who are *submissive* to His will.

There are many ways of telling if a person has been marked by the Presence of God:

- In the Lord's Presence is **"fullness of joy" (Psalm 16:11).**
- Set free from anxieties and fears, this person will be governed by peace (see John 14:27).
- Love is the distinguishing mark on this person (see Matthew 5:44).
- In Jesus, this person is made a light that illumines dark places (see Matthew 5:14).
- This person will bear the hope of His Presence (see Romans 5:1–2).
- He or she will discover Jesus as the One who heals all sickness (see Exodus 15:26). God's Presence always results in healing: spirit, soul, and body.
- Such believers will bear the Holy Spirit's fruit: love, joy, peace, longsuffering, kindness, goodness, faithfulness, gentleness, and self-control (see Galatians 5:22–23).

There are many other descriptions I could list of those who are marked by the Lord's Presence. Those who are *branded* by the Lord's name will manifest an amazing quality of life—a life filled with God's Presence.

The Mark of Authority

Authority can be inherited along the lines of a name, because a person's name includes the authority associated with that person's position and place. If we are marked by the name of the Lord, we will bear the authority intrinsic to His Presence. This, however, brings up an issue with the use of the Lord's name.

Often we have heard people passionately praying for things from God. They fervently pray and at the end of uttering all their requests, they simply say, "In Jesus' name." Sadly, sometimes such zealous ones do not maintain a lifestyle that reflects Christ's character. They have inadvertently reduced the Lord's name to a kind of lucky rabbit's foot. However, when a believer's life reflects the character of Jesus, that person's life is able to lay hold of God's authority. The source of authority is not merely in the name but in the character represented by the name. If we are marked by the Lord's name, then we will also be marked by the character and authority of Jesus.

The Mark of Humility and Brokenness

The apostle James wrote that "**...God resists the proud, but gives grace to the humble**" **(James 4:6).** Jesus was the ultimate Servant; the Gospels say He was meek and lowly of heart (see Matthew 11:29).

Those who are marked by the name of God have embraced the value of humility and have discovered the mystery of God's grace. Grace speaks of God's supernatural endowment to help us be what we are not, and to do what we cannot. Those who are humble shall be great in the kingdom because they have learned to keep themselves within the scope of God's work. They have learned to deny themselves in order to serve Christ more fully.

Jesus Himself spoke of the value of the humble in His Sermon on the Mount: **"Blessed are the poor in spirit, for theirs is the kingdom of heaven" (Matthew 5:3).** One of the greatest dangers in God's kingdom is the sin of spiritual pride. Those who wear the mark of humility find a potent shield of protection against this vice. Such people no longer worry about having to prove anything to anyone—they are totally secure in the Father's love and acceptance. They bear the mark of humility because they bear God's name.

Why is it important to list these components of a life marked by the name of the Lord? Because God's names are at stake in us; people will see God through the manifestation of His names in our lifestyles.

What an amazing God we serve! How could anyone ever want anything more than the gift of His name? Remember what King David sang:

> **Some boast in chariots, and some in horses, but we will boast in the name of the LORD, our God (Psalm 20:7 NAS).**

In Hebrew, the phrase to **"boast in"** means "to have confidence in, to trust in." Boasting in God's name indicates that we have confidence in His character, His attributes, and His nature—who He is.

God longs to free us from our sinful tendencies of doubt and self-promotion and our habit of trying to draw our confidence from our own resources or those of the people around us. This is the way of the world, but God's way is different.

God offers us a level of confidence and assurance that far surpasses any confidence the world could ever know. The world's confidence can be shaken because ultimately it is dependent upon human strength. The confidence God wants to give is never-ending; it cannot be disappointed; it cannot falter; it cannot fail because it is rooted in the very foundation of God's sovereign Presence, character, and nature. It is rooted in the unshakable foundation of His hallowed name!

God is extending the fullness of His name to you today. He is offering to put His name on you and give you *every* bless-ing that comes with it. How will you respond? Are you ready for the fire of preparation necessary for all who desire to receive His name?

For further reflection, ponder these questions before God:

1. Where do your affections lie?
2. What consumes your thoughts?
3. Do your actions glorify God or satisfy your own personal desires?
4. Do you do things that steal your time away from God?
5. Which characteristic listed in the Beatitudes (see Matthew 5:3–11) would you most like to flourish in your life?

As you embark on the adventure of knowing God, let Him show you the amazing mystery and wonder reserved for those who have chosen to receive and bear His name. Truly His name is above all names! ■

Adapted from *I AM: Inheriting the Fullness of God's Names* by John Paul Jackson. Copyright 2004. Used by permission. For more information, visit www.streamsministries.com.

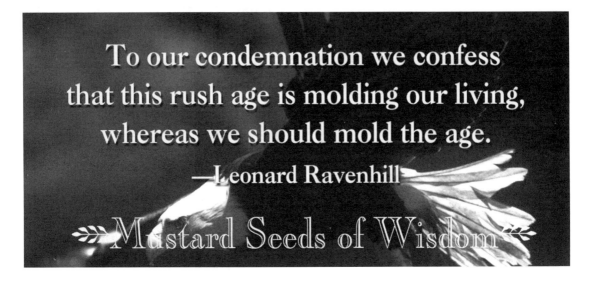

To our condemnation we confess that this rush age is molding our living, whereas we should mold the age.
—Leonard Ravenhill

Mustard Seeds of Wisdom

The GREAT LIBERATION

by Rick Joyner

One of the most controversial doctrines throughout the church age has been the place of women in the church, especially whether they should be allowed to teach or exercise authority in the church. This is no small matter, and must be settled before we can come into our full purpose as the church. When it is settled, it will release one of the greatest overall advances in the church since the giving of the Holy Spirit.

Like any true doctrinal resolution, this must be done without compromising the Scriptures, but rather basing our doctrine on them, rightly dividing the written Word that has been given to us for that purpose. In this article, I intend to agitate two major controversies, not for the purpose of creating more division, but so these issues are confronted until they are resolved.

First, it is my position, which I will base on Scripture, that women must not only be allowed to teach in the church, but that a great and crucial teaching ministry has been deposited by God in women. It is also my position that there should be no ceiling on the authority that a woman can exercise in the church, including apostolic authority, which is also established in the Scriptures.

Second, it is also my position, based on studies and observation, that the church has become so feminine that most men feel uncomfortable or bored. Even though the majority of the church is presently led by men, about 75 percent of the church are women who want their husbands, sons, and brothers to be attracted to the church. In general, this will not happen until there is a place for the masculine nature in the church.

How could the church, which is so predominantly led by men, have such a tendency to make the church overly feminine? To some degree, this is a result of the devil's overwhelming assault to blur the distinctions between men and women. It is also, at least partially, the result of women exercising illegal influence over the church because they have not been allowed to do it legally.

> **True men are never intimidated by true women, and true women are never intimidated by true men.**

This is not to imply that there should not be feminine influence in the church, and even a feminine identity. In fact, I believe there should be even more than there is now, but it should not exclude the masculine. We should have both. This, too, must be corrected for the church to come into its full purpose.

The church should be the foremost place on earth where men are free to be men, women are free to be women, and everyone is completely free to be who God created them to be, using all of their gifts and talents for His glory. Such a place would be one of the most attractive societies to all people on the earth, which is why the devil is so intent on blurring the distinctions that God made between men and women.

True men are never intimidated by true women, and true women are never intimidated by true men. When both are real about who they are, they set others free to be who they are. It is actually the wrongful compromises that are causing the divisions because anyone who is compromising who they truly are will always be insecure. One of the greatest revolutions in Christianity is about to come because the Lord is going to set the men free to be who He created them to be, and He is going to set the women free to be who He created them to be.

The Great Teaching Ministry

It is basic to Christianity to understand that the Lord came to give us life and to give it more abundantly. Life is our primary business. The word "father" means "life-giver" because the sperm seed of life comes from the man. However, let us think for a minute. What would happen to that seed if there was no woman present? Who is it that carries the seed, nurtures it, brings forth the life, and does the biggest part of the job of raising that life to maturity? Basically, until the child is born men do the fun part and the women do all the work. After the child is born, and through its most important formative years, the mother will usually continue to be the greatest source of nurture and teaching.

I am not advocating changing this. In fact, it is, I believe, a divine order of things. However, I do advocate giving honor to whom honor is due. I believe motherhood is possibly the highest calling that one can have on this earth. Every mother is a "queen mother," and should be treated like one and given the highest place of dignity and respect.

A Prophetic Experience

The next three paragraphs came from a prophetic experience. I do not believe prophecy should be used to establish doctrine in the church; only the written Word of God can be used for that. I am not trying to establish a doctrine here by sharing this prophetic experience, but I am sharing how I came to the following conclusions. Prophecy is sometimes given to illuminate doctrine and illuminate the Scriptures, but if we do not see it in the written Word it should not be accepted. I was given these prophetic experiences in order to see where the true spiritual authority often comes from and how much more we should be devoted to prayer and to honoring, even celebrating, mothers on the earth. In this I am speaking of both natural and spiritual mothers.

I have had several prophetic experiences in which I was standing before the throne of the Lord in heaven. In two of them I was able to observe that many, if not a majority, of those who were close to the Lord's throne were women. There are things in such experiences that you just know you are supposed to see or understand; I knew that most of these were mother intercessors who were the ones truly responsible for some of the great moves of God upon the earth. Most of these moves were led by men, who are known for them on the earth, but in heaven these women were known for them. They were the ones who carried the spiritual seed, nurtured and protected it until it matured.

It was then that I began to understand that many who are the most well-known on earth are not well-known in heaven, and many who are not well-known on earth are some of the most well-known in heaven. The hidden ministry of the intercessor was intended to be hidden, even in Scripture, until the day of judgment. In fact, this ministry loses its power when it becomes too well-known on the earth. However, those who "see" should recognize where true authority comes from. Having authority with God is much more important than having authority with men.

> I knew that most of these were mother intercessors who were the ones truly responsible for some of the great moves of God upon the earth.

After these experiences I started to believe that when John and Andrew came to Jesus and asked to sit at His right hand and left, He could not grant this because it was reserved. Many of those for whom it was prepared are women. Prayer can have more authority on the earth than the United Nations and all other seats of authority combined. For the most part, women have chosen this "best part" far more often than men.

Even so, the Lord is about to display true womanhood in all of its glory through the church. This will compel women to see and understand all that they were created to be. The Lord is also about to display true manhood in all of its glory and all that it is called to be through the church. This, too, will cause all men to understand who they were created to be. This will also make it possible for both men and women to accept and respect the place of the other. This world was not made to be either masculine or feminine, but the place where both could thrive as they were created.

> **Could there be a ministry more worthy of honor and support than the ministry of being a mother?**

It is also in this that true unity will come. The way I become one with my wife is not by making her into a man, but by honoring and appreciating her differences, seeing them as complimentary, not conflicting. Now let's look at the teaching ministry God has given to women, and how essential it is to a healthy church life. Then we will address the authority issue.

The Great Calling

In Proverbs 6:20-23 we read:

> **My son, observe the commandment of your father, and do not forsake the teaching of your mother;**
>
> **Bind them continually on your heart; tie them around your neck.**
>
> **When you walk about, they will guide you; when you sleep, they will watch over you; and when you awake, they will talk to you.**
>
> **For the commandment is a lamp, and the teaching is light; and reproofs for discipline are the way of life.**

Here we are told to observe the commandments of our fathers, and not forsake the *teachings* of our mothers. It is said that our basic character traits are set by the time we are four years old. Therefore, this is when teaching and instruction are the most critical. The mother's teaching has its greatest impact on the child during these most formative years, and this can have the greatest impact on the course of a person's life. Is there any teaching ministry more important than this? Could there be a ministry more worthy of honor and support than the ministry of being a mother?

In Exodus 20:12 we read the commandment to: **"Honor your father and your mother, that your days may be prolonged in the land which the Lord your God gives you."** In Ephesians 6:1-3, Paul restates this commandment, ensuring that it would receive the same compliance by those under the New Covenant: **"Children, obey your parents in the Lord, for this is right. Honor your father and mother (which is the first commandment with a promise), that it may be well with you, and that you may live long on the earth."** All of the commandments reveal God's standards for righteousness. Except for the ones commanding us to love, the commandment to honor our fathers and mothers is emphasized more in both the New and Old Testaments than all of the others. As Paul pointed out, this is actually the only commandment with a promise attached, and that promise is longevity.

The church has done a fair job of honoring spiritual fathers, but having been a Christian for almost thirty-five years now, I have not heard spiritual mothers even mentioned more than a couple of times. The commandment is that we honor both, yet I do not believe that much of the church even understands what a spiritual mother is. A good case can be made that the primary reason why so many churches and movements become spiritually irrelevant so fast, not having longevity, is because they do not honor both. If we are going to be the church that we have been called to be, we must recognize and honor both our spiritual fathers and mothers.

I confess to having a deep and growing love for Catholics, while at the same time having a great and deep grief for many of their doctrines and practices. The one that I especially consider an extreme is the degree to which the veneration of Mary has been taken. This was seared in my heart when I walked into the great cathedral in Cologne, Germany, and saw what I estimated to be more than a thousand candles burning under the picture of Mary, but just one flickering little candle burning under the picture of Jesus! However, I also think that Protestants and Evangelicals do not honor Mary, the mother of Jesus, enough, even though we are told in Scripture that she was to be honored so that all generations would call her blessed (see Luke 1:48). Maybe this is an overreaction to Catholic practices, but both are extremes.

> **If we are going to be the church that we have been called to be, we must recognize and honor both our spiritual fathers and mothers.**

Certainly that young girl who risked all that she did to carry and give birth to the Son of God is deserving of being considered one of the greatest heroes of the faith for all time. However, she did not just carry the seed of the Holy Spirit and give birth to the Son of God, but persevered with Him through the cross, and remained faithful to Him until the end, even when all but one of His apostles had fled in fear.

Though I consider it the most anointed movie ever made, I could hardly endure watching Mel Gibson's movie, *The Passion of the Christ*. Even knowing that it was a movie, and knowing that they were all actors, it was still almost unbearable to watch a portrayal of our King being tortured the way that He was. Yet Mary stood by her Son, beholding the real torture and crucifixion, which lasted many more hours than the movie, and she stayed with Him until the very end. Why? Because she was a mother.

> **Most of the great men and women of God can point to their mothers, like Solomon did, as the real reason behind their success.**

Mary is worthy of honor, not worship, and maybe more than any other person in the Gospels except her Son. God has deposited faithfulness and faith into motherhood, and it deserves such honor. However, we must now ask: How is it that Catholics would go to such extremes in honoring Mary, and not even allow women to be priests? This seems remarkably incongruous, but there are similar contradictions in the practices of much of the rest of the church concerning the place of women.

This is a matter that must be addressed and rectified if we are going to fulfill our full purpose. This is why Paul reminded Timothy that it was because of his mother and grandmother that he was in the faith (see II Timothy 1:5). We will also see how Paul, contrary to what many assert, gave such honor to women, their teaching ministry, and their authority. We will do this without in any way bending the Scriptures, but we will have to straighten out a few wrong interpretations, which are easily revealed as such.

Who Is the Priest?

This leads to another issue. There was a doctrine promulgated in the 1970s that the man was "the priest of the home." I felt at the time that this would be a devastating doctrine in the church, and I think we can see clearly now just how devastating it was. As stated, Timothy's mother and grandmother were responsible for him being in the faith. Most of the great men and women of God can point to their mothers, like Solomon did, as the real reason behind their success.

First, all Christians are called to be priests, not just men. This doctrine seemed to be an attempt to instill the importance of men being the spiritual heads of their homes, but it was very misguided. Priests are intercessors, and the fact is that, in general, women tend to be much better intercessors than men, and because of this doctrine, some of the best intercessors were neutralized.

Many people like to point to the failures of highly visible ministries during the 1980s as the reason for the great slide of moral integrity in the church, but I think at least a good part of this can be traced to some of the doctrines in the 1970s that took prayer, one of our greatest weapons, out of the hands of many who knew best how to use it.

If this doctrine was taken from the Old Covenant, the perpetrators should have followed the model to its conclusion. There was a division of authority between the kings and priests under the Old Covenant. The kings held secular authority in order to allow the priests to be devoted to the divine service and to teach the ways of the Lord to the people. Likewise, in the New Testament the man is the head of the home, but this is in order to take care of the management of the affairs so that the woman can be free to do that which is more important. In the Lord, those in authority are the servants of those under them.

What women are called to do in the home, in intercession, and teaching the children, is far more important than going out and making money. If we look at it from a worldly, human perspective in these times, in a society that scores value so much according to possessions and wealth, it is understandable why women staying at home with the children might think of themselves as second-class citizens. However, this will not be the case for anyone looking from the more important, spiritual perspective.

I personally have no trouble with women having careers and professions, and believe that they should be rewarded with both money and authority commensurate with their accomplishments, equal to men who do the same things, but that is a low calling, not the high calling that motherhood is. Even so, the real issue is: Are we doing the Lord's will? I have no doubt that many women are doing the Lord's will in the profession, but I also have no doubt that many, who may still be doing a great job and accomplishing much, have settled for less than they could have attained in this life by not esteeming their calling as mothers far above any secular profession. It is what we do for eternity that really counts. Many of the accomplishments that may have received the accolades of men will look very shallow on the Day of Judgment. The real issue is whether we were seeking first the kingdom of heaven in our pursuits, or our own interests.

In the Lord, those in authority are the servants of those under them.

The Greatest Wisdom

King Solomon was said to be the wisest man who ever lived, except of course for the Lord Jesus. After writing the book of Proverbs, which is the only book in the Bible devoted exclusively to wisdom, Solomon concluded it was: **"...the oracle which his mother taught him" (Proverbs 31:1).** The wisest man who ever ruled on earth was taught his great wisdom by his mother!

Solomon's mother knew that he was destined to be king, and she saw and devoted herself to preparing him for his destiny. It was an awesome calling to prepare the future king, but our children have a greater calling than Solomon; they are called to rule and reign with Christ. Therefore, every mother of a Christian child is a true "queen mother" who deserves even more honor than any queen mother of a mere earthly kingdom.

> **It is probably the intercession of mothers, in the natural and spiritual, that enable more people to assume their callings and purposes...**

The following statement by Solomon in the Song of Solomon is also quite enlightening:

> **Go forth, O daughters of Zion, and gaze on King Solomon with the crown with which his mother has crowned him on the day of his wedding, and on the day of his gladness of heart (Song of Solomon 3:11).**

Solomon was the son of David, the greatest king of Israel. He was the heir to the throne because of his father, yet here he confesses that it was his mother who crowned him.

If we read the story in Scripture, we see that one of Solomon's brothers was trying to seize the crown for himself when Solomon's mother went and interceded for her son with King David, and Solomon was then crowned. Likewise, it is probably the intercession of mothers, in the natural and spiritual, that enable more people to assume their callings and purposes than we will probably ever suspect until it is revealed to all on the Day of Judgment.

Again, we need to consider why there has been so much attention given to honoring spiritual fathers, but so little to spiritual mothers. It is probably because so much of that ministry is hidden, carried out in prayer before the Lord. Such ministry is still not esteemed in the church the way that it should be.

Some may have the argument that Solomon ended up falling, so his foundation must not have been as strong as it should have been. That is true, but I do not think it was because he honored his mother too much, or did not honor his father enough. The fact is Solomon did have longevity and was allowed to remain king for many years after he introduced apostasies into the nation. An argument could be made that this was actually the result of him honoring his father too much. By this I mean that Solomon only had his father's vision and when he finished building the house of the Lord, he did not have a vision of his own, so he drifted from the faith.

To truly honor our fathers and mothers does not mean that we cannot go farther than they did, or have a vision for things that they may not have had. In fact, if you listen to a truly loving father or mother, they delight in seeing their children go farther than they did. Our ceiling should be the floor of the next generation. The way they can honor us most is by taking what we leave to them and going much further.

The Lord Is Masculine

Another issue that must be settled is the fact that the Lord is masculine. Again, one of the devil's ultimate intentions to thwart the purpose of God is to blur the distinctions that God made between men and women. One of the ultimate conclusions and delusions of this apostasy is to try to make God into a woman. It is not "our mother in heaven," He is our Father in heaven. He did not create us Adam and Steve, but Adam and Eve. Jesus was a man and is *the man* Christ Jesus. As the Scripture makes clear, He continues to be the One as the mediator between God and man (see I Timothy 2:5). This cannot be compromised, and those who try to erode this clear teaching of Scripture are on the path to a profound deception and bondage, not liberty.

It is the delusion of the pretenders to true authority, who obviously know of their own inadequacy, to suppose that for them to ascend to their purpose they have to bring others lower. No true woman, who is confident in her own purpose, is in any way intimidated or offended by God being masculine or by any man being masculine. It is only the weak, insecure, or deceived who think that for them to advance they have to change others, or anything external for that matter.

Let us also consider this—the Lord is so secure in who He is that He is not intimidated by His bride, the church, doing even greater works than He did. In fact, He wants her to. Likewise, no true man who is secure in his manhood is intimidated by his wife doing even greater things than he has done. In fact, a true man will applaud, support, and encourage her, just as the Lord does His bride.

The bride of Christ may do greater works than the Lord did while on the earth, but she will do it through His power and authority. Likewise, every husband and wife team is a partnership. However, some of the great men of God and great men of faith are those who allow their wives to be all that they are called to be, and do all that they are called to do.

Women do not have to emasculate the men to be able to minister or take the authority that men are called to walk in, but rather the reverse is true—they need to find men who are men and who are secure enough to let them be who they were created to be. The only freedom that any of us will ever know is to be who God created us to be and allow others to do the same.

Women in Business

It is fitting that Solomon concludes his great book of wisdom, the book of Proverbs, with an entire chapter devoted to the perfect woman. It is also noteworthy that some of the most esteemed characteristics of this woman were her business skills. She was into real estate, developing, manufacturing, and was a remarkable manager. Her husband delighted in her for it.

If you want a New Testament reference, Lydia was a businesswoman in Phillipi, the first to receive the Word of God in Asia, and it was in her house that the disciples met (see Acts 16:14, 40). God has given to women some of the greatest gifts for business and management, and the truly wise men appreciate it, and not only free them to do it, but honor and appreciate them for it.

> **One thing we are committed to is basing our doctrines and practices on Scripture above all things.**

The Great Controversy

All of this brings up an important and controversial issue: What about the New Testament Scriptures that say women should not be allowed to teach or even speak in the church? That is a good question. One thing we are committed to is basing our doctrines and practices on Scripture above all things. First let us look at I Timothy 2:11-15:

> **Let a woman quietly receive instruction with entire submissiveness.**
>
> **But I do not allow a woman to teach or exercise authority over a man, but to remain quiet.**
>
> **For it was Adam who was first created, and then Eve.**
>
> **And it was not Adam who was deceived, but the woman being quite deceived, fell into transgression.**

> **But women shall be preserved through the bearing of children if they continue in faith and love and sanctity with self-restraint.**

Now let us consider that many have taken this statement as a conclusion that because Eve was deceived, women are more prone to deception than men. How many wars were started by women? How many cults, sects, or false teachings? How many false religions? Now answer these same questions about men. So do you still think women are more prone to deception than men? These obvious facts have made this an issue for many over the years. Then why would Paul say this? That is a question that deserves an answer. Even if this statement is true as intended, if only Eve was deceived, then Adam knew what he was doing! How smart was that?

Before addressing this let us look at I Corinthians 14:34-35, which says:

> **Let the women keep silent in the churches; for they are not permitted to speak, but let them subject themselves, just as the Law also says.**
>
> **And if they desire to learn anything, let them ask their own husbands at home; for it is improper for a woman to speak in church.**

These Scriptures are so clear and straightforward. How could we possibly doubt that this was exactly what the apostle meant? I will give you six reasons:

1) It is in contradiction to other Scriptures.
2) It is contrary to the entire weight of Scripture.

3) It is in contradiction to Paul's own practice.

4) Nowhere does the Law say this.

5) The fruit that has come from this interpretation is bad.

6) If we are to honor our mothers, what could possibly be more dishonoring than to tell them that they are not even able to speak in church?

The main reasons why these two verses have been challenged by sincere Bible-believing Christians is when they are taken literally, they stand in contradiction to other Scriptures, which cannot be overlooked. A basic principle of biblical interpretation is found in Psalm 119:160: **"The sum of Thy word is truth, and every one of Thy righteous ordinances is everlasting."** If there is ever an apparent contradiction in Scripture, there is a reason for it.

A basic principle of biblical interpretation is even if you do not understand the reason for such a seeming contradiction, you never base your doctrine on the one or two Scriptures that stand in contradiction to the rest of the Bible, but always go with the **"sum"** of the Word or the weight of Scripture. Even so, this does not justify overlooking any Scripture. If there is a seeming contradiction in Scripture, we can be assured it is intended to be there by God. The tension between seeming contradictions is meant to drive us to a deeper understanding. I say here "seeming" contradictions because even in those that seem the most apparent, I have learned there is always a higher perspective that will bring both into light

and into harmony with each other, regardless of how impossible this may seem.

> **The tension between seeming contradictions is meant to drive us to a deeper understanding.**

Another problem that scholars and leaders of the church have had in literally interpreting these two verses is that nowhere in the Law does it say that women are not permitted to speak in the congregation. Paul, who had been the "Pharisee of Pharisees" would have known this better than anyone. This seems to confirm what theologians have asserted, that Paul was quoting here a letter or a report *from* the Corinthians concerning practices they had adopted and was replying to them. These consider the next verses to be Paul's reply to the Corinthian practice of not allowing women to speak:

Was it from you that the word of God first went forth? Or has it come to you only?

If anyone thinks he is a prophet or spiritual, let him recognize that the things which I write to you are the Lord's commandment.

But if anyone does not recognize this, he is not recognized.

Therefore, my brethren, desire earnestly to prophesy, and do not forbid to speak in tongues.

But let all things be done properly and in an orderly manner (I Corinthians 14:36-40).

> Paul named Priscilla first, indicating by the clear protocol of the times that Priscilla was the preeminent one instructing Apollos.

My wife and daughter recently visited the church in Corinth, Greece, and were given another interesting explanation for these verses. It was explained to them that many of the temple prostitutes had been converted in Corinth, and by custom, had their heads shaved. To protect them from more scorn in the church, Paul issued a decree for the church in Corinth that all women should wear head coverings. Also, because of the heated bickering between the women of the church and these converted temple prostitutes, Paul also mandated that all of the women should keep silent in the church. They asserted that this was only for the church in Corinth

because of this special circumstance, which is why Paul did not mandate this practice in any other churches. It is true that none of the other churches in the New Testament were given this instruction or had this practice.

There have been many other interesting and sometimes convincing explanations given to these verses by some of the great teachers in history. Probably the best reason why these verses are not to be taken as a doctrine that Paul intended for the whole church is that it is in contradiction to Paul's own practice.

Paul acknowledges in Romans that Priscilla and Aquila instructed Apollos, who himself became one of the greatest teachers in the first century church. Paul named Priscilla first, indicating by the clear protocol of the times that Priscilla was the preeminent one instructing Apollos. It was even considered in the first century to have been an intentional statement of liberation for women in the church to teach men. Paul further established this at the end of this letter to the Romans. When he listed those that the church in Rome should greet, Priscilla was again named first as if to verify his intention in this (see Romans 16:3).

In Romans 16:7 Paul writes, **"Greet Andronicus and Junias, my kinsmen, and my fellow prisoners, who are outstanding among the apostles, who also were in Christ before me."** This clearly names a woman among the apostles. We are also told that the apostolic office was given to be a "witness of the resurrection" (see Acts 1:22, 4:33).

It is noteworthy that the very first witness of the Lord's resurrection was a woman. She actually bore witness of it to the apostles, who were at the time cowering in fear and did not believe the witness!

Obviously it takes far more bending of Scripture to hold to the doctrine that women should not be allowed to speak in church, or have authority, than it does to accept that they should. However, both positions or conclusions can leave unanswered questions for those who are sincere seekers of truth and genuinely desire to obey the Word of God. I, therefore, do not believe that either position should be held so dogmatically that we allow it to divide us. We must so esteem the Scriptures that we would never rationalize a text we do not agree with. Having heard and read a multitude of teachings on this subject, and having examined it myself, I base my doctrine and practice on what I consider to be the weight of the Scriptures rather than a single text that seems in contradiction to it, while remaining tolerant of those who see it otherwise.

There are many other ways in which both the Lord and the apostles honored and elevated the status of women in bold departures from the practice of the times. As stated, the Lord chose a woman to be the first to see and declare His resurrection, which was in fact the apostolic mandate. As He promised in Psalm 68:11, **"The Lord gives the command; the women who proclaim the good tidings are a great host."** Without question, some of the greatest evangelists in history have been women,

and some of the greatest today, who I think merit being considered true apostles, are women.

A third major, theological problem of not allowing women to speak in the church is that we have women named as prophetesses in both the Old and New Testaments. This includes Miriam and Deborah in the Old Testament (see Exodus 15:20, Judges 4:4) and Anna and Philip's daughters in the New Testament (see Acts 21:9). We are also told in the books of Joel and Acts that when the Lord pours out His Spirit, our sons and daughters will prophesy (see Joel 2:29). Would God give someone the gift of prophecy, but not allow them to speak?

> I base my doctrine and practice on what I consider to be the weight of the Scriptures rather than a single text

It should also be noted that just before Paul seemingly mandated in his letter to the Corinthians that women should not be allowed to speak, he wrote that if they prophesied, they should do so with their head covered. How could they prophesy if they could not speak?

Another major problem that we have if we do not allow women to teach or speak in the church may be the most important of all. Could there be anything more dishonoring to our mothers than to tell them that they are not even allowed to speak in church? These are the ones who have probably been our most important teachers. These are the ones who not only gave life to us, but nurtured and taught us from the beginning. The Lord thought it was so important for us to honor them that it is the only commandment He gave with a promise attached to it—the promise of long life, which to most would be one of the greatest promises of all.

> We must rise up and preempt the enemy by taking the high ground on every important issue of our times.

Summary

We will be limited in our spiritual advancement until this matter is resolved in the church. This involves more than half of the present citizens of the kingdom, more than half of the members of the body of Christ. Until women are allowed to function in the place to which they have been called, the body of Christ will be at best like a stroke victim that is half paralyzed.

The church is called to be the light of the world. This implies that we must have the answers to the world's pressing problems. **"Where the Spirit of the Lord is there is liberty" (II Corinthians 3:17).** Yet the church in our times has not only failed to lead the great liberation movements of recent times, we have often been their greatest enemies. This must change.

When we fail to lead with sound biblical truth, the enemy will fill the vacuum with every form of perversion. Many leaders in the church have mistaken the nature of those who filled the vacuum as the nature of the whole movement. The primary reason why there are such perversions and extremes in the women's liberation movement is because the church did not take the lead in setting women free from the oppression they had been subject to. This movement should not have to be led by women; godly men who have the heart of God for His children and household should have led it long ago!

We must rise up and preempt the enemy by taking the high ground on every important issue of our times. Even if we are starting late, as much of the church is doing in relation to women's liberation, it is not too late to seize the high ground of sound biblical truth, take our stand, and push the darkness back.

One of the great problems that we have in the church today is that there are many teachers, but not many fathers. Most whom I have heard described as spiritual fathers are older men who have served faithfully for many years, and are not spiritual fathers, but just old teachers. A father is not just someone who is old, but someone who reproduces. Most men become fathers when they are young, not old. A spiritual father is someone who reproduces his ministry and the grace that he has been given in others. However, for a man to become a father, there must be a woman present. For a man to become a father, a woman must also become a mother. We must start recognizing and honoring both our spiritual fathers and mothers.

We need to recognize and honor the women who carry the seed of the Lord through intercession, and then nurture the young with words of life and a constant vigilance. These spiritual mothers will be some of the best teachers of newborn believers, just as mothers are the best teachers of young children. This is not to negate the place of the men in this, but God made men and women to be different and did divide the labor required to propagate the race. This does not negate the place of women teaching on the highest or more advanced levels either, but the foundations are more important to lay properly. This is a great gift and honor that the Lord has given especially to women.

When the world sees godly women of the church in their God-given roles, being fulfilled to the uttermost because they are being who they were called to be, motherhood and womanhood will be esteemed as the glorious callings that they are.

The Lord wants to display womanhood just as He wants to display His bride, the church. The church is a bride, and is referred to in the feminine because that is the nature she is called to reveal. The church will never be able to do this without women being in their place.

> **We need to recognize and honor the women who carry the seed of the Lord through intercession, and then nurture the young with words of life and a constant vigilance.**

We also need to understand that the bride is to be like "an army with banners," which is quite masculine, and we will not be that until men are in their place. These may seem to be contradictory natures, but the male and female natures perfectly compliment one another when they are right. When the Lord is finished with His church, the world will see in it the perfect glory of both the man and the woman. Men will look at the men in the church and say, "That is what I am called to be." Women will look at the women in the church and say, "That is what I am called to be." True unity will only come when men are men and women are allowed to be women. There would be no Jezebels if there were no Ahabs. Until we are both free, neither can be free. ∎

Humble HEART

by Sally Boenau

Jesus, You have given me a most
important part—
A sharing of Your precious yoke—
a meek and humble heart.

The rage of all that's worldly in my
thought and word and deed
Cannot destroy Your living Words—
Your incorruptible seed.

A union of our spirits, an adoption
of my soul,
An ever-increasing knowing of just
how You make me whole.

Jesus, how surprised I am to find
what makes for life—
What God must cut away of me with
His ever-living knife.

The pain, the strain, conflicting thought
of what is really right;
The shame, the blame one must endure
to exercise new sight.

When passion and my indignation
explode at what's unfair,
And standing firm and loving are the
things I can hardly bear,
I think of You and how You felt when
You were in a garden,
And how your path through darkest
night was one that led to pardon.

Oh thank You, thank You faithful
Witness, for showing me the way—
Humbleness of heart and mind will
be my choice this day.

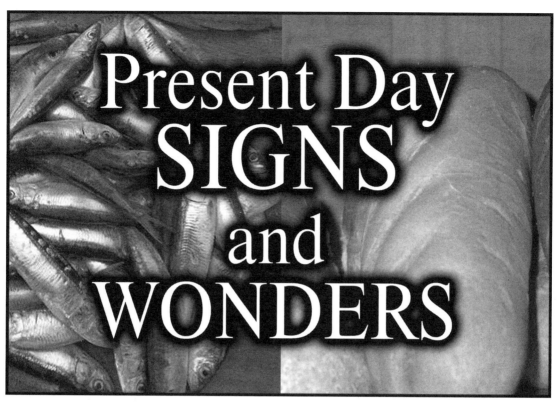

Present Day SIGNS and WONDERS

by Paul Keith Davis

A. W. Tozer said it best with the title of his classic book, *The Pursuit of God*. The ultimate adventure for this generation is the pursuit of the Lord Jesus Christ. There can be no greater endeavor than to know Him as personally as He may be known. The Scripture promises, if we draw near to Him, He will draw near to us.

The "one thing" that characterized King David's life was his hungry heart. David loved the Lord's presence more than anything else, and for that the Lord loved and trusted him (see James 4:8). Devotion to becoming God's "friend" is our most noble pilgrimage (see John 15:15).

Even so, we are also given clear and concise biblical affirmations of the functioning of His victorious church. There is a mandate placed upon the latter-day church to gather the harvest and awaken a misguided generation to its righteous destiny. To accomplish this mandate, we must be endowed with heaven's virtue and empowered with the overcoming victory of the Lord's redemptive work. The Lord's example and demonstration of mighty works are necessary for this inevitable responsibility, and as He promised, even greater works (see John 14:12).

The gospel of the kingdom is the power of God leading to salvation. This gospel does not merely consist in Words, but also in God's sovereign power. The ministry of signs and wonders does not diminish the supernatural nature of God's written Word; it confirms it.

God's revealed Word is plainly established by the Holy Spirit's endorsement. He demonstrates approval or affirmation through signs, wonders, and manifestations of the Spirit.

According to the writer of Hebrews, the Lord's Spirit works with His people by: **testifying with them, both by signs and wonders and by various miracles and by gifts of the Holy Spirit according to His own will (Hebrews 2:4).**

> **There must be a balance in our personal endeavor to know the Lord and our mandate to win this generation through the Spirit's demonstration of power.**

God's power and witness are fundamentally necessary for us to accomplish heaven's blueprint. We simply do not posses the ability within ourselves to accomplish God's ultimate plan. We need God and the embodiment of His Spirit that provides power. Even so, as wonderful and necessary as incredible displays of the Spirit are, we cannot allow them to supersede our quest to know Him as the Living Word.

A Word of Wisdom

John G. Lake was a man used powerfully as a missionary to South Africa and healing evangelist throughout America. History now documents wonderful miracles and spiritual wonders that the Lord performed through this humble servant. Nevertheless, in 1925 he discerned that his generation "missed the mark" by being more captured by the phenomena of God than the Person. The same was true in the days of Moses when he said:

> **You have seen all that the LORD did before your eyes in the land of Egypt to Pharaoh and all his servants and all his land;**
>
> **the great trials which your eyes have seen, those great signs and wonders.**
>
> **Yet to this day the LORD has not given you a heart to know, nor eyes to see, nor ears to hear (Deuteronomy 29:2-4).**

Consequently, there must be a balance in our personal endeavor to know the Lord and our mandate to win this generation through the Spirit's demonstration of power. Through fellowship with Him, our spiritual senses become keenly sensitive to His voice and the message being confirmed through signs and wonders. These prerogatives must be maintained in the proper biblical order.

The Original Model

The ministry of the early church was profound on many levels. By natural standards, the credentials of the individuals utilized were not impressive.

For the most part, their personal abilities left them unqualified for their pioneering assignment. Even so, they received an impartation from God that validated their mission and facilitated the revelation of God's kingdom. They believed God and trusted not in their own strength, but in His.

The Bible plainly outlines the many signs and miraculous wonders that accompanied the early church in their task. The Scripture tells us that reverential awe fell upon many as miraculous wonders took place. People were added to the church daily and God's name was notably glorified (see Acts 2:41-43).

These are the same results we need today. Our task is no less important or difficult than the one given to the early apostolic church. In fact, in many ways ours is even more intense. Therefore, we need all that the early church had and in multiplied fashion.

The early disciples preached the gospel of the kingdom and ministered to people's spirits, souls, and bodies. They did not "shrink from declaring the whole purpose of God" (see Acts 20:27).

Furthermore, in the midst of persecution and an unbelieving generation, their message was confirmed with the Holy Spirit's power imparted to them on the Day of Pentecost. It was their prayer that the Lord would:

> ...grant to Your servants that with all boldness they may speak Your word,
>
> by stretching out Your hand to heal, and that signs and wonders may be done through the name of Your holy Servant Jesus (Acts 4:29-30 NKJV).

God's power is a witness to the gospel. That is why the early church passionately prayed to be empowered with signs and wonders as an instrument to convey the good news of the kingdom and win the lost.

The early disciples preached the gospel of the kingdom and ministered to people's spirits, souls, and bodies.

A Twentieth Century Token

In each expression of spiritual outpouring throughout church history, God's presence was authenticated with various expressions of His Spirit. During the early twentieth century, Maria Woodworth-Etter's ministry was characterized by wonderful manifestations of spiritual signs and miraculous wonders like those done by the early apostolic believers. Marvelous displays of healing and deliverance were prevalent in her meetings. Additionally, it was not uncommon for many people to "fall under the power" and remain in that condition for many days. The Bible promised to "bear witness" to the kingdom message with diverse and various miracles and gifts of the Holy Spirit (see Hebrews 2:4).

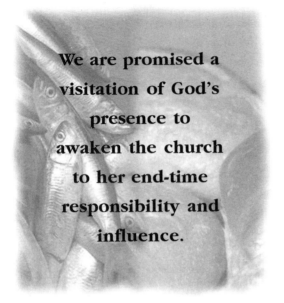

We are promised a visitation of God's presence to awaken the church to her end-time responsibility and influence.

Oftentimes doctors would examine the people while in this condition to determine their heart rate and other vital statistics. In each case it was reported that every individual was in a perfectly healthy state. They were overshadowed with God's Spirit and prostrate before God without food, water, or movement. It was reported that in some cases people remained in this condition for as long as seven days. This was confirmed by both the secular and Christian media.

Tremendous testimonies of healing, deliverance, and divine commissions were reported following the encounters. During these experiences it was well-documented that many people would be commissioned to foreign lands and come out of the experience able to fluently speak the language of the nation

to which they were sent. Furthermore, many accounts report the spirit of conviction that accompanied these manifestations to such an extent that the most hardened characters melted into weeping repentance.

This was a token of the heritage of God's people and the empowerment of His presence essential in the fulfillment of our latter-day mandate.

A Present Sign and Wonder

There exists an elevated atmosphere of anticipation and encouragement for this generation to experience profound expressions of God's power. We are promised a visitation of God's presence to awaken the church to her end-time responsibility and influence. We are now beginning to see more evidence of this in the Western church. God's strategic plan is unfolding at an escalated pace.

This past February, David and Donna Kelly hosted a conference in Cincinnati, Ohio. Wanda and I joined Rick Joyner, James Goll, and Patricia King as the speakers. At this conference the Lord granted a wonderful affirmation. It was indeed a sign and a wonder that has generated fruitful results and mobilized faith in countless believers. The theme was "Engaging Heaven." It has been the quest of many individuals and fellowships to be awakened with acute spiritual eyes and ears that provide hearts of understanding and cooperation with heaven. During the conference, the Lord's Spirit provided specific endorsement to the importance of this theme and its current relevance.

According to Proverbs 29:18: **"where there is no vision, the people are unrestrained"** and perish. This phrase conveys the necessity for the spirit of revelation to exist in God's people in order for there to be advancement. The Hebrew word used for **"vision"** implies "open vision" for communicating God's heart and strategic design. Revelation provides spiritual eyes that see and ears that hear, thereby facilitating hearts with comprehension.

On the first evening of the conference, the host pastors, along with numerous other workers, friends, and technicians visibly saw and spoke with an individual whom they have known for years. This brother is an itinerant minister from Nashville who had planned to attend the conference. The people at the registration desk assisted him with his name badge and conference information. Also, several people spoke with him on the opening evening of the conference, and most said that his short response was merely a word or blessing. The interesting thing is, this brother was in Nashville, Tennessee at the time these appearances occurred.

An Extraordinary Appearance

Weeks earlier, the Kelly's leadership team and intercessory base felt compelled to initiate a forty day fast leading up to the conference. There seemed to be a weightiness associated with heaven's mandate for the gathering. The Holy Spirit encouraged them by releasing a prophetic word expressing His desire to deeply impact the attendees and the region's spiritual atmosphere. The battles have been long and wearisome, but these prophetic messages of hope and destiny provide encouragement to leadership and the Lord's body. The Lord is granting wonderful tokens of confidence to position us for our spiritual release.

> Revelation provides spiritual eyes that see and ears that hear, thereby facilitating hearts with comprehension.

The decreed fast ended on February 16 and the conference began on Thursday, February 17. During the opening evening, someone with the identical appearance of the brother from Nashville was clearly seen in the balcony. The host pastors acknowledged his presence during the opening session prompting others in the balcony to embrace and greet him.

The following morning, February 18, this brother came to the meetings, but disclosed that he had departed Nashville at 2 a.m. in order to arrive in time for the morning session. Naturally, the Kelly's attempted to correct this and acknowledged that he was actually in the service the previous evening. He had been publicly acknowledged and greeted by many friends.

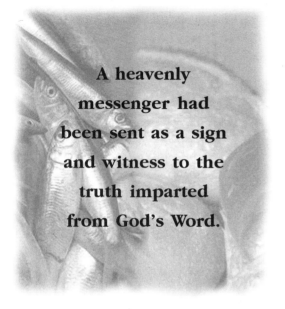

A heavenly messenger had been sent as a sign and witness to the truth imparted from God's Word.

Surprised at their insistence, he adamantly denied being in the service the previous evening. He had been in a fellowship gathering in Nashville with other believers until 11 p.m. This fact has been confirmed and documented by witnesses. It was then that the Kelly's realized that something extraordinary had occurred. A heavenly messenger had been sent as a sign and witness to the truth imparted from God's Word.

Fruitful Results

Naturally, these unusual signs and wonders do not occur needlessly. There must be some fruit or affirmation that is generated which advances God's kingdom. The Lord very often allows manifestations of His Spirit with signs and wonders as:

1. A witness to the messages presented and their present emphasis.
2. An encouragement to the faith of His people.
3. Mobilization of His body into His plan and into their destiny.
4. Spiritual awakening to the lost and lukewarm.

This was the fruit of the sign and wonder in Cincinnati.

Numerous witnesses have been interviewed on tape verifying their encounters with the messenger from God who took on the appearance of this brother as an affirmation of the spiritual realities being imparted during the conference. There has been a great surge of faith birthed in God's people as a result of this sign.

(More information and documentation on this occurrence can be obtained from David and Donna Kelly: http://passionandfire.org).

Entertaining Angels

This was quite an unusual occurrence but one that has been extensively scrutinized and validated. The Bible provides the only source of genuine affirmation of such an encounter. The Scripture admonishes us to:

Let love of the brethren continue.

Do not neglect to show hospitality to strangers, for by this some have entertained angels without knowing it (Hebrews 13:1-2).

The Bible records countless instances of angelic appearances that marked seasons of transition and advancement. This is especially true in the early apostolic church. There is an essential cooperation between heaven and earth.

We discover the Lord Jesus walking along the road to Emmaus in "another form" in the Gospel of Luke. The two disciples did not recognize Him until He came into their home and broke bread before them (see Luke 24).

In the book of Acts, we also notice Peter's supernatural deliverance from jail. As he came to the home of the disciples, the young girl who opened the door was startled to see who she perceived was Peter. Upon reporting this to the other disciples, they responded that it must have been his angel. This clearly implies that there were spiritual messengers working with them who took the form and appearance of the disciples.

This gospel of the kingdom was first declared by the Lord, evidenced by the Holy Spirit, and endorsed by God. He showed His approval of the gospel of power through signs and wonders and miraculous manifestations of the heavenly realm. Angelic appearances and supernatural signs awaken people from apathy and lethargy and re-ignite hearts that have grown cold or lukewarm.

God's Motivation

It is not my intent to overly emphasize signs and wonders, but rather the messages they convey. There must also be a genuine fruitfulness that comes from the manifestation of the Spirit. To more fully understand our mission and function on earth, we must also comprehend God's motivation. Our heavenly Father's desire is to display His glory and bring the full measure of His reward to His Son. This is accomplished through the preaching of His Word and the testimony of His power.

> **Angelic appearances and supernatural signs awaken people from apathy and lethargy and re-ignite hearts that have grown cold or lukewarm.**

When our motivations are firmly planted in the Lord's heart, then we are biblically justified when we long to see manifestations of His Spirit that glorify His name and convey salvation to the lost. The book of Acts alone records as many as seventeen instances of conversions birthed out of supernatural encounters.

Ultimately, our highest purpose is to delight in God and display the essence of who He is to a needy generation. We simply cannot accomplish this mandate in our own strength. We need His empowering Presence and the vindication of His Spirit. ∎

BORN FOR BATTLE

All Scriptures are New International Version unless otherwise indicated.

by Colin Brown

A line has been drawn! An epic spiritual battle is looming larger by the day. Those who know they have been born for battle have been summoned to fight the good fight. Arising is a corporate **"man after my own heart; he will do everything I want him to do" (Acts 13:22).**

Armed with the grace of God, a valiant and uncompromising new leadership is emerging—an army and family devoted to the Lord and truth. A common proclamation among their ranks echoes David's valor: **"For who is God besides the Lord? And who is the Rock except our God?" (Psalm 18:31)**

An acute awareness among them is that the kingdom of God is near. With boldness and humility, they are standing firm and moving in step with the Spirit. Wisdom guards their focus for they are mindful of their weaknesses, agreeing, **"But we have this treasure in jars of clay to show that this all-surpassing power is from God and not from us" (II Corinthians 4:7).**

Power Lines

An irrepressible force for advancing the kingdom of light is in the making. There are strategic and vital connections among the troops being put in place. These "power lines" are the result of sincere and heartfelt relational connections.

These powerful points of contact between the troops, while profound, usually occur with a quiet simplicity and little fanfare. To experience this work of the Spirit is to know the very real difference between the yoke the world places on us to make things happen as distinct from how Jesus does it. This yoke of the call to His service, as a call to battle, and to revive the battle weary, is: **"Walk with Me and work with Me—watch how I do it...Keep company with Me"** (Matthew 11:29-30 The Message).

No soldier of the Lord Jesus Christ is called to be isolated or out on his or her own. We are each remarkably interwoven together in our union with the Lord, as a tapestry of extraordinary handiwork. Each of us are enlisted as a vital part of a great family, army, and fellowship on earth, intimately related to the great company of witnesses and veterans in heaven, who have fought the good fight of faith before us.

This present greatest of movements among the troops ever to be witnessed is progressively gathering momentum and generating a synergy of the Spirit where: **"Five of you will chase a hundred, and a hundred of you will chase ten thousand, and your enemies will fall by the sword before you"** (Leviticus 26:8).

The Blessing of Strong Opposition

Opposition sharpens and defines us! Politically speaking, it has been said, "Strong opposition always leads to good government." This is true for the church where in the wisdom of God, a powerful and unrelenting enemy does us much good. Facing such opposition keeps us on our knees, on our toes, and on the edge of our seat in the very best sense.

We are being made to be **"dressed ready for service"** (Luke 12:35).

Developing the character of the Lord Jesus in the church through such tough spiritual warfare, even on our own soil, is integral to this calling in being born for battle. Remember that this fight is not against flesh and blood, and that the weapons of our warfare are not the weapons of this world (see Ephesians 6:10-18; II Corinthians 10:3-5).

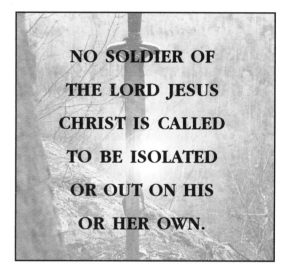

NO SOLDIER OF THE LORD JESUS CHRIST IS CALLED TO BE ISOLATED OR OUT ON HIS OR HER OWN.

Joseph's ability to govern with wisdom in Egypt was learned this way. In the face of fierce opposition, so very close to home, the true character of his heart was solicited to be strong. In summary of the tremendous conflict he endured, he nobly declared, **"You intended to harm me, but God intended it for good to accomplish what is now being done, the saving of many lives"** (Genesis 50:20).

Paul likewise sought to encourage his Corinthian friends, openly sharing the difficulties confronted on the battlefield of our calling, and the importance of prayer for each other, especially when the heat is on.

We do not want you to be uninformed, brothers, about the hardships we suffered in the province of Asia. We were under great pressure, far beyond our ability to endure, so that we despaired even of life.

Indeed, in our hearts we felt the sentence of death. But this happened that we might not rely on ourselves but on God, who raises the dead.

He has delivered us from such a deadly peril, and he will deliver us. On him we have set our hope that he will continue to deliver us,

as you help us by your prayers. Then many will give thanks on our behalf for the gracious favor granted us in answer to the prayers of many (II Corinthians 1:8-11).

> RETREATING AS A RESULT OF FOCUSING ON OUR INADEQUACIES OR FAILURES IS NOT AN OPTION.

Faithfulness through thick and thin is a powerful and telling sign of the love of Christ having worked deeply in the hearts of the sons and daughters of the King.

These overcomers triumph through Him against the pride filled notions of another god. Like Habakkuk, they have received the revelation: **"See, he is puffed up; his desires are not upright—but the righteous will live by his faith"** (Habakkuk 2:4).

Retreating Is Not An Option!

Retreating as a result of focusing on our inadequacies or failures is not an option. Turning to the Lord is always and the only right thing to do. Faith is the resolute focus in the eyes of Abraham's offspring. **"Against all hope, Abraham in hope believed ...Without weakening in his faith, he faced the fact that his body was as good as dead...Yet he did not waver through unbelief regarding the promise of God, but was strengthened in his faith and gave glory to God, being fully persuaded that God had power to do what he had promised"** (Romans 4:18-21).

In this theater of great spiritual conflict, God's power is seen in the grace we are given to rise above the darkness and troubles of the hour. These include both inward and outward turmoil and troubles, like those that Job faced.

His very great and precious promises found in His Word, along with the grace of the prophetic that stands in keeping with the Scriptures, spur us on beyond the thought of ever retreating. **"And let us consider how we may spur one another on toward love and good deeds. Let us not give up meeting together, as some are in the habit of** doing, but encouraging one another—and all the more as you see the Day approaching" (Hebrews 10:24-25).

In Rick Joyner's book, *The Torch and The Sword*, an extraordinary and very wise young girl (see Chapter 3), emulates the character of Abraham's faith, in view of the battles she faces personally and otherwise. She imparts some great gems of wisdom, like: "They have us completely surrounded now. But anyone with courage to keep moving even when they are attacked can make it through their ranks...I was told that when they saw my resolve that they would give way before me, and they did."

In speaking lovingly, yet soberly about her mother, the young girl said, "She taught me very well, but she could not do what she taught me to do... When she hesitated and started to retreat she was quickly overcome. She then began ridiculing me with the rest of them. Once you begin to retreat before the evil ones, you are easy prey for them. She is now one of their prisoners...I could not let that stop me."

This young girl showed a wisdom that surpassed her mother's. How sobering that what our mouths declare that we wholeheartedly believe is only of real substance in how we live, especially in the theatre of battle. Our Christlike courage is most evident in the face of great difficulty and adversity. Be assured, what we say we believe will be thoroughly tested. Testing will surely come!

Even when those who are dearest to us stumble, our focus must remain primarily on the Rock. **"You will keep in** perfect peace him whose mind is steadfast, because he trusts in you. Trust in the Lord forever, for the Lord, the Lord, is the Rock eternal" (Isaiah 26:3-4).

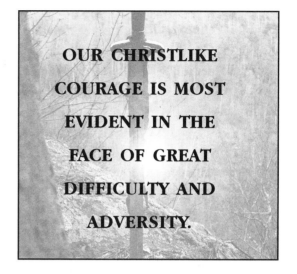

OUR CHRISTLIKE COURAGE IS MOST EVIDENT IN THE FACE OF GREAT DIFFICULTY AND ADVERSITY.

A Soldier's Prophetic Dream

The landscape of the church is completely changing! A very different outlook from what we have known will emerge. I came to understand this in a dream I had in October 2002, which helped me to appreciate what God is doing with His church, to conform us to the image of His Son.

I had gone to sleep very tired. I dreamed that I was riding with a good friend in his car. Eventually, we found ourselves at a beach that was very familiar to me because I had spent much time there when I was younger.

I got out of the car and walked toward an elevated view of the beachfront. Its landscape had changed significantly, and it was clear that a powerful storm had altered it.

As I stood there, I observed various types of heavy machinery on the sand. The workers were determined to recover the familiar old landscape to which they were so accustomed. I realized that this was a picture of how many in church are resistant to change, even while the Lord is reshaping the church as seems best to Him (see Jeremiah 18:1-6).

THIS EXTRAORDINARY AND AWESOME WORK WAS AN ACT OF LOVE AND GREAT KINDNESS, AS WELL AS JUSTICE AND MERCY.

I was then shocked to see another storm in the form of a powerful, sandy whirlwind, bearing down upon these workers and their man-made devices. They had no knowledge of or sensitivity to the danger they were facing. Yet, even more gripping was the closeness and direction of many more of these powerful whirlwinds out of the sea that were headed straight for the beach. Beyond a shadow of a doubt, these winds of the Spirit again would totally and radically change the landscape of the beach.

As I stood there seeing what those on the beach could not, I was consumed with a profound sense of the fear of the Lord. This extraordinary and awesome work was an act of love and great kindness, as well as justice and mercy. The kingdom of heaven was at hand.

All the same, as much as I wanted to, I could not make those on the beach see that their efforts were working against the Lord's purposes. Nor could I alert them to the great danger they faced because of the noise of their machinery.

As I considered this insight after waking, I realized how much the fear of change makes for such resistant hearts, and seeks to incapacitate a new and fresh movement, even the movement of God. However, when the Lord is moving and recovering His domain as He is now doing, nothing can alter what He has decreed. A line has been drawn!

The wisdom of Gamaliel remains by addressing those who stand in opposition to the very One they think they defend. **"Leave these men alone! Let them go! For if their purpose or activity is of human origin, it will fail. But if it is from God, you will not be able to stop these men; you will only find yourselves fighting against God"** (Acts 5:38-39).

The Maturity of a Soldier's Character

Those who were born for battle and have an understanding of the times must focus their attention primarily on the Lord Himself, not their opposition, inwardly or outwardly. As one senior officer put it to a younger fellow soldier: **"Endure hardship with us like a good soldier of Christ Jesus. No one serving as a soldier gets involved in civilian affairs, he wants to please his commanding officer"** (II Timothy 2:3-4).

Rick Joyner has said, "Our first goal must be to confront and overcome our personal demons and our personal fears, so that we can grow in the authority to take on bigger demons and set other people free... We can win this war if we grow in faith. True faith...is the result of a living relationship with the God who loves us, has called us, and will empower us to do all that He created us to do" (*Breaking the Power of Evil*, pgs. 40-41).

The apprenticeship of faith and the maturity of the soldier's character of heart warrants more attention than most other matters and things. The real changes at hand are related to the condition and health of the human heart. Maturity is deeply connected to the wisdom that says, **"Above all else, guard your heart, for it is the wellspring of life"** (Proverbs 4:23).

Finishing Well

These are both exciting and sobering days. To have been born for battle at such a time as this is ranked among the highest of honors. How blessed we are! All the same, we are called to walk a narrow path indeed. Our personal and corporate vigilance is as crucial as David's, where our choices have eternal implications. Let us together, before the Lord, choose well!

"His (God's) **intent was that now, through the church, the manifold wisdom of God should be made known to the rulers and authorities in the heavenly realms,**

according to his eternal purpose which he accomplished in Christ Jesus our Lord" (Ephesians 3:10-11).

For those born for battle, this unique day is an opportunity for embracing the worth and surpassing greatness of knowing Jesus our Lord, Savior, and Friend. What a privilege and honor to know the power of His resurrection and to participate in the fellowship of His sufferings, by becoming like Him in His death (see Philippians 3:7-11).

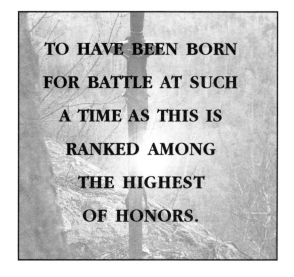

TO HAVE BEEN BORN FOR BATTLE AT SUCH A TIME AS THIS IS RANKED AMONG THE HIGHEST OF HONORS.

Those who fight the good fight and finish well will see the glory of God revealed, the holiness of His Name restored, and the manifold wisdom of His ways exalted. With His fire and passion dwelling in our hearts, flowing forth as words of life, we will know this: "'**My name will be great among the nations, from the rising to the setting of the sun. In every place incense** (prayer) **and pure offerings** (expressions and gifts of sincere gratitude) **will be brought to my name, because my name will be great among the nations,' says the Lord Almighty"** (Malachi 1:11). ∎

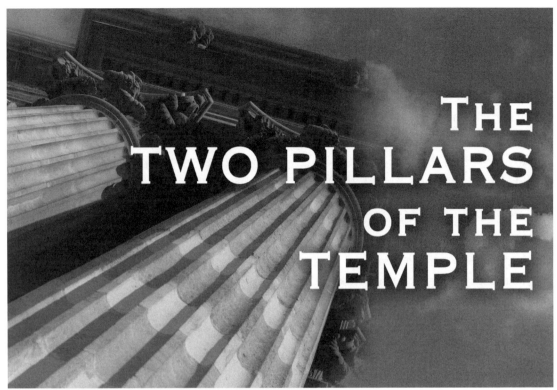

THE TWO PILLARS OF THE TEMPLE

by Rick Joyner

Thus he set up the pillars at the porch of the nave; and he set up the right pillar and named it Jachin, and he set up the left pillar and named it Boaz (I Kings 7:21).

Jachin was a priest and Boaz was a businessman (see I Chronicles 9:10, Nehemiah 11:10, Ruth 2:1). That these were chosen to be the two pillars of the temple is a prophetic statement that these are to be the two foundational ministries of the church, "the temple not made with hands." How can this be? Understanding this is crucial to understanding the church as it is intended to be. This is because the purpose of the ministry of the church is to reach people in everyday life. Business or commerce is the place of the most basic human transactions with one another, and this is where God wants to do some of His greatest works.

It is a false concept many have that most biblical heroes were priests, or those who we would see today as being in full-time ministry. The fact is that the overwhelming majority of the great men and women in Scripture were either farmers, businessmen, military men, or government officials, not priests. These include: Abraham, Isaac, Jacob, Joseph, Moses, Joshua, all of the judges, David, Daniel, Nehemiah, Esther, all but a couple of the prophets, all of the apostles when they were called, Cornelius, and almost all of the other ministries named in the New Testament.

Most of the great heroes of the faith in Scripture continued to work in their "secular profession" or trade the whole time they performed their work for the Lord. Even the great apostle Paul continued to make tents from time to time. He was not doing this as a hobby or because he needed the money, but to keep himself in touch with the practical issues of life that are essential if one is to have a truly relevant ministry. It is for this reason that the Lord will only entrust with the heavenly riches those who have been faithful with earthly riches (see Luke 16:11).

Also, this is the reason that some of the greatest heroes of the faith were also very wealthy and/or powerful, such as the patriarchs, Joseph, David, Daniel, and others. Without question, the pursuit of riches can be a major spiritual stumbling block, but when kept in their proper place, which means to use them properly for the kingdom as stewards who have been entrusted with them, learning to manage them properly can help us to be prepared for the **"true riches" (Luke 16:11).**

The fact remains true that almost any profession or trade seems to be the best platform for being launched into a life of extraordinary accomplishments in the Lord, just as the Lord Jesus Himself chose all of His own apostles from among the everyday trades and businesses of the time. These trades and businesses were their seminary, and it trained them up in such a way that they would never be out of touch with the common man.

The true temple of authentic Christianity is life itself. A factor in the coming great revolution of the church age will be when we break out of the prison of the modern concept of what church is. Church is not something we go to—it is our life and must be as real to us on Monday morning as it was on Sunday morning.

> ...the Lord will only entrust with the heavenly riches those who have been faithful with earthly riches.

Though our times of corporate worship, teaching, and ministry are important, true church is 24 hours a day, 7 days a week. The services and church meetings are where we get much of our spiritual food and equipping for going to the frontline of the battle, daily life. Therefore, the Lord does not judge His church by how good the meetings are Sunday morning, but how good the people are doing Monday morning, Tuesday afternoon, and so on.

We should worship God as much Monday morning as we do Sunday morning. This does not mean that we need to sing choruses or hymns at work, but everything we do should be done as unto the Lord as worship to Him.

Consider this: It was said of many that the Holy Spirit came upon them, but who was the first one in Scripture to be *filled* with the Holy Spirit? We read about Him in Exodus 31:1-3:

> Now the LORD spoke to Moses, saying,
>
> "See, I have called by name Bezalel, the son of Uri, the son of Hur, of the tribe of Judah.
>
> And I have filled him with the Spirit of God in wisdom, in understanding, in knowledge, and in all kinds of craftsmanship.

> We must start to see every job that we have as worship done for the Lord.

As Robert Frazier points out in his excellent book, *Marketplace Christianity,* Bezalel was not filled with the Holy Spirit for the purpose of miracles or prophecy, but for craftsmanship! Have you considered that your job, your skill, is holy to the Lord? Consider Colossians 3:23-24:

> Whatever you do, do your work heartily, as for the Lord rather than for men;
>
> knowing that from the Lord you will receive the reward of the inheritance. It is the Lord Christ whom you serve.

If we are doing our work for our boss, the corporation, or whoever else makes out our paycheck, then we are not living as we should, but have a thick veil over our eyes. If we work for men, then it will be from men that we receive our promotions and rewards. If we do our work as unto the Lord, then it is from Him that we will receive our rewards. Who would you rather work for? Who do you think can take care of you better?

We must start to see every job that we have as worship done for the Lord. Therefore, everything we do should be of the highest standards of excellence. We should have a vision of growing in our skills and the knowledge of our jobs so as to continually improve our performance. As Martin Luther King, Jr. once said, "If you are a street sweeper then sweep streets like Michelangelo painted!"

It should not matter to us if men give us credit for it or not, as we have a greater confidence that God will. This can bring a liberty and peace to our lives that helps us to overcome the stress and problems that many suffer in their jobs. Then we can focus on something even greater, helping to save the souls of those who work with us.

We need to see our jobs as "holy unto the Lord," and that He will even fill us with His Spirit for the purpose of excellence in our profession or trade. One of the greatest inspirations of my life was not a Christian, but he was considered one of the greatest pilots in the world. Every time he got in an airplane, he did so with the resolve to fly it better than he did the last time. He was an unrelenting perfectionist, and flying with him in the cockpit was one of the most intimidating jobs I have ever had. But he instilled in me a passion for excellence and to continually improve whatever I did, which I have honestly not seen in another Christian to that degree. This is a tragic irony. Certainly those who serve the King of kings should be this!

We should also learn how to use our spiritual gifts in our job. Some might consider it profane to use the gift of prophecy for helping us in our jobs, but the Lord wants to be involved in everything we do, and He also wants to prosper us in everything we do. Just as the Israelites in captivity were told to pray for the peace and prosperity of the nations to which they were scattered so that they would live in peace and enjoy prosperity, the Lord wants to use us as a blessing wherever we go. Isn't that what He did with Joseph, Daniel, and others? Did they not use their gifts in this way?

The prophetic gifts are especially useful in everyday life and can get the attention of many others quickly, just as a single word of knowledge about the woman at the well ended up stirring a whole city. Ask the Lord to give you words of knowledge, words of wisdom which is a supernatural wisdom, discernment of spirits, and prophecy for your job. Like

Joseph and Daniel, such can turn even the heart of the most powerful kings, which means they could certainly touch your boss.

When we do this we should also use the kind of discretion that the Lord Himself used with the woman at the well. He did not thunder "Thus saith the Lord!" at her. He gently let her know that He knew more about her, and she started asking the questions. We do not need or want the religious bombast that many seem to believe prophecy must come with. That is really more demeaning to the gift than helpful.

> The Lord wants to be involved in everything we do, and He also wants to prosper us in everything we do.

Of course, we need wisdom and discretion in how we use any gift of the Holy Spirit, always keeping in mind that He is holy. Do this, but also keep in mind that you are there as a Joseph or Daniel to help guide maybe even heathen leaders with the wisdom supplied by the Lord. This is not just to give you an edge in your job, though it certainly will do that, but it is to be a blessing and help to those the Lord has sent us to. As the Lord Himself explained in Matthew 5:43-45:

"You have heard that it was said, 'You shall love your neighbor, and hate your enemy.'

"But I say to you, love your enemies, and pray for those who persecute you

in order that you may be sons of your Father who is in heaven; for He causes His sun to rise on the evil and the good, and sends rain on the righteous and the unrighteous.

> **Good management is one of the most essential needs and greatest lacks within the church.**

The Lord was even willing to heal those who did not even return to thank Him. He will actually do many great miracles for people who will not even acknowledge Him or the miracles. Why? Because most of what He does He does just because He loves people and wants to help them. We are called to be a light to the world even though most of the world will reject it. He wants us to be a light to people even if they do not acknowledge it or give Him the glory for His goodness. That is the nature of love, and God loves the whole world.

The Good Steward

Good management is essential for accomplishing anything of significance. Good management is one of the most essential needs and greatest lacks within the church. Anyone who is entrusted with anything of value, who does not develop good leadership and management skills for stewarding it, will either lose or bury their talents.

There is a great delusion that managers are born and not made. After nearly twenty-five years of studying leadership and management, I am convinced that some are born with either of these gifts, but also either can be acquired and developed. We may be born with the calling and gifts, but if we do not proactively develop them, they will decrease instead of mature.

Basic management skills and knowledge are the same whether they are applied to a business, a team, an army, or the church. Good pastors assess the people and resources they have been entrusted with and use them the most effectively for the kingdom. They also help equip their people to overcome in life, in all that they do, for the sake of the gospel.

As a pastor I feel that my greatest success will be to see every soul who I have been entrusted to help oversee stand before the Lord on that great day and hear **"Well done, good and faithful servant!" (Matthew 25:21 NIV).** I therefore have to look at each person as a sacred trust, the Lord's own children who He entrusted me to watch over and equip for their purpose. I cannot possibly do this without using good management skills.

I oversee eight ministries, each of which I could devote all of my time to and not feel that it is enough. One day when I was feeling the pressure of this almost to the breaking point, I cried out to God. He immediately answered, "You know, I uphold the universe with My power. I can help you with this." Of course I knew the doctrine very well about how His yoke is easy and His burden light, the one that He gives to us is light, and even had some great teachings on them (see Matthew 11:30). But I was just not doing it in the very place where it is needed the most— the ministry to His church! It was because of this I started studying how He managed the universe, and I saw the glory of God in a way that radically changed my life.

Good management principles are essential for using the talents that He has entrusted to us for the maximum return for His kingdom. His good management principles are what uphold the universe, and it is a common grace that is available to all men, whether they acknowledge Him or not. They can be used for good or evil, but to date they are mostly used for evil. Instead of shying away from them because of this, we need to start using them for good! We do want to take the kingdom to the marketplace, and there is a lot from the marketplace that we do not want to bring back into the church.

However, there are some things we can learn from those who are successful in any field about management and leadership that the church desperately needs. Even though common grace is available to all men, it is still from God.

> Good management principles are essential for using the talents that He has entrusted to us for the maximum return for His kingdom.

It is for this reason that I require everyone on our leadership team to read at least two books a year on management and leadership. It does not matter how gifted one is, those who excel in any field, whether it is business, a trade, a sport, or even the military, are the ones who are continually reviewing and practicing the basics of their profession. They also seek to improve and further develop whatever gifts and skills they have been given.

In the Parable of the Talents, it was the slave who buried the talent that he was entrusted with which was called a "wicked, evil slave" (see Matthew 25:26). I think this is the last thing anyone should want to hear on that day when we must all stand before the judgment seat of Christ. The slaves in this parable who were told to **"enter into the joy of your master,"** (Matthew 25:23) were the ones who multiplied what they were entrusted with.

> **When the church fully matures it is going to be like Christ, doing the works that He did, like He did them, and where He did them.**

Now if all of the gifts and ministries of the Spirit were only to be used in church meetings, and if we truly equipped the saints to do the work of the ministry, where would they do this? It would not be possible for everyone to function in their gifts and ministries in just the few hours each week that are usually devoted to church meetings. Even with all of the home groups this is not possible. It is also essential we understand that the Lord does not want to be limited to just using us a few hours each week! The gifts and ministries we have been given are obviously to be used in everyday life.

I have come to believe that at least 85 percent of the gifts and ministries that have been entrusted to the church are not for use in our church services, but rather in everyday life. Isn't this where the Lord did the great majority of His own ministry? When the church fully matures it is going to be like Christ, doing the works that He did, like He did them, and where He did them.

Summary

We must understand how the two pillars of the temple are both the priestly ministry that we have all been given, and the ministry in business that we have also been given. Business is the place of basic human transactions, and God wants into all of them. These two pillars fit together, work together, and are both needed if the church is going to become what it is called to be. Billy Graham said, "I believe that one of the next great moves of God will be in the workplace." This is a true prophecy. We need to understand it and prepare for it.

This article is simply intended to stir you to hear the trumpet call that is being sounded almost universally now in the church about marketplace ministry. This is not a low calling. Ministry in the church, or what we now think of as church, is the high calling. The ministry in our church services is intended to feed, supply, train, and equip the soldiers who are on the frontline of the battle, which is the true ministry, which is everyday life. Until the very end of this age all but a few of the great men and women of faith, and the great exploits of the faith, will be found among these frontline soldiers of the kingdom. ∎

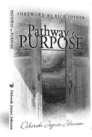

THE FELLOWSHIP OF THE

Knights of the Cross

PASSING THE MANTLE TO THE EMERGING GENERATION

The Knights of the Cross is a unique approach to fulfilling the mandate to disciple and raise up from among this emerging generation of children and youth, those who will do all things for the sake of the gospel of Jesus Christ and who will live their entire lives on a mission for the King and His Kingdom.

The Knights of the Cross currently consists of boys and girls between the ages of 9-12 (Children of the King) and 13-17 (Soldiers of the Cross).

To find out how you can start a local fellowship of the Knights of the Cross or apply to become a member through correspondence, or to have someone come and speak to your group about this exciting discipleship ministry, contact:

THE KNIGHTS OF THE CROSS
PO BOX 440, WILKESBORO, NC 28697

E-Mail: koc@morningstarministries.org

LET HIS KNIGHTS ARISE!

MORNINGSTAR | *School of Ministry*
Ephesians 4:1 Live Worthy of the Calling

MSM is a one or two year curriculum, depending on your needs and experience. Graduates of the first year curriculum can go on to an internship program with the MorningStar leadership team.

The MSM curriculum is intended to raise up a new generation of radical Christian leaders who are committed to sound biblical truth, to being like Christ, doing the works that He did, and never retreating before the enemies of the cross.

Housing available for 2005-2006 term.

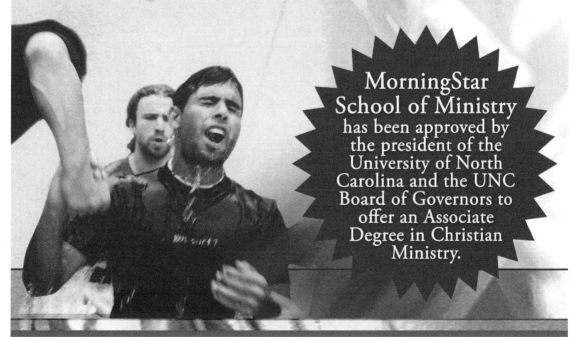

MorningStar School of Ministry has been approved by the president of the University of North Carolina and the UNC Board of Governors to offer an Associate Degree in Christian Ministry.

For more information or to request an application call 803-547-9655 or write to MSM, P.O. Box 19409, Charlotte NC 28219

This school is authorized under Federal law to enroll non-immigrant students.

MorningStar Strategic Team

MST FINANCES

MST IS

our partners' fellowship – those united with us in prayer and support of our strategic missions.

are invested in missions of strategic importance, such as the restoration of H.I.M. and the equipping and sending out of powerful and effective missions.

MEMBERS CONTRIBUTE

$15.00 per month, $150 per year, or more.

JOIN THE TEAM

Please send completed form to:
MorningStar, P.O. Box 440, Wilkesboro, NC 28697
Fax: 1-336-651-2430

Contact MST:
1-800-542-0278
mst@morningstarministries.org

Name _____ Date _____

Address _____

City _____ State _____ Zip _____

(   ) _____
Phone   E-mail

Here is my contribution of $_____ to MST in the form of:

☐ Cash ☐ Check ☐ Money Order (payable to MST) ☐ Credit Card

MSJ0605

Charge my:
☐ Master Card
☐ Visa
☐ Discover
☐ AMEX

Credit Card ☐☐☐☐ ☐☐☐☐ ☐☐☐☐ ☐☐☐☐   *Expiration Date* ☐☐/☐☐

Signature: _____ (Credit Card contributions will not be processed without a signature)

☐ Please automatically deduct $_____ from the above credit card each month.
Deducted the first business week of each month. Though we do not encourage debt, automatic deduction is a reliable method of supporting ministries conveniently. You may cancel at any time.

Note: MorningStar will never sell or give away your personal information. If for any reason you would like to stop deductions from your credit card or withdraw from MST, you can call 1-800-542-0278.

JOIN US IN A HISTORIC RESTORATION

MorningStar purchased the former Heritage USA Grand Hotel and Conference Center, along with fifty-two acres of property, and established Heritage International Ministries (H.I.M.).

HOTEL ROOM AT H.I.M.

THE NEHEMIAH PROJECT
RESTORE A HOTEL ROOM

You, your family, church, business, or group can restore a hotel room at H.I.M. Each room you help to restore will be named in your honor or as a memorial to the one you choose.

For more information, visit the H.I.M. section of www.morningstarministries.org. You can also contact Tiffany Taylor at HIM@morningstarministries.org or by calling 336-651-2400, ext. 113.

TAKE A SECTION OF THE WALL

Please send completed form to: The Nehemiah Project, P.O. Box 440, Wilkesboro, NC 28697

☐ **$5,000 to restore a hotel room**
For each $5,000 a room will be named in your honor.
(You can pay installments of $500/month)

☐ **$1,000 or more**
For $1000 or more your name will be placed on our Nehemiah's wall.
(You can pay installments of $100/month)

☐ **Any size donation**
Your name will be placed on the Permanent Register.

Name _____ Date _____

Address _____

City _____ State _____ Zip _____

( ) _____
Phone _____ E-mail _____

Here is my contribution of $_____ in the form of ☐ Cash ☐ Check ☐ Money Order ☐ CreditCard

Charge my:
☐ Master Card
☐ Visa
☐ Discover
☐ AMEX

Credit Card ☐☐☐☐ ☐☐☐☐ ☐☐☐☐ ☐☐☐☐   *Expiration Date* ☐☐/☐☐   MSJ0605

Signature: _____ (Credit Card contributions will not be processed without a signature)

☐ Please automatically deduct $_____ from the above credit card each month.
Deducted the first business week of each month. Though we do not encourage debt, automatic deduction is a reliable method of supporting ministries conveniently. You may cancel at any time.

Note: MorningStar will never sell or give away your personal information. If for any reason you would like to stop deductions from your credit card, please call 1-800-542-0278.

Statement of Ownership, Management, and Circulation
(Required by 39 U.S.C. 3685)

1. Publication Title: The Morning Star Journal® 2. Publication No.: 0129-03
3. Filing Date: October 1, 2005   4. Issue frequency: Quarterly
5. No. of issues published annually: 4   6. Annual Subscription Price: $16.95 U.S.; $24.95 Int'l
7. Complete Mailing Address of Known Office of Publication: 1605 Industrial Drive., Wilkesboro, NC 28697
   Contact person: David Hart, Telephone: 336-651-2400, ext. 105
8. Complete Mailing Address of General Office of Publisher: same as #7
9. Publisher: MorningStar Publications, P.O. Box 440, Wilkesboro, NC 28697
   Editor: Rick Joyner, P.O. Box 440, Wilkesboro, NC 28697
   Managing Editor: Deborah Joyner Johnson, P.O. Box 440, Wilkesboro, NC 28697
10. Owner: MorningStar Fellowship Church, P.O. Box 440, Wilkesboro, NC 28697
11. There are no Bondholders, Mortgagees, or Other Security Holders.
12. The purpose, function, and nonprofit status of this organization and the exempt status for federal income tax purposes has not changed during the preceding 12 months.

	Average No. Copies Each Issue During Preceding 12 Months	No. Copies of Single Issue Published Nearest to Filing Date
13. Publication Title: The Morning Star Journal®		
14. Issue Date of Circulation Date Below: October 2005		
15. Extent and Nature of Circulation		
a. Total No. of Copies (Net Press Run)	15,000	15,000
b. Paid and/or Requested Circulation		
(1)Paid/Requested Outside-County Mail Subscriptions	10,203	10,007
(2)Paid In-County Subscriptions	20	27
(3)Sales Through Dealers and Carriers, Street Vendors, and Counter Sales, and Other Non-USPS Paid Distribution	98	85
(4)Other Classes Mailed Through the USPS00		
c. Total Paid and/or Requested Circulation	10,321	10,119
d. Free Distribution by Mail		
(1) Outside-County	0	0
(2) In-County	0	0
(3) Other Classes Mailed Through the USPS	0	0
e. Free Distribution Outside the Mail	77	77
f. Total Free Distribution	77	77
g. Total Distribution	10,398	10,196
h. Copies Not Distributed	4,602	4,804
i. Total Sum of 15g. and h.)	15,000	15,000
j. Percent Paid and/or Requested Circulation	68%	67%

16. This Statement of Ownership will be printed in the Vol.15-4 issue of this publication.

David Hart, Office Business Manager, August 4, 2005

V JEAN TY____

GOING it ALONE

Seven January Adventures

Edited and Published
d'Arblays Press

ALSO by V Jean Tyler

FLASHBACK   - December 2002
GRAINS OF SAND   - January 2004
RELEASE   - January 2005
SURVIVAL   - March 2008

This Edition first published in 2008 by

d'Arblays Press
23 Brookbank Close
Cheltenham, Gloucestershire
GL50 3NL

Printed and Bound in England by

Creeds the Printers
Broadoak
Bridport, Dorset
DT6 5NL

ISBN: 9780954864644

Dedication

to Samuel, my first guide,
who looked after me on Kilimanjaro

Acknowledgements

to Margot Collingbourn-Beevers of
d'ARBLAYS PRESS
for her professionalism and friendship

to Torrington First Thursday Writers' Group
for their camaraderie and encouragement

CONTENTS

Foreword

I've had this book in mind for the last ten years. As I have explained in the introduction to the Kilimanjaro diary, my husband became seriously ill after we had booked what we intended to be the first of an annual long-haul travel experience in our maturing years. We cancelled and he died of cancer just a year later.

So here I am, sixteen years on, having had fourteen adventures on my own. When I write 'on my own', it is the planning and choice of holiday and the leaving home which I do alone. After that, I'm never alone. There are the air travel companions en route, and then the joining of a scheduled group with a special interest, or the moving from one group to another when the travel company has responded to my wish to include various places of interest while I am in some far-flung location. On one occasion, when I was the only taker for an advertised excursion to Madagascar, in fact the company did not cancel - as did one such when there was a minimum uptake - but treated me like royalty, and I enjoyed the unforgettable services of the exceptional guide all to myself!

Many of the fellow travellers were alone as I was, and this itself provided a kind of unspoken bond. During the first couple of days I would choose to release as much, or as little, of my life history as the antennae told me was sensible. Some were wonderful company and a few of us still remain in contact, usually at Christmas with "Where have you been this year?" interest. Half a dozen or so have visited each other's homes.

All the guides associated with the trips have, without exception, been incredible: well informed, tolerant, charming, and with a consuming passion for, and interest in, their particular area or country. Adam in Tanzania, one of those superb 'natural' naturalists if you see what I mean, had the eyes and ears of a hawk; Samuel, my sole carer on Kilimanjaro, urged me persistently to go "slowly, slowly", but could forge ahead at an amazing rate in spite of being a chain-smoker! Andrew, naturalist, author, lecturer, photographer, and environmental site manager, was obsessed with Darwin's finches on the Galapagos Islands, initially an irritating trend but by the end of the two weeks, we became as excited as was he when the final finch came into view. The local naturalist, Juan, was a charmer, always questing for more knowledge - and a good guitarist into the bargain.

On the Kunene we had the attentions of five young, strapping South Africans: Andy, Shane, Gavin, Chris and Dave. Their five charges must have seemed like comparative geriatrics.

Alex had a deep love for the Philippines and a rare rapport with the Filipinos. Wallie, a charming young Frenchman married to a Filipino, assisted us on the demanding Cresta Trail. Rodney was my star guide in Zimbabwe, and the way he transmitted the mood of the Rock Paintings in the Matopos Hills was very special.

In India, the family were my guides, and they lived there: what could be better? Tika looked after us in Nepal, a perfect gentleman with an expressed love for his family and a deep gratitude for being able to earn a living sharing with others his knowledge and affection for his homeland. Ben was guide, provisions organiser, cook, driver and mechanic in Botswana and Namibia, answered all our questions but also asked us about life in the UK. He was a good listener.

Reading through the diaries for the 1993-1999 holidays, I see I've moaned a bit about early mornings (these have never been my strong point), looking for loos, gastric turbulence, and the mandatory fall per adventure, but these are trivia which pale into insignificance when I'm reminded again of magical, heart-stirring moments which have taken up permanent residence in the senses: the three young, fit Namibian men on the way down from Kilimanjaro who suggested that my husband would have been proud of me: he was, I knew; the self-inflicted dehydration in the Galapagos, when I'd hallucinated and seen litre bottles of water in the trees on the way down from Alcedo crater; the acoustics in Tagus Cave; the Palo Santo tree aroma; the last night by the Kunene, sleeping under Palm Trees, with the sounds of the breeze, the Epupa Falls and the bird song - the best bedroom in the world; the drinking of fresh milk from a coconut prepared by the Mangyans in the Philippines; Zimbabwe sunrise at Malalangwe with a Klipspringer spectator; a visit to the Amritsar Golden Temple with very pregnant younger daughter; the Nepali reed women on Koshi River Bridge; and, finally, the breathtaking dawn over Dune 45 in Sosussvlei in Namibia.

I could never have embarked on the very first, the Kilimanjaro adventure, if it had not been for a very successful left hip replacement, and I am everlastingly grateful to Mr Christopher Mills for his orthopaedic skills. Even with that new hip I think I was lucky to survive some of the adventures, comparatively unscathed. I did have the benefit of ignorance at the time! I am writing this during convalescence following a right hip replacement by the same surgeon eight weeks ago, and at 75 I still intend to have my holiday thrills, possibly of a less physical nature.

I have had the irrepressible urge to share these travel experiences and, should they be enjoyed, I intend to treat the 2000-2006 annual 'fixes' in similar vein.

September 2007

KILIMANJARO

KILIMANJARO

and a

TASTE OF TANZANIA

with **AFRICA EXCLUSIVE**

January 1993

KILIMANJARO and a Taste of TANZANIA
The Reason Why

John had booked us an African safari holiday for the autumn of 1990. He became ill with what eventually proved to be an incurable cancer and had died by the following autumn, so that for him the excursion was cancelled. At his insistence, with some lack of heart on my part but in an effort to please him, I had promised him that for me it would be merely postponed.

It was in July 1992, when I was halfway through a morning GP surgery, and uncharacteristically keeping to time, more or less, that a patient failed to show (as they do) and I decided to make a phone call.

The previous weekend I'd read in the Naturetrek newsletter of a holiday in Tanzania, which included going up Kilimanjaro. I couldn't get it out of my mind. I tried to dismiss the idea. The previous November I had had a left hip replacement and suspected that the contemplation of such a holiday might be considered crass stupidity. Some of my friends would certainly think me mad. But what about Christopher Mills - the approachable and charming orthopaedic surgeon who had given me this new, pain-free lease of life?

As luck would have it, I got through to him at our local hospital where he was in the middle of an out-patient session. I said something like "I've got this opportunity to go up Kilimanjaro: what do you think?" There was a long pause and I imagined he might be considering a suitably polite rejoinder to one who should have known better. To my surprise and delight he said "Give it a go, and bring back a picture from the top!".

So I booked a place and, with advice from my much-travelled family, collected a kit list, had all my jabs and arranged for others to cover my clinics. Just three weeks before my scheduled departure on January 1st, the trip was called off because it was undersubscribed and I was devastated. But, amid contemporaries' comments such as "It's probably for the best", "You might not have coped", and "It could have made you ill", I became all the more determined to get there on time.

I scanned all the weekend travel supplements and left messages on every Africa travel firm's answerphone. Briefly, Africa Exclusive came up trumps (admittedly more expensive) with an almost identical package, and the first day of 1993 found me on a bus from Exeter to Heathrow. I have to confess to serious anxieties the night before: this was a big adventure and I was on my own. In fact, if I'm truthful, had the whole thing been called off at the eleventh hour, my disappointment could well have been vying with a sense of relief.

2.1.93   The KLM flight was prompt and comfortable. The only slight blip was when the metal component of my Exeter Hospital hip produced a very definite 'bleep' on the security scan during the transfer at Amsterdam airport. The plane landed at Kilimanjaro just after midnight (9 pm UK time) and I waited for some while for my borrowed blue haversack to appear on the luggage carousel: I grabbed it with a sigh of relief and went looking for the Ranger Safari driver. He was a tall, handsome Tanzanian in an immaculate khaki safari suit and although he was holding aloft a card with my name written in large letters, I had to show him my passport to convince him that I was Dr Tyler: he had been looking for a man.

Police with guns boarded the vehicle at one point and poked them about under the seats. It was a bit unnerving but an hour and a half later we were turning into the Mountain Village Lodge on the outskirts of Arusha, an oasis of light, and coloured foliage, in the black African night.

3.1.93   I awoke with the dawn to a glorious, full-bodied cacophony of stirring Bulbuls, Babblers, Coucals and many others I wished I could identify. My room was a charming African roundavel, thatched with banana leaves and overlooking Lake Duluti. The entire lodge nestled between Mounts Meru and Kilimanjaro. It was breathtaking - and it was warm!

Later in the day the Ranger Safari "boss man", called Abba, introduced himself and two young Italians, Wilma and Francesco - both doctors, two young Swiss - Daniela, a nurse and Stefano, a train driver, and a Tanzanian-born Indian, Sibtain, who worked for Alfa Travel in London, but had returned to Tanzania for his cousin's wedding.

These five were to be my travel companions on the safari. They were all quite charming, fun to be with, included me in everything, and I succumbed quite happily to being addressed as 'mother'. Apart from Sibtain, who spoke excellent English, we understood little of each other's language and yet, in retrospect, I cannot recall that was a problem.

Our Tanzanian driver, Adam, was a keen ornithologist, which pleased me no end. The six-day safari commenced at Lake Manyara National Park and in some ways that day was the most exciting, seeing our 'firsts' of Wildebeest, Buffalo, Giraffe, a yawning Hippo, and Impala, as well as vast numbers of water birds including Sacred Ibis and Crowned Crane. We spent the night at the Lake Manyara Hotel, perched on the escarpment of the Great Rift Valley with a bird's eye view of the lake below, plus an uncomfortably close view of the Olive Baboons outside. They stalked up and down, piggy-backing their youngsters, in the hope that a careless tourist might have left her window open!

The safari vehicle was comfortable, being built for nine passengers but, including Adam, we were just seven so there was reasonable breathing space, much appreciated in the mid-day sun. We travelled with all the large windows open and the roof up, except when the dust was excessive.

Stunning Serengeti and Ngorongoro with Moonscape

4.1.93 For two days we toured the endless plains of the Serengeti. We saw early a soft-eyed (Kirk's) Dik-dik, a shy Klipspringer, smart agile Thomson's and Grant's Gazelles, Common Waterbuck and Reedbuck, conspicuous Zebras which melted into the background at a hundred yards, an elusive Golden Jackal and, quite unexpectedly, a lion with its Wildebeest kill and two hungry cubs waiting patiently for their turn at the feast.

Another excitement towards the end of the second day was to have a clear sighting of a magnificent Cheetah striding purposefully away, her two young following closely in her wake. Two female Ostriches shepherded their crèche of about fifteen youngsters across the horizon, and a family of Warthogs, heavy-headed and with legs going like clockwork, swerved away from our approaching vehicle. I like Warthogs: the very thought of them makes me smile.

The last thrill of the Serengeti was to see a Leopard draped over the fork of a leafless tree in the slanted evening light. I have to admit I would never have spotted it if it hadn't been for Adam's direction. He had eyes like a hawk - and of course he did know where to look. It was a pretty distant view but we studied it through binoculars for some minutes. My photograph needed the eye of faith and a subsequent 'blow-up' to be really convincing.

Adam had also brought to our notice, earlier in the day, the form of a silent, still-sleeping crocodile which had been very much nearer!

We spent a night each at both the Seronera Wildlife Lodge and the Lobo Lodge while in the Serengeti. They were both built imaginatively into the massive rock, providing unforgettable views of the plains below. Attractive Rock Hyrax stopped and started in the natural habitat around and between parts of the hotels, and provided easy photo opportunities; they are (unbelievably) related to the elephants. A bright red and blue Agama Lizard, obligingly sun-bathing at Lobo Lodge, made another good camera shot.

En route for the Ngorongoro Crater we called at Olduvai Gorge, where a majestic and colourful Masai man gave us a brief rundown on the extraordinary, and comparatively recent, archaeological finds: these ranged from fossils of an extinct three-toed horse found in 1911 by a German professor while butterfly hunting, to Mary Leakey's discovery, in 1959, of an ape's skull from 1.75 million years ago. The research continues.

This was a very dusty day and Wilma draped a voluminous georgette scarf round most of her slim body, but especially over her face and head.

It was a good day for large birds such as Secretary Birds, Hamerkops, and Kori's Bustard - although I was tempted to change one of the vowels in the latter when my camera battery died just in time for me not to get a good picture.

The Ngorongoro Wildlife Lodge gave a wide and deep view of the crater. At night this became an enormous weird moonscape, which continued to fascinate me well into the early hours. The following morning we changed to a four-wheel drive to go down into the crater. It was misty and damp and cool, the road very steep and unmade. The weather improved as the morning wore on and we saw great Elephants stripping Yellow-barked Acacia trees, Coke's Hartebeest, herds of Buffalo, and a Black Rhinoceros with her baby. The Rhinoceros slotted into the 'strange shape' brigade, to my way of thinking, along with the Warthogs, Hippos, and Humpy Wildebeest.

The birds were spectacular: Blacksmith Plover; White-headed Buffalo Weaver; Black-headed Heron; Black-winged Stilt; very Yellow Wagtail; Yellow-billed Goose; and the amazing, pink-flushed Flamingoes en masse. I cannot possibly mention all the birds. Even in my novice-ticking class, I identified (with help) over 130 birds. There are over 1,300 species described in Collins Guide of 'The Birds of East Africa', and in the preface one of the compilers says how difficult it had been to decide which ones to include. There are more?

The ride up out of the crater was made hazardous by heavy rain, and I mean heavy, which started about 3.30 pm. A couple of mud-entrenched abandoned vehicles ahead of us were pushed unceremoniously out of the way to let us through. The same squelchy red mud put a stop to our regular safari vehicle the following morning when, after an hour's slow ride towards Arusha, Adam was forced to put the chains on the wheels. Stefano was very practical and made himself chief assistant, getting spattered red-patterned legs and shorts for his trouble.

8.1.93 This was where we parted. I said good-bye to the young five: Sibtain was returning to his cousin's house in Arusha before going back to London, and the others were spending a relaxed week in Zanzibar. (I was beginning to think this might have made more sense than starting on the Kilimanjaro lark.)

Time to think and then act - Upwards!

9.1.93 I had another day in Arusha and took a walk around Lake Duluti, where I was rewarded with the sight of a masterful Fish Eagle. The following day I had a tour of Arusha National Park and saw Black and White Colobus Monkeys, white-chested Sykes' Monkeys, Sable and Roan Antelopes, and another collection of birds.

I sorted my luggage. My safari clothes were to stay at the hotel so that the porter would have a lighter pack to carry on the climb. It still seemed pretty heavy, being comprised of such 'essentials' as sleeping bag, bed roll, waterproofs, and extra sweaters for the top.

That evening I was expecting to dine alone and was wishing that my young companions had not left, but along came one of the 'boss' men and said, "These are your group for Kilimanjaro." They were three Frenchmen, Jean-Didier, Claude and Felicien, who were 40, 46, and 50 respectively, I discovered later. I am supposed to be reasonably conversant in French but these three came from Corsica and it took me a while to get used to their accent, which seemed to have almost a Scots lilt. John and I had once holidayed in Corsica, and had found it a wild and wonderful place. These three seemed to me to match the landscape of their homeland exactly.

10.1.93 The climb started from Kilimanjaro Park Gate. We were driven there by a cheery chap called Jonathon. We trekked for four hours through lush rain forest to the first overnight stay, Mandara Hut at 8850 feet. It was a pleasant sunny day and we walked in shorts and T-shirt.

Our guide was called Samuel: he was 45, had six children (he volunteered the information that Family Planning made his wife ill - I resisted the temptation to ask for details), and was extraordinarily fit in spite of chain-smoking. The only time he became short-tempered was one morning when he discovered he had lost his cigarettes. He was very anxious that we did not try to hurry up the mountain: we were to give ourselves time to adapt to the altitude. "Poly-poly mamon" was his oft-uttered advice.

Our hut had four bunks, three at ground level, and an upper one, which was distinctly shorter, to accommodate the sloping roof. Being the smallest I was allocated the latter, which was fine really. I liked having my private space above the rest, but it was unusually high and there was no ladder! I managed and felt oh, so thankful, that I had had my hip done. I slept well and felt quite refreshed when we got our 6 am call.

11.1.93 We made a good start, and Samuel followed and caught us up later. The Frenchmen went on ahead: they were very fit. It was about now that I discovered they were all members of a volunteer mountain rescue team in Corsica. I expressed my feelings of horror and inadequacy to Samuel, who said it was irrelevant and told me to "poly-poly" on. I must admit I was feeling tired by the end of the morning. We were climbing steadily all the time and the weather had turned distinctly cold and damp.

We lunched by one of the five small rivers we had to cross. I saw a Scarlet-tufted Malachite Sunbird on one of the sentinels of Giant Lobelia. Tree Groundsel towered over us to a height of at least 20 feet. Apart from these two tall plants, the vegetation was like moorland. We reached Horombo Hut at 3.30 pm. The three 'Corsairs' had got there at 1 pm. We were now at 12,200 feet.

12.1.93 I had been advised (because of my age, I guess) to spend an extra night at Horombo to get better acclimatised. In fact I felt very well and had no headache or other symptoms of altitude sickness.

The Frenchmen left early the next morning, and I spent the day writing up my diary, taking short walks and trying to photograph what I thought was an immature Verreaux's Eagle. (Not a brilliant picture but good enough for one of my twitcher sons to say how lucky I was to see an 'immature Lammergeyer'. I agreed!). The Horombo four-striped mice scuttled about everywhere, asking to be photographed.

KILIMANJARO

Jean-Didier - Samuel - Claude and Felicien

Going Up and Giving Up ...

13.1.93   The next day we struck out for Kibo Hut, at 15,400 feet. It was a very tough walk for seven hours across the saddle in blizzard conditions. (It's not supposed to snow at this time of year.) Kibo was covered in over a foot of snow and everyone was talking about the 'bad conditions'. It was extremely cold and I began to wish I'd not wasted the comparatively better weather for a night at Horombo. I envied the Frenchmen who had made the summit on a clear night before the snow.

Samuel served some stew at 6 pm, and then I went to bed with my clothes on until I was called at 1 am with "Shall we try, Jean?" The snow had stopped but the dark sky was heavy and moonless. White stretched everywhere and gave a feeling of timelessness and limitless, unstructured horizons. The going in the deep snow was incredibly hard. Samuel led with his torch and I followed with mine. Other guides led their charges above and below us.

We climbed for four hours by which time we'd got to over 17,000 feet and it had started to snow again. I knew I'd had enough. "I think perhaps I'd better go back," I said. "I think we should both go back," he replied. I hadn't thought of going back on my own! Going down was slippery and I was so grateful for Samuel's arm. The snow had obscured all the leg-breaking stones and rocks. I think we got back about 6.30 am and I was surprised to find how many others were already back in their bunks, asleep. In fact, a mere handful had made it to Gillman's Point (18,600 feet) and no-one was allowed to continue to Uhuru Peak (19,340 feet). I got higher than the majority and I was certainly the oldest, but it would have been great to have got to the top and taken those photos.

14.1.93   I slept in my clothes again until 8.30 am, when Samuel arrived with a cup of tea and a sense of urgency in his voice. We had to start down before the snow or rain came. We retraced our steps across the tedious cold saddle to Horombo Hut, where I was billeted with two young English chaps who'd acquired South African accents while working in Kenya, and a Japanese girl called Marika who spoke no English and painted delightful miniature flower pictures amid all the damp and grime of the, now very muddy, huts.

Wet Descent

15.1.93   I slept the sleep of the dead and had to be woken up at 7 am the following morning. I breakfasted near three young men from Namibia: not only had they carried all their own gear, including food, and done all their own cooking, but they had also reached Gillman's Point. They asked me in kindly terms, more or less, what I was doing on this expedition and I found myself telling them my recent life history. "Well, I think you've done remarkably for your age (!)" said one. "Your husband would have been proud of you." said another. A cord twanged deep inside and I put on my sunglasses. The rain came down really heavily, with thunder, and lightning struck the ground ahead. I felt fear for the first and only time during the holiday, and recalled the death of a friend struck by lightning in Malaysia. Samuel sensed my anxiety and took my hand, with "I will lead you", until the time interval between the flash and the thunder clap had extended to several seconds, and the rumble became less harsh and more distant.

It was a long hard trek from Horombo to The Gate, and those charming little footpaths through the woodland glades had become young red rivers, the flow obscuring the stones and slippery roots beneath. I slipped two or three times and wallowed in the mud like a hippo. I was glad I had a minimum of clothes on and wasn't trussed up in heavy waterproofs and gaiters as some of the others were.

By the time we reached the bottom it was difficult to see where my shorts finished and my legs began. I wondered at the porters, especially on the ascent, some with no shoes and balancing great loads on their heads. Once the luggage was delivered at the appropriate huts, they were required to go and gather heavy heaps of firewood for the cooking. This involved going further and further down the mountain as their tourists approached the summit. My porter was called Lonki, but 'Lanky' would have suited him better, he was so tall and angular. I made a Freudian slip on a couple of occasions and called Samuel "Sambo" but he either didn't hear or didn't mind!

HOROMBO   FOUR-STRIPED   MOUSE

We had to sign the book and identify ourselves and say how far we'd climbed. Samuel and Lonki and the cook, who was a very silent older man and whose name I never did get to grips with, wanted their photographs taken so I took out my little camera in the pouring rain and obliged. I thanked them from the bottom of my heart: Samuel distributed the money I had given to him for the three of them and they seemed well pleased.

Comfort and Convalescence

The smiling Jonathon was a welcome sight at the wheel of the safari vehicle and I climbed its high side, apologising for my muddy state. He laughed and didn't seem too upset. The clouds were rolling away and the road to Arusha seemed to be full of brightly-clad Africans walking the steaming grass verges. A couple of Hamerkops rose reluctantly from the middle of the road as we approached. "They're eating insects after the rain", said Jonathon.

On arrival at Arusha Mountain Village Lodge, I felt set solid at right angles in my seat, my clothes wet, and my legs caked with the now dry, lumpy mud. I roused myself and managed to negotiate the high step. I registered and went to my allotted delightful room, where I stripped and stood under a gloriously hot shower for nearly an hour until I was in danger of falling asleep. It was the first hot water I'd enjoyed for ages, for this luxury had been either cold or absent at the safari stopovers, never mind the Kilimanjaro huts where an outside tap trickle had had to suffice. During these minimal ablutions one morning, I'd been fascinated by a young German girl who balanced a small mirror on the back of the stone trough while she replaced her contact lenses with cold trembling fingers.

I sorted my mucky clothes, collected the cleaner ones from the hotel office, changed and went sleepily into dinner. I was very happy to see 'my' three French Corsicans sitting in the bar: I'd forgotten they were now to do the safari I'd done the previous week, starting off from Arusha. They hailed me like a long lost friend and I had to give a detailed account of my failure to reach Uhuru Peak. Felicien went to find his calculator to convert 'over 17,000 feet' into metres. He came back and announced whatever was the answer and they all cheered and bought me a drink. I ate with them and felt that my French had suddenly improved!

Last Leg

16.1.93   I had twenty-four hours of luxury before I was to leave for home. I slept well and late, the sun shone and I sat in the opened French windows of my room and cut all my nails. I put my pack and my washed boots in the sun to dry, and went out with the camera, looking at butterflies and some of the exotic garden flowers. The English lady manager of the hotel said "You do look relaxed". I felt it.

Lunch, more sun, packing, dinner with a very talkative German guest who was not into listening, and it was time for Goodip to take me to the airport. This was a nightmare ride. The rain had played havoc with the surfaces and all the vehicles seemed to be driving in the middle of the road, flashing their offside indicator lights. I asked Goodip about this. "A lot of them drink and drive," he said "and the light makes it easier for them to see the edge of the vehicle." "What if they're actually turning right?" I ventured. He laughed showing his perfect white teeth: "I don't know, I don't know".

The airport was a very relaxed, casual place except when it came to asking for money, such as the airport tax. I was a dollar short somehow, so ended up paying some sterling and consequently more overall. The man who studied my passport asked about the British Royal family and did I know the 'latest royal scandal'. He seemed disappointed at my apparent lack of interest: I did wonder what had happened in my absence.

The plane was two hours later than billed because of going to Nairobi first for fuel, but we finally arrived at Heathrow, via Amsterdam, on schedule. My luggage was actually second off the conveyor belt and I came through the 'nothing to declare' channel to see the smiling faces of my younger son and his wife. After an overnight stop at their house, which was followed by a slow Sunday ride through some of the nicest parts of dear England, I eventually arrived in Barnstaple just after 5.30 pm. And so, finally, a taxi home and then a walk up the drive to a neighbour's house to collect the mail, etc - where I became enveloped, very comfortably, in a Sunday family tea party.

Retrospection

After a week or so, I was back into the home-and-work routine but my mind was still full of the crêpe paper colours of the flowers, even on the trees. I could see the uncanny shapes of the Termite hills, the dead tree perches populated by brightly-coloured Bee-eaters, Sunbirds, Weavers, Rollers, Starlings and others. It's the colours and the shapes that linger: flat-topped Acacia, dangling 'Sausage' trees, Euphorbia Candelabra, tall Lobelias, Tree Groundsel and enormous ancient Baobabs and the stature and movement of the long-necked Giraffes, erect Herons, Crane, Storks and Flamingoes, hurrying Bustards and Secretary Birds, weird little Warthogs, creepy Crocodiles, and large, lumbering Elephants.

So much was new. I had memories and ideas to live on for months. Maybe I'll go back but I doubt whether I'd attempt Kilimanjaro again. It might just be pushing my luck too far. In retrospect I think I was very fortunate to get down in one piece. Two fit young men damaged themselves on the way down, one sustaining a nasty-looking ankle fracture and another probably just a bad sprain.

My Exeter hip had served me well and I sent a card to my orthopaedic surgeon, Chris Mills, to express my gratitude - and to blame the weather rather than the hip for preventing me from getting my summit photograph. I wondered whether I had shortened its life with so much activity but, for the fortnight's quality of experience, I reckoned it was worth the risk.

I felt fighting fit when I got back home and, as I walked up the drive to the tea party, I felt as though I could walk for ever. I'd been worried about my knees which sometimes give me creaky pain when I'm swimming but they'd made superb brakes all the way down the mountain. I'd taken two aspirins a day to help the circulation and deter thrombosis so maybe these had limited my joint discomfort as well. I had lost half a stone, which no doubt was partly accounted for by the exercise, but a loss of appetite must surely have contributed also. This is often put down to altitude but the woodsmoke smell and taste of everything, initially novel and quite pleasant, eventually palls.

I managed not to lose anything of importance. I realised in the bus to Heathrow that I had left my itinerary at home but fortunately others knew where I was supposed to be each day! I left my facecloth at the Ibis Hotel at Heathrow and lost two unused films in the safari vehicle: I guess they were on the floor and rolled out somewhere when the door opened.

I would not be afraid to travel alone again, although I doubt I'd go in for any totally freelance and unstructured holiday. It's easy to feel sexless and role-less (which has its advantages) when living alone, but on this holiday I slipped happily into a friendly, maternal situation during the first week with the younger people, and enjoyed a sense of femininity and sexual equality because of the very natural, relaxed way I was treated by the Corsicans. My self-esteem and self-confidence went up a few notches.

I read Kuki Gallmann's "I Dreamed of Africa" before I went away and, even after only a fortnight there, I think I have an embryo of understanding of her addiction. She has turned personal tragedy into a triumph and was one of the first to initiate protection for the, then, much-hunted Rhinoceros. We saw a memorial in one of the parks to some of the people who had lost their lives in the early days of this campaign.

Equally impressive was a tribute, at the foot of Mount Kilimanjaro, to all the porters who had made possible the original ascents. And so say all of us, now and ever after.

Postscript:

A few months after my return, when I was doing a GP surgery, a pleasant, older man, who was scheduled for a hip replacement the following month, mentioned 'his' surgeon, Chris Mills; (I had not previously discussed my operation with him for, generally speaking, patients are not particularly interested in their doctor's medical history).

He continued: "He's done a lady doctor, who has since climbed Everest!".

"Amazing!" I volunteered.

It has been suggested that the surgeon in question has since dined out on that story. Well, he never did get the photograph!

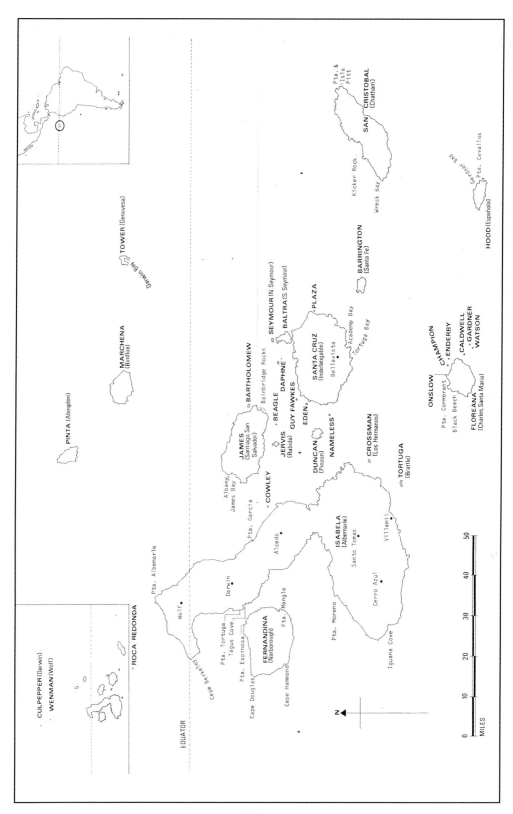

CULPEPPER (Darwin)
WENMAN (Wolf)

"ROCA REDONDA

PINTA (Abingdon)

MARCHENA
(Bindloe)

TOWER (Genovesa)

Darwin Bay

EQUATOR

Pta. Albemarle

Wolf

Cape Berkeley

Darwin

Pta. Tortuga
Tagus Cove
Pta. Espinosa

Cape Douglas

FERNANDINA
(Narborough)

Pta. Mangle

Cape Hammond

Alcedo

Pta. Moreno

Santo Tomas

Cerro Azul

Iguana Cove

ISABELA
(Albemarle)

Villamil

Albany,
James Bay

Pta. Garcia

JAMES
(Santiago,San
Salvador)

• COWLEY

Bainbridge Rocks

BARTHOLOMEW

• BEAGLE
JERVIS
(Rabida)
GUY FAWKES
DUNCAN
(Pinzon)

EDEN
NAMELESS°

DAPHNE
SEYMOUR (N.Seymour)
BALTRA (S. Seymour)
PLAZA

SANTA CRUZ
(Indefatigable)

Bellavista

Academy Bay

Tortuga Bay

CROSSMAN
(Los Hermanos)

TORTUGA
(Brattle)

BARRINGTON
(Santa Fe)

SAN CRISTOBAL
(Chatham)

Pta. &
Isla
Pitt

Kicker Rock

Wreck Bay

ONSLOW

CHAMPION
° ° ENDERBY
CALDWELL
• GARDNER
WATSON

Pta. Cormorant
Black Beach

FLOREANA
(Charles, Santa Maria)

HOOD (Española)

Pta. Cevallos

Gardner Bay

N

0   10   20   30   40   50

MILES

DARWIN'S EVOLUTION

December 1993 – January 1994

The

GALAPAGOS ISLANDS

with **NATURETREK**

The GALAPAGOS ISLANDS

Darwin nostalgia : Meeting 'le Groupe'

Quito - Here we come

The Encantadas, or 'bewitched' islands, (so-called because of the testing, variable strong currents) is an alternative name for the more pragmatically-named 'Galapagos' Islands, derived from the Spanish word for tortoise - 'galapago'. When I first announced my intention to visit the archipelago in the Pacific Ocean, I found myself trying to explain its geographical position with such phrases as "600 miles left of Ecuador", but by the time of my return to England, in mid-January, there had been two TV holiday programmes about the islands. Everyone was extremely well informed and was telling me what I ought to have seen!

Many years ago I had been fascinated by a Higher School Certificate project on 'Darwin's theory of evolution'. His erudite but controversial paper had been published twenty years after his voyage on HMS Beagle and was inspired by just a five-week stay on the Galapagos Islands. I found his accounts of the animal and plant life, and their adaptation to variations in their particular immediate environment, both fascinating and seductive, and ever since I had nursed a yen to see them for myself.

Between three and five million years ago the tips of the successive eruptions from the older Galapagos Platform emerged from the sea and the barren volcanic islets came into being. Hence, in geological terms, they are comparatively 'recent' and provide a rare opportunity for the study of the colonisation, and give room for endless speculation on the mysteries of how all the species arrived, and adapted specifically to the variant conditions on each island, in order to survive.

My adventure began when my younger daughter, Helen, left me at Heathrow, on 29 December 1993, with seven total strangers with whom I was to spend the next eighteen days - for the most part on a 96ft Brigantine Schooner. I arrived at 7.35 am, just five minutes after the recommended two and a half hours before the scheduled flight time. I was the last - apart, that is, from the Naturetrek leader (yes, they had come up trumps this time), Andrew Cleave, "naturalist, author, lecturer, photographer, environmental site manager" - who appeared twenty minutes later, very relaxed and laissez-faire. He'd done it all before, three times I think.

The rest of the group comprised Liliane, a blonde Jewess from Rye, who it soon became apparent was interested but not adventurous; Wendi and Kate, two well-spoken middle-aged lady cousins who were well informed in all areas of natural history, and particularly well equipped, especially in the region of first-aid; Ferdi, a Cockney Indian solicitor in his forties from Woodford Green, now managing his mother's, largely Asian, General Medical Practice; and two younger couples - Joan and Graham, who had travelled widely through Graham's employment in the oil business; and Sheelagh and Chris, who had had numerous foreign holiday adventures and worked in the field of spectrometers.

The flight to Miami seemed a long nine hours; then, after a two-hour wait, we flew on to Quito - when the day became even longer as we put back our watches five hours. From the airport an over-laden, overcrowded mini-bus took us to the Hotel Chalet Suisse, where I rearranged my luggage, wallowed in a hot bath, and slept fitfully.

30.12.93 Thursday Daylight revealed that although we were nearly 9,000 feet up, we were nevertheless in a valley flanked by high mountains, which exhibited glimpses of snow-capped peaks as the misty clouds rolled about.

A 6.30 am call made sure we were all ready for the trip to the Cotopaxi National Park. We drove along the Pan-American Highway, aptly named the 'Avenue of Volcanoes', and up to the high slopes of Cotopaxi. Our guide, Isabella, intimated that she had climbed as high as the snowline: it took us all our time to drag ourselves in slow time round the lake. The 12,000 feet altitude was taking its toll. (Cotopaxi reaches 20,000 feet and is the highest active volcano in the world.)

The vegetation warranted at least a week's study. Thriving Acacias and Eucalyptus contrasted noticeably with the less vigorous, introduced pines. Green Alchemilla, Stag Moss, and an infinite variety of attractive ferns gave an impression of lush, comfortable vegetation. A colourful carpet of tiny sprawling plants spread over the higher ground. The blue blooms of the Jacob's Ladder were quite stunning.

A preponderance of very keen (obsessive?) 'twitchers' in our group drew the attention of us lesser mortals to the Tyrant Flycatcher; Plumbeous Sierra Finch - Finches were to become something of a holiday theme; Cinclodes; Andean Tit-spinetail; the impressive Carunculated Caracara; and, around the lake, the Andean Lapwing; Black Hawk; Great Thrush; Slate-coloured Coot; Blue-winged Teal; Rufous-coloured Sparrow; an unnamed duck; and, just as we were leaving, the Black-headed Andean Gull. There may well have been others but my natural history receptors were satiated for the time being.

We took a longish drive to a delightful sixteenth century Spanish Hacienda, where we enjoyed a substantial meal of ham salad, soup, fried chicken, and delicious bananas - another holiday theme. Liliane was a vegetarian and opted for the salad and the soup. I had half a chicken carcass (more or less) floating in my soup but managed to prevent young Chris from voicing his observation on the subject to his wife, within Liliane's earshot. Liliane did not feel very well afterwards and complained of a headache, but I imagine it was the altitude, not the soup. Against her homoeopathic principles, she accepted a Migreleve tablet and soon recovered.

We came out to pouring rain, the sight of a wet little man up a home-made, alarmingly flexible ladder, minus a safety harness, singing as he painted the roof, and the quick flash of a humming bird enjoying the nectar of a large Datura shrub. During the drive back to Quito, I sat on the back row of the minibus with Ferdi and Graham, who dived enthusiastically into the 'Birds of Columbia' and discussed the environment, conservation, and lack of government motivation, in relation to ornithology.

Liliane and I had changed traveller's cheques at the hotel that morning and apparently cleared them out of the local mucky, multi sucre currency notes, so Andrew led us on a lengthy trail to a hotel, for those who needed money for the Galapagos: he also wanted others of us to get our bearings for two weeks hence, when he, Ferdi, Kate, and Wendi would be going off on the 'Jungle Extension'. The route did seem unnecessarily long for weary, under-oxygenated tourists, and led one of the party to suggest that Andrew was brilliant and charming, but an academic and practically useless. I reserved judgement!

I washed and changed and re-packed, putting warm travelling clothes in a bag to leave at Hotel Chalet Suisse. Andrew, Chris, Sheelagh, Liliane, and I went out for a light meal at a local crêperie and enjoyed getting to know each other - and the currency - a little better. I was in bed by 11 pm and anticipated the morrow's journey to the Galapagos with mounting excitement.

GALAPAGOS

Palo Santo : Red Mangroves : Great Blue Heron

Angelique boarded New Year's Eve

31.12.93 Friday   The flight to the Galapagos was via Guayaquil, the commercial capital of Equador. We were surprised on our arrival at Baltra (an air base built by the US in the Second World War for patrolling approaches to the Panama Canal) by an extra tax. And also by the first sight of the yellow-flowering Prickly Pear Cactus, conspicuous above the arid desert vegetation all around. An airport bus of sorts took us to the ferry from the south of the island and, as we sailed over to Santa Cruz, the silver-grey of the dry zone gaunt Palo Santo 'holy stick' trees contrasted strikingly with the shoreline's dense Red Mangroves, among which stood an authoritative Great Blue Heron.

Another bus drove us down the length of Santa Cruz, but we had a stop and walked near impressive caldera (sink holes) at the summit of the volcano, admired tall Clubmoss, and an infinite variety of unusual ferns. We were charmed by a male Vermilion Flycatcher and educated in painstaking detail to observe the subtle differences between the umpteen species of Darwin's sparrow-like Finches. One such, male and 'Ground', (at this stage I had not seen enough to distinguish 'small' from 'medium' from 'large', never mind 'Ground') came and perched obligingly on Andrew's hand as we ate a very welcome alfresco meal at sunset, near the end of our ride to Puerto Ayora on the south coast of the island.

We piled our luggage on the busy quayside, admired the Flame Trees as they glowed in the artificial lights, stocked up with wine and then waited for the panga. It took twenty minutes for the little vessel to reach our boat, the Angelique, out in the bay. As we went out further and further into the dark, and beyond all visible craft, bobbing up and down on the quiet black water, Chris murmured "We're running out of boats!".

The Angelique was anchored, we realized later, in the vicinity of the house belonging to the captain, Franklin Angermeyer, son of a German father and an Ecuadorian mother, early settlers in the Galapagos. We were welcomed aboard by Sarah, the captain's friend, and housekeeper for the cruise, who had a surprisingly penetrating Sloane Ranger voice (for this neck of the woods, anyway). The captain himself did not appear but members of the crew presented themselves, whom we later came to know as Edy, the smiling chubby cook, Vincente, the panga and anchor man, Camillo, who looked after our creature comforts, and Enrique, who climbed to the top of the rigging like a monkey. All nodded their heads and looked pleasant, although I suspect they understood as little English as I did Spanish. We were shown to our cabins (I had one to myself in spite of not paying a 'single' supplement), and then enjoyed a delicious buffet supper of fresh fish and exotic fruits on deck, and watched the moon rise and talked of the morrow. It was wonderful: the scene was set.

At about 3 am there was a knocking on my cabin door. I aroused myself sleepily, remembering just in time that I was on the top bunk. I opened the door to Camillo, who had come to check that I had closed the porthole, as we were to start sailing. I hadn't, and I couldn't, so he obliged. I am not sure, in retrospect, how I understood all this!

SANTA FE

Red legs, red carapaces : Juan with guitar

1.1.94 Saturday   Now, the next morning, it was New Year 1994, and during the night we had sailed to Santa Fe. After a good breakfast at 7 am, the panga took us ashore for our first wet landing, that is, we paddled from the little boat to the sandy shore, where we saw our first Sea Lions, watched by Galapagos Hawks. We walked through a forest of Palo Santo trees and smelt the heavy, aromatic, resinous sap from a damaged trunk. Land and Sea Iguanas observed us, often without twitching a muscle as we studied them. It was easy to imagine that their faces expressed human emotions such as pleasure (some looked as if they were smiling), severity, or plain bad temper. Galapagos Pigeons (doves) with soft blue eye rings, comfortable brown bodies, and red legs, reminded me of partridges but they came much closer. The Sally Lightfoot Crabs moved their conspicuous red carapaces swiftly and smoothly over the rocks, sometimes giving a glimpse of powerful blue underneath.

We swam from the Angelique, then had lunch, and retired to our cabins for a siesta, but I spent the time trying to take pictures of the Sea Lions and Brown Pelicans which swam right outside my open porthole. We walked again in the afternoon and returned to tea and banana cookies.

Later, a vegetarian supper was followed by Juan's nightly talk. He was the mandatory local guide travelling with us and preparing us for the morrow. He was a dapper little chap, perpetually smart in pressed shorts and shirt, with unlimited enthusiasm for his beloved islands. His grasp of the local natural history was impressive but he was not too proud to ask Andrew to update or improve his knowledge. His skill on the guitar was an added bonus.

ESPAÑOLA

Noisy Sea Lions and Mockingbirds
Blue-footed Boobies and Red-billed Tropicbirds

2.1.94 Sunday It had taken longer to sail to Española (Hood) than expected. The night had brought cross-winds, which had necessitated a fair amount of tacking. We went ashore at Punta Suarez, where noisy Sea Lions competed for our attention with the Hood Mockingbirds, whose persistent, strident calls, together with their purposeful, sizeable beaks, more than made up for their insignificant, mottled-grey plumage.

We walked through densely-populated Booby territory, Masked and Blue-footed, easily identified, as their names suggest: the blue seemed strange and unnatural. The sea was not rough enough to demonstrate a local blowhole but we enjoyed the large numbers of Marine Iguanas everywhere, some of the males very handsome in unexpected and striking colours. Swallow-tailed Gulls, and exotic Red-billed Tropicbirds, with their incredibly long tail feathers, gave grace and elegance to the scene.

A Masked Booby was hatching its chick, or 'giving birth', as an American tourist advised us! Most of the Waved Albatrosses had gone, leaving a weird guano-spattered landscape, but we saw one at close quarters, and then another with its ungainly, single, unevenly-fledged chick. The weather was very hot and even I resorted to a hat and sunglasses. Wendi had a heavy fall, and her metal water bottle, which got caught between her and the hard stone, was dented, and cracked a rib - confirmed after she returned home. I was relieved that she had not fractured her hip, for the fall looked as if she could have done just that. She moved gingerly for days but made little fuss and joined in all the excursions. As we tried to board the panga, the mother of a very young Sea Lion became exceptionally aggressive and, when she realized she was outnumbered, turned her frustration on the pup.

The wind got up and it turned really cold that evening (all a matter of degree). The water supply - always fickle and only expected from 6.00 am to 6.30 am, and between 6.15 pm and 6.45 pm on any day - diminished from a fine trickle to a drip. Wendi was shocked and in considerable pain, Chris had the flu and looked awful, and Juan said he felt 'very ill'. Not a very happy evening. However, Juan did manage to give us the usual briefing, after an excellent supper.

FLOREANA : Early settlers - Margaret Wittner

Birds Crabs Turtles : Goggling delights : Pumpkin soup

3.1.94 Monday Floreana was our next port of call, an island steeped in the mysterious history of disappearing early settlers. Margaret Wittner, one of these, had certainly not disappeared. Well over 80, and with younger members of her family, she still ran the post office and shop. Joan had quite a conversation with her in German and we all took pictures. Several of us wrote cards, and paid over the odds for them to be sent back home from Frau Wittner's emporium, but very few had reached their destinations about four months later!

3 January 1994

SALLY LIGHTFOOT CRABS on FLOREANA

We saw pale Winter Sanderling running with the tide like clockwork toys; the larger mottled Whimbrels; a 'peet-weet-weet'-ing Solitary Sandpiper; long-legged Flamingoes; a yellow-bellied Large-billed Flycatcher; a Yellow Warbler (local name Canario!); Wedge-rumped (Galapagos) Storm Petrel - aptly called the Sea Swallow; Cactus Finch; and so on. Anyone who would like to read my 'twitcher-assisted tick list' is very welcome. Spider Crabs and disappearing Ghost Crabs scuttled about, as well as my favourite Sally Lightfoots. The grey ground cover was relieved by the now-familiar yellows of the Parkinsonia Aculeata and 'bush' Scalesia.

Heavy grey clouds gathered as we walked along Turtle Bay, where the Green Sea Turtles mostly hovered near the edge of the water, presumably waiting for dusk when they would track up the beach to lay their eggs. Later, we swam near the Devil's Crown and, with the goggles, I saw Blue-striped Snappers, King Angelfish, Yellow tailed Surgeon Fish, Black Trigger Fish, and a blue Sea Urchin. Who needs to scuba dive?

As for the day's food, the most mouth-watering memories are still the pumpkin soup, the sweet papaya fruit, and the mint tea.

ISABELA ISLAND

Dolphins : Galapagos : Penguins

4.1.94 Tuesday   This morning we were allowed to sleep until 6.30 am, and, after a leisurely breakfast, enjoyed a long day's sail. Sweeping round the south of Isabela Island, a whale was spotted in the dim distance. Someone saw it blow. I just caught sight of what I think was a fin. We all sat with eyes peeled and binoculars at the ready for ages but the large unnamed mammal eluded us. There were Shearwaters, Gulls, Brown Noddies, and Phalaropes in plenty. We saw the crazed body of a Risso's Dolphin, then a Bottle-nosed Dolphin, and after a little while, a whole school of Common Dolphins.

Late afternoon, the Angelique anchored in Elizabeth Bay, halfway up Isabela Island's west coast, and the panga took us through the mangrove swamps and round the islets of colonized lava. The red of the mangrove contrasted conspicuously with a leaden sky. With the panga's engine switched off, we watched flying fish, Flightless Cormorants with tatty wings, the white-fronted Galapagos Penguins looking ready for a formal dinner date, prehistoric-looking Brown Pelicans and an insinuating Octopus. Large Iguanas looked as if they were a product of the lava rocks on which they were spread. I remember this place as strangely quiet and wonderful. A goat (introduced) popped up its head and surprised us at one juncture, its mouth overflowing with untidy vegetation.

The Finch fanatics were anxious to spot the Mangrove variety but it didn't show - even for them.

HERMIT CRABS MOVE HOUSE

Turtles : Mating, Stranded, and Skeletal : Darwin's Crater

5.1.94 Wednesday   A second panga trip to the Mangroves the following morning still did not track down this elusive little bird, but we did have a wonderful view of a Striated Heron, obligingly exposed as it sat among bare Mangrove branches. The water was quite shallow and the many rocks provided a perpetual hazard for Vincente and, in spite of his skill, we hit one of these and let in water. Chris bailed vigorously with the only container on board, but it was decided we should return to the Angelique.

We sailed further up the coast to Bahia Urvina, where the repaired panga took us for a wet landing on a steep shore which was strewn with the most beautiful shells. We watched two Hermit Crabs inspect one each of these and then move their soft little bodies out of their current shell homes and back them gingerly into the selected larger accommodation. We walked along the dark lava rocks, saw Turtles mating, assisted a stranded Turtle (after much discussion as to whether it was the right thing to do) and studied a well-seasoned Turtle skeleton. This, together with Crayfish and Coral skeletons, is the legacy of the 1954 uplift of the marine reef, which left many creatures stranded and doomed. Noisy,and very-much-alive, Pelican families squawked loudly in a clump of tall vegetation. Small sturdy Mangroves were already beginning to colonize the inhospitable disturbed coastline. It had been a fascinating afternoon.

There was an on-going discussion about the proposed route. We all (including Andrew) were very keen to go to the less-visited Tower Island, home of the Red-footed Boobies, but Captain Franklin was stone-walling the idea: difficult currents, it would take too long, had been known to take over forty hours and so on. The previous Galapagos trip which Andrew had led had been disappointed. The dispute rumbled on between the Captain, Sarah, Juan, and Andrew: the crew wore expressions of mock seriousness, which broke into mischievous smirks when their boss was out of sight.

In the meantime we sailed further up Isabela's west coast to Tagus Cove, by which time it was dark. All the lights were extinguished while Captain Franklin made the difficult manoeuvre into the narrow deep entrance. It was pitch black, piratical, surrounded by very high cliffs, in fact a crater - Darwin's Crater. Only the left-over Christmas decorations, the flashing Santas, kept twinkling on the Angelique until we were safely anchored. Juan and Edy played and sang love songs after dinner, outside on deck. The music resounded round the crater as if we were in some small theatre with wonderful acoustics.

6 January 1994   ISABELA ISLAND

DARWIN'S CRATER - viewed from above Tagus Cove

31

FERNANDINA : Rope lava, Iguanas, Lizards

Mangrove Finch : sick Sea Lions

6.1.94 Thursday The water and the electricity were late coming on, and thus the associated generator did not wake us until 7.45 am. We accomplished a difficult dry-landing on to irregular rocks, and then walked for four hours into the island. Here, the spectacular views of the insignificant Angelique resting in Darwin's Crater below, the higher inland salt lake reflecting the morning's clear blue sky, and the brilliant yellow-flowered vegetation, were far more impressive than the wild life, which was thin on the ground, in the air, and in the water. The getting-back-into-the-panga exercise was particularly difficult, and another member of the crew accompanied Vincente to assist, so that it was necessary to make two trips.

The Tower undercurrent rumbled on but the immediate programme continued as planned. We sailed on to Punta Espinosa on the north coast of Fernandina, a smaller island to the west of Isabela. Here we had a less acrobatic dry landing and walked comfortably on the Rope Lava, except over one expanse which resembled an unyielding ploughed field. There were Marine iguanas everywhere, fighting, resting, swimming, bobbing their heads and doing mini press-ups. Occasionally one obligingly provided a resting place for a lizard, some of which were strangely pale against the darker host. Twisted, sea-washed trees produced a similar effect against the sinister lava.

Whimbrels, Ruddy Turnstones, Herons and the occasional Galapagos Penguin were easily seen and appreciated: these are the kind of birds I enjoy! A row of Blue-footed Boobies lined up on a distant long ridge of lava rock and resembled the back of an enormous male Iguana, or a skyline of Palo Santo trees. I found a smooth bit of rock and watched the snow-white waves crashing over the black lava, and knew that John would have loved this place.

We walked back and saw more contrast between the dark-leaved Black Mangroves and the paler white Mangrove Shrubs. Here there were two bits of excitement. An American Oystercatcher was seen to do to death a colourful, fully-grown Sally Lightfoot Crab, with its matching stout red bill. The crab escaped temporarily more than once and made desperate bids for freedom across the dark rock, but was finally outwitted. The Oystercatcher continued its violent stabs to get at the tasty meal inside. The second piece of ornithological interest was provided by the much-sought-after Mangrove Finch. This (dare I say?) comparatively dowdy little bird was seen, as one might expect, in the Mangroves, shuffling round a tree - something like a Treecreeper I thought, olive-green in colour and somewhat foreshortened. Andrew said it had "lost a few feathers".

A few sick Sea Lions lay around in the shelter of the Mangroves. Juan said they had a virus carried by the mosquito and that this was a 'natural' disease, and as the Sea Lion population was increasing, it was 'no problem'. The poor things were pretty wretched with what could have been a painful panophthalmitis. After tea on the Angelique, we went out in the panga on a Penguin search but saw just one swimming.

That evening the Tower dispute was finally settled with a most important result - we were definitely going. We were to sail at 4.30 am, not at 4.30 pm as one faction had wanted, nor later the following morning, which had been another arguable option. I suspect this compromise meant that nobody had lost face.

Whales and Sharks : Volcanoes : Housekeeping

7.1.94 Friday The morning was spent on deck whale-spotting. Distant but distinctive fins were identified as belonging to Bryde's Whale and a False Killer Whale. Isabela's Darwin and Wolf Volcanoes provided stable landmarks as we sailed up that island's west coast. According to the map we crossed the Equator when we were more or less parallel with Isabela's Ecuador Volcano. Roca Redonda was visible far away to the north.

Tuna Fish was served for lunch: not fresh but out of a tin. Andrew refused to eat it because of the method of catching, which is said to unnecessarily damage and kill other species.

We continued to look for fins rather than finches in the afternoon (almost as difficult), and some brownish fins associated with appropriate tails were said to belong to Hammerhead Sharks. By 5.15 pm we had rounded Isabela's north coast and started down its east side. The little Pinta Island, which hadn't seemed to move its position well over to the north east for hours, eventually disappeared from view. I never did see its neighbour, Marchena, probably because it is only half Pinta's height. We could now see the other side of the Wolf and Darwin Volcanoes, with Santiago (San Salvador) ahead.

It had been a great trip with time for talking, tidying, writing notes and just thinking. Joan cut down her shorts, Sarah painted some dress fabric and I enjoyed talking to Andrew about the ordination of women, and church organs!

As the sun set, we looked for Alcedo Volcano. Tomorrow was the long trek to its crater and back. That night I thought I could see the Great Bear hovering at a strange angle on the horizon.

ALCEDO DAY

Breathtaking colours : Breathless trekkers

8.1.94 Saturday We were called at 4.40 am. Everyone was excited and even apprehensive. Our day packs were heavier than usual with the extra water, in addition to which three of the men carried yet more water to be left at strategic points on the upward journey in readiness for those who had drunk themselves dry on the way to the top, before the downward journey (like me). It was just getting light as we accomplished our wet landing, and pleasantly warm, but by 8.30 am, the temperature was set for a long, cloudless day and it was already really hot.

Andrew led with Joan, followed by Graham and Ferdi, then Chris and Sheelagh and me. Juan brought up the rear with Wendi, who was still suffering, and Kate. Liliane had opted to stay on the Angelique. The other seven of us eventually made it to the top. Selfishly, I was not sorry that young Sheelagh had a problem with altitude, so that her frequent rests coincided with mine, when my pulse went up to more than twice its usual rate.

Brilliant yellow Acacia flowers, set off by the plant's equally startling green foliage, cheered the stark background of Palo Santo trees and dusky green of the arid landscape. The occasional Vermilion Flycatcher added another welcome brilliant splash of colour. At the breathless top, hawks circled the sky and I studied them as I lay on my back in my own personal recovery position. The enormous Tortoises were even larger than I had imagined, their feet like those of an elephant. One had its rear end raised as if to allow air to pass under the shell from one end to the other: I knew how it felt.

We walked a short distance along the top, taking pictures and marvelling at the distant fumarole in Alcedo's caldera (four-and-a-half-hours' walk away - not today!). The descent started at 12.15 pm and, to my surprise, proved to be almost as wearing as the ascent. I have never been so hot in my life and felt my shoulders and calves burning - but dared not stop to apply any inadequate factor 6 for fear I would not be able to get going again. I kept imagining I could see the longed-for relief water in the forks of trees but most of them faded to nothing as I approached: I was hallucinating. I was more than grateful to Graham for a swig of his water supply when we were between refuelling points.

Somehow I stumbled down to the shore and, removing only my walking boots, staggered into the sea in my shorts and top. My whole body loved it, but especially my feet. The panga seemed to be going off in the opposite direction as we waited on shore (having returned by 4 pm as instructed). We discovered later that the anchor had become wedged between rocks and Franklin had dived down 60 feet (goggles only) to recover it. No wonder he does not like sailing round this neck of the Archipelago.

It was difficult getting back into the panga on a very choppy sea with heavy packs and tired limbs. The Angelique set sail almost as soon as we were aboard. Sarah greeted us with cookies and oh-so-welcome tea. The water supply seemed better than average so I showered and did some washing. Edy had really gone to town on the meal and produced four courses, but sadly most of us were too tired to do it justice and just wanted to drink. We asked Juan to explain: the last thing we wanted to do was to upset the chef! I was in bed by 8.10 pm. The sail that night was evidently as rough as it had been but I was only vaguely aware of any movement.

There had been plenty of scope for casualties, but the only serious sufferer was Ferdi, who had the most appalling blisters covering most of his soles. He took it easy for the next couple of days.

SANTIAGO ISLAND

Sea Birds and Sea Lions

9.1.94 Saturday   Bacon and egg for breakfast! Everyone's appetite seemed to have returned. We were now anchored at Puerto Egas, Santiago Island, on the east side of the Canal Isabela, opposite to and a bit north of yesterday's Alcedo.

We walked along the coast in a welcome breeze, studied the Galapagos Poisoned Apple, an Oystercatcher with two young, Semi-palmated Plover and Black-bellied Plover, Ruddy Turnstones, Whimbrels, Wandering Tattlers, and then some delightful groups of playing, basking and suckling Sea Lions. There was just one Golden Fur Seal dozing in a well-shadowed crevice, its blunt nose pressed up against a rock. A Yellow-crowned Night Heron was similarly photographically inaccessible. Groups of young Iguanas sat motionless in their press-up positions, facing the sun. We swam from a dark gritty beach with powerful rollers and got our costumes full of sand.

A sail along the west coast of Santiago - north, past Playa Espumilla with its spectacular geological interest - brought us to Caleto Bucanero: the very name gets the imagination going. We swam from the Angelique, which was not anchored. It drifted away and Franklin set the engine going but the wash then swept Kate and me even further away. Everyone else was back on board by now, looking anxiously over the side and becoming more distant by the second. One of the crew threw a rope which fell a long way short, but then better placed a tethered lifebelt, and pulled us in. I never imagined they'd leave us for good but it was quite a relief to be back on board. We sailed around to Santiago's east coast, to a point between it and Isla Bartolome.

BARTOLOME

Parrot Fish : Turtles : and Tourists

10.1.94 Monday   Beautiful anchoring. Panga to Bartolome, Pinnacle Rock, where we walked up steps over the extraordinary lava formation for part of the way, and then on the ash-covered slopes to the top whence there were great views of a submerged crater and of both sides of the tailpiece of the fish-shaped Bartolome. Silver grey Tiquilia Nesiotica colonised the dark talus slopes.

A second trip out in the panga took us to the 'tailpiece', where we walked along the shore and saw sharks, black fish with yellow tails, and brilliant-coloured Parrot fish, the latter momentarily suspended in incoming waves like something in aspic. There were Turtles and their tracks in abundance - and tourists, more than we had seen before. This was not surprising when we considered how many boats we had seen in the area: none as good as ours to look at, of course. We'd labelled one a 'floating gin palace'. I have to admit there was the occasional moment when I wouldn't have minded a decent gin and a comforting hot water supply.

We walked back across the Mangroves and swam from the lovely beach on the shark-less side. The heat was terrific and we were glad to submerge ourselves: even Andrew went under. We basked like the Sea Lions. After lunch we panga-d down the east coast of Santiago, where it was too rough for either a wet or dry landing. Graham and Juan swam from the panga, while we had a successful search for the Galapagos Penguins and watched two blue-footed Boobies doing their comic courtship dance.

We were due to sail (for Tower) as soon as we got back to the boat, but Sarah's cousin arrived with Franklin's cousin - they seemed to be another Sloano-Galapagos item, which Andrew said was bad news. They descended into the private nether regions of the Angelique with bottles of wine, but left about 5.30 pm, and by 5.45 pm we were on our way.

11 January 1994   The Angelique : Tower Island

TOWER ISLAND

Frigates : Red-footed Boobies : Yellow-crested Night Heron and other colours

11.1.94 Tuesday I had been badly bitten in the night by mosquitoes in spite of a firmly-closed porthole: at least the experience reminded me to take my malaria tablets, Avoclor - two once a week, on a Tuesday - plus two Paludrine every day. We had sailed into Darwin Bay of the elusive Tower Island, and were surrounded by greyish cliffs and Palo Santo Trees. Lava Gulls, immature Boobies and Swallow-tailed Gulls flew around and settled on the boat, while the rigging gave perch for several Frigate birds.

The pale yellow sand where we landed was spattered with the same birds, especially the Red-footed Boobies: it was a magic place. We walked along the coastal lava looking at nesting birds, and lingered round a small pool full of attractive little fish. Here were grouped no less than seven Yellow-crested Night Herons and one Striated Heron, all obviously replete, for none of them was feeding on the fish. We sat on the rocks at the end of the walk and watched sharks in the bay a long distance below. Some blessed clouds covered the sun and the walk back was a little cooler. Large Ground and Sharp-beaked Ground Finches were noted.

A party of chattering Germans and Americans arrived on the beach from one of the 'gin palaces' and set up a drinks apparatus. They left before us without some of their rubbish. Our conscientious Juan collected it up and said he would be reporting 'that boat'. We had a refreshing swim on the now deserted island.

I curled up in the shade on deck after lunch and actually slept. Later we landed near Philip's steps and were glad of 'his' handrails as we negotiated the boulders. There were Boobies everywhere, Masked on the ground, and Red-footed (mostly immature) sitting in the stunted Palo Santo trees which created an extensive silver landscape. The Masked Boobies' nests were interspersed with those of the Frigate Birds, on each of which sat a lone immature Frigate looking even more ungainly and out of proportion than most young birds. They are fed for three months by both parents and then for a further eight months by the mother. Small wonder their nests look so untidy and soiled; another consequence being that successful breeders cannot nest every year.

We left the Palo Santo forest and walked along the foot-trying lava on the coast. There were swirls of Red-billed Tropic Birds, Boobies and, most notably, Wedge-rumped Petrels (alias Galapagos, Storm) which were never still and from a distance resembled a swarm of locusts. We had been hoping to see a Short-eared Owl, for Andrew had seen these on previous visits, taking their pick of the Wedge-rumped Petrels, but we scoured the cliffs in vain. However, on the return lava walk, he spotted one, well back from the cliffs: this was the find of the true professional. I would never have seen it, and even if I had I would not have recognised it for what it was. A long-directed gaze through the binoculars convinced me. A small movement of its head and a slight ruffling of the feathers on its dark brown speckled chest changed it from a small log to a Short-eared Owl. It looked quite puffed up and furry. We were half an hour late back to the boat with all this owl-spotting. Franklin was waiting and we sailed immediately.

SEYMOOR ISLAND : ISLAS PLAZAS

Lots of yellow : Last night's sailing

12.1.94 Wednesday　　　　　I awoke to find we were already at Seymoor Island, a tiny piece of land just north of Baltra. This was good news for we would not have to rush. We went ashore early and saw many nests of Blue-footed Boobies along the pathway but very few were sitting. We did see an impressive display by a male Great Frigatebird, with his brilliant red pouch inflated to enormous proportions. I suspect his reaction may have been heightened by the exhibition, full length, of Ferdi's equally startling red waterproof trousers, shaken about by Chris, (Ferdi was still nursing his feet!) - possibly invoking a spirit of competition. Anyway, it provided a great photo opportunity.

The Prickly Pears and Palo Santo Trees were all stunted, presumably by the prevailing wind, although there was no wind for us as we walked back for the panga pick-up. Vincente had not arrived but another more luxurious panga (from a 'gin palace'?) had just dropped off its passengers so its boatman took us back. Franklin was champing at the bit to be on his way and we sailed immediately for the Islas Plazas. These are more or less off the middle of the east coast of Santa Cruz. We arrived at the south island just after 2 pm, having had, during the sailing, a detailed discussion about tipping and what to do with our time in Quito.

South Plaza is a long bare strip of an island. The cacti sported brilliant yellow flowers (and a Cactus Finch) and the Sesuvium formed a carpet of green, ranging through yellow and rust to red. The Land Iguanas were 'trimmed' with yellow and blended with the cacti, as did a tuneful Yellow Warbler. Flocks of Audubon's Shearwaters swooped above the steep cliffs along the southern edge of the island. Chris was anxious to get a really good picture of these birds and was reprimanded by Sheelagh for walking so close to the 50 foot drop, carrying tripod and other heavy camera paraphernalia. Juan informed us cheerfully that "two people were lost down there".

Land Iguana holes were pointed out and groups of Marine Iguanas sat on the cliffs. Walking back along the 'other' edge, Sea Lions were everywhere. One female was feeding two young, which would have been born two years apart! Two males seemed to be having a practice fight, but another very large male seemed aggressive for real when we approached the little landing stage.

We sat on deck on the Angelique, hoping to see the 'green flash' as the sun disappeared below the horizon from a clear blue sky, but at the last moment a small cloud gathered itself together, very inconsiderately, and we were denied even the possibility.

This was to be the last evening's sailing and we felt quite sad. Many of the party also felt quite sick when a heavy swell came up, and they opted to eat outside in spite of the weather. I was grateful for my marine heritage: my father was a marine engineer and both grandfathers and their fathers went to sea.

13 January 1994

Juan and - LONESOME GEORGE - at the Darwin Centre

Puerto Ayora : Santa Cruz : Darwin Centre

Finch Fanatics Fulfilled

13.1.94 Thursday We had now arrived back at Puerto Ayora, the port on the southern shore of Santa Cruz, whence we had started the cruise. We visited the Darwin Centre, read the displays on the boards and studied all the illustrations. I thought the whole layout was excellent and it meant so much more at this end of the holiday. A stifling heat gave us all very wet T-shirts.

We saw young tortoises being reared for reintroduction into the wild. Even the five-year-olds looked very small after seeing those on Alcedo. A very large one - known as 'Lonesome George' - was thought to be between a hundred and a hundred and fifty years old - so may well have met Darwin himself.

We walked to the shopping area next, where Andrew, Juan, and I had a very welcome coke. While we were enjoying our refreshment, Andrew pointed out Franklin's mother, Frau Angermeyer, who recognized him immediately and came and spoke to us. She was a strange-looking lady with her weird headgear and rah rah skirt but very pleasant and said how 'good' it was for Franklin and Sarah that we had had the two-week cruise on their Angelique. I bought a couple of T-shirts for presents and some ear-rings, and then went to the spacious, air-conditioned bank to change some more traveller's cheques.

The panga collected us and we went for a last swim from the Angelique, followed by a good lunch on board. We went ashore in the afternoon and were driven up into the hills, where we saw a variety of finches, including the Woodpecker Finch and the Vegetarian Finch, which made the finch fanatics very happy because the latter 'completed' the tick list. We walked through a green, damp, lava tunnel and emerged just ahead of a large, noisy Ecuadorian school party. Lucky children, I thought.

The last night's dinner was accompanied by copious wine, plus an outsize bottle of Southern Comfort provided by Chris and Sheelagh. Juan sang and played very well - sometimes with Edy - before, during and, for a long time, after dinner. Sarah chose this moment to produce the bar bills (I had also bought one of her hand-painted Angelique T-shirts). Most of us eventually went to bed by 11.30 pm - very late by Angelique standards.

Crew farewell : Last panga

Final dinner in Quito with a Margay

14.1.94 Friday Like most people I suspect, I had what might be called 'a slight head' for the 6 am reveille the following morning, but everyone was packed and on parade in time for breakfast. We panga-d for the very last time, bade our farewells to the crew and handed over the tips, and at Puerto Ayora boarded the bus which took us north across Santa Cruz.

I played about with some doggerel on the group personalities en route. The ferry carried us and our luggage to Baltra, where the dusty airport bus traversed that island and along the runway to the airport. We had a long wait, during which Juan entertained all and sundry in a not entirely sober fashion on his guitar.

At Quito we were met by Bert, a Dutch courier from the agency, and driven, in a more spacious minibus than we had used on arrival a hundred years ago, to the Hotel Chalet Suisse. Juan changed his shirt, splashed around his aftershave and more or less sobered up, so that by the time his lovely wife (also a guide) arrived to take him home to their young son, everything was in order. Nevertheless we handed over the not inconsiderable sum of tip money to the wife: she had a handbag!

Eventually I got to my room and, after tracking down my luggage which was not there but in the room next door, I had the long-awaited bath and wallowed in an extravagant level of piping hot water. I wrote out the doggerel 'in neat' while the jungle extension party - Kate, Wendi, Ferdi, and Andrew - were busy re-organising their gear.

We all assembled, clean and tidy, in the entrance hall and went out to dinner at Bentley's, where we had a room to ourselves, live entertainment, attentive service and an excellent meal for under £20. The bills were presented with the prices for the men and without the prices for the ladies, but we each paid for our own. Good old Ferdi paid for the lot with his credit card and then amassed a variety of currency from everyone, dollars, sterling and sucres. I enjoyed spare ribs as the main course. The doggerel went down well and I promised to send everyone a copy.

Finally, the proprietors presented the hotel 'pet' which looked a bit like an ocelot but which they called an Amazon Tiger (identified later as a Margay) - a magnificent, powerful animal, said to be young. I wondered how large it would grow. We were late to bed again: 11.30 pm.

Park shopping : 'Listed' Buildings

Chinese supper

15.1.94 Saturday   Breakfast was at a civilised 8 am, and was followed by farewells to the jungle four. Those of us remaining felt quite sad and depleted. Joan and Graham went off to shop and then bird-watch on their own, while Chris, Sheelagh, Liliane and I went searching for a particular cooperative, probably in the wrong direction. We got side-tracked into a book shop and it was Liliane who got talking to a local business woman and negotiated a lift for all of us: the cooperative was closed.

Liliane and I went off on our own and shopped in the park and thoroughly enjoyed ourselves. We bought attractive Ecuador ear-rings which looked so fragile I imagined they'd have a brief, bright life. They are still intact twelve years on and more than once I've wished I'd bought more. From a nearby vendor I bought hand-knitted woollen hats for the three granddaughters. We moved on to the street stalls, where Liliane negotiated a price for a woollen tabard, a beautifully soft light-weight alpaca garment. I cashed in on her business skills and bought one for myself for the same price. Years later, when I'd become acquainted with an expensive catalogue called 'Peruvian Connections', I saw something very similar at many times the price. The original is still going strong.

We enjoyed a pasta lunch at a roadside café and then took a taxi, with Chris and Sheelagh to Gonzalez Square in the old town, and walked to the plaza where the San Francisco Monastery was situated. An unkempt exterior belied the wealth of baroque carving inside, much of it covered in gold leaf. We wove our way through the crowded street markets and saw the Church of La Compania with its green and gold domes, and then discovered the Cathedral in the Plaza de la Independencia on which a large plaque commemorates Quito's founder, General Sucre.

We opened occasional doors from busy, noisy, side streets and found quiet deserted cloisters which were like another world. We had decided to walk back the couple of miles in the pleasantly cool cloudy weather but large raindrops began to fall. We imagined this 'shower' would soon stop, but we were wrong. It rained steadily all afternoon, evening, night and into the next morning. We got to the state where we were too wet to get into a taxi if we had happened to see one, which we didn't. For the first time in 1994 I felt really chilled. Back at the hotel I had another luxurious bath, a change of clothes and packed ready for the morrow.

Liliane and I decided to try the Hotel Paladrina recommended by Bert, the Dutch guide. We got a taxi in the rain but the driver didn't know of it. We got him to drop us at the Hotel Colón (Spanish for Columbus and nothing to do with the large bowel!) where we had changed money, and which we understood to be near our intended destination. We found the place, went to take the lift up to the seventh floor, only to be told it was closed on a Saturday. We eventually ran down an excellent Chinese restaurant where we had a tasty meal, some more than palatable Chinese wine, talked about the holiday and many other things, and got a taxi back.

Quito - Flooding

Miami : Heathrow : Barnstaple - Flooding

16.1.94 Sunday   Bert got us to the airport by 8.45 am but there had been flooding with the heavy rain, when Quito airport had been closed, so that flights were still 'catching up'. We flew out at 1.15 pm, two hours late. I was asked to change seats to oblige a heavily pregnant lady who wanted to sit next to her husband, and then again, so that a young Ecuador couple could sit with their small child. I was more than happy to finish up next to Graham and Joan. The wait at Miami was shorter because of the Quito delay and I travelled the second, longer, leg of the flight with Liliane. The night felt somewhat foreshortened as we kept putting on our watches - six hours in all. I slept very little and found myself already anticipating the schedule for the next few days at home.

We landed at Heathrow at 9 am and I was not one of the unlucky ones to have my luggage searched. I felt a touch of envy when I saw Liliane being greeted by her husband. I bought a road-rail ticket, caught a bus to Reading within half an hour, and had only a ten-minute wait for the Exeter train, which went out from the nearest platform: my luggage was getting very heavy.

At Exeter I discovered that Quito was not the only place having its transport disrupted by floods. Devon had had a very wet fortnight and no trains were running to Barnstaple. I was madly extravagant and had a taxi all the way home. An unexpected bonus was being able to talk to a taxi driver who knew all about Darwin's Theory of Evolution and had interesting opinions of his own.

All was well at Heronslake and I finished off a film by taking a pale winter sunset over the lake. It would take a lot to drag me away from here for any length of time. I took a couple of weeks to settle down. I kept having my Darwin's Finch brain cells alerted every time I saw a sparrow and, more ridiculously, was reminded of the fumaroles when I passed the smoking chipboard factory at South Molton. I had brought back a few sticks of Palo Santo wood for the vicar, thinking he might be able to use them in the church, but I kept a couple of them for myself and their heavy scent could bring back the Galapagos ambience in seconds. I posted off the music for "Fiddler on the Roof", as I had promised, to Juan, and some photographs of the crew.

I missed the company and not having anyone with me to talk to about the holiday, but I managed to bore most of Torrington. I don't expect to go to the Galapagos again. Nothing could be as fresh and new a second time and it would be tempting providence to expect everything to go so well again: the journeys, the weather, the boat with its pleasant and competent crew, the well-informed but unobtrusive leaders, and the good companionship of the other travellers.

I do hope that tourists like me continue to be properly directed, and that tourism in general is so controlled that the Galapagos Islands stay the unspoiled paradise that I have seen.

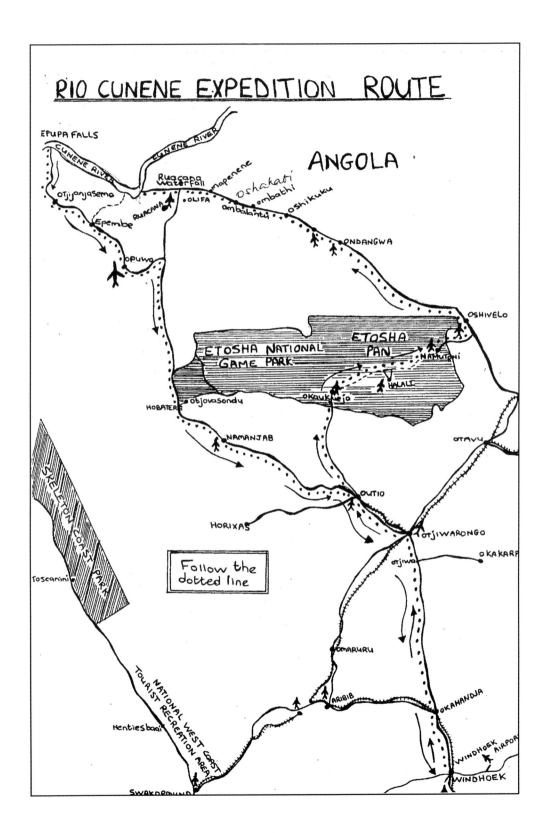

RIO CUNENE EXPEDITION ROUTE

ANGOLA

EPUPA FALLS

CUNENE RIVER

CUNENE RIVER

Ruacana Waterfall

mopenene

Oshakati

Otjijanjasema

RUACANA

OLIFA

ombathi

ambalantu

Oshikuku

Epembe

ONDANGWA

Opuwa

OSHIVELO

ETOSHA NATIONAL GAME PARK

ETOSHA PAN

NAMUTONI

HOBATERE

Otjovasondu

OKAUKUEJO

HALALI

NAMANJAB

OTAVY

OUTJO

SKELETON COAST PARK

HORIXAS

OTJIWARONGO

Follow the dotted line

OKAKARA

Toscanini

otjiwa

OMARURU

NATIONAL WEST COAST TOURIST RECREATION AREA

ARIBIB

OKAHANDJA

Hentiesbaai

WINDHOEK AIRPORT

SWAKOPMUND

WINDHOEK

CONQUERING the KUNENE

January 1995

NAMIBIA

with **World Wildlife** *and*
Wilderness Safaris

NAMIBIA

CONQUERING THE KUNENE!

A Tedious Start

12.1.95 Thursday   During the preparations for this, my third lone, long-haul, January adventure, I felt more apprehensive and more aware of being alone. Maybe my mother's death just before Christmas had had something to do with these emotions, coupled with the fact that the trips to Tanzania (1993) and the Galapagos (1994) started during or immediately after the festive season, so that I was excessively occupied, and had company, until the moments of departure.

I opted for a taxi to take me to Barnstaple for the National Express London-bound bus. Roy, the driver, had been to Africa when he was in the army and had climbed Kilimanjaro "and beyond". I was quite surprised at this revelation, probably because he is now a phlegmatic, somewhat overweight middle-aged man, more than filling his driving seat, but then we've all had other lives.

I almost fell up the pavement at the bus station (only when re-writing this twelve years later did I realize my careless footwork had started so long ago). I was looking upward for the appropriate stop and wearing my walking boots for the first time in twelve months, and a small, sad-looking girl saved the day by putting her arm out and almost dropping her cigarette. Contact thus made we talked while we waited. She was going to the funeral of a forty-three-year-old girlfriend who had died of breast cancer. I found myself telling her about John's and Mum's funerals.

The coach was half empty so everyone had a window seat. The sun shone on a lovely green and pleasant England, making the countryside look more inviting than it had done for weeks, and I wondered why I was going so far away. At Heathrow it was two hours to go before check-in, so I located the comparatively insignificant, unmanned Air Namibia desk, with its attractive yellow and blue sun and flamingo logo, and sat in a comfy seat within easy reach.

I watched and wrote and listened to the family next to me, who were returning home to Johannesburg after spending Christmas in England with relatives. A lively lad with this party, aged about eleven, kept studying me openly. I smiled, wondering whether it was the incongruous combination of my walking boots and a long skirt (my travelling 'uniform') which attracted his attention. Eventually he came up with "Are you a doctor?" "Yes," I admitted, "do I look like one?". He nodded. Well, I suppose ultimately we look like what we are if we've been at it for long enough!

The flight left promptly and in no time we were up to 43,000 feet and travelling at over 600 mph. I was seated next to a young couple, John and Louise, who were returning to Cape Town, both having been born in South Africa. They, too, had spent Christmas in England with relatives. They were very attentive and I was grateful to John for assisting with my recalcitrant meal tray, which kept sticking at a 45-degree angle.

Louise could not stand the crying of a pretty little coloured baby and became extraordinarily aggressive towards its parents. I murmured about the difficulties of its broken routine etc, and felt very uncomfortable. I fell into a fitful doze, dreamt I was pregnant, and came to in time for the end of 'Forest Gump'.

I never did get really comfortable. I took my boots off, my feet swelled and I had difficulty getting them on again; a passenger who boarded at Frankfurt took the seat in front of me, stored hand luggage underneath where my feet would have liked to have been, and tipped back the seat as far as it would go. He had more hand luggage in the overhead locker and woke with a start when I inadvertently took out his small rucksack (almost identical to mine) which was so heavy that it took my shoulders by surprise and brushed his head during its precipitous descent. I then could not get the weighty thing back, and he was obliged to assist, muttering all the time in German.

Holiday Bonding : Norma and Peter

13.1.95 Friday   We made a soft landing at 8.45 am - 6.45 am UK time - so it was a short night anyway. Fortified by a bacon and egg breakfast, we disembarked, awaited the arrival of the reluctant luggage, and boarded the bus for the forty-minute drive to the Safari Hotel in Namibia's capital, Windhoek. The heat was welcoming and relaxing and I took off my sweater.

I had been told by Chris Breen of World Wildlife, through which company I had booked my trip, that there would be an English couple travelling on the same flight, but I hadn't identified them among all the Germans and South Africans. The airport bus was sparsely populated so I plucked up courage and approached and asked a likely-looking couple if they were Norma and Peter Smith. They were indeed and I was quite relieved to see that, although they appeared to be around the same age as myself, they too had committed themselves to what promised to be a physically demanding 'holiday'.

The bus journey gave an immediate taste of the dry dusty landscape which was to become so familiar, relieved by Acacia and Palms. Near the end of the drive, on the outskirts of Windhoek, blossoming Flame Trees startled the eyes with their hotspots of colour, and a purple-blooming Jacaranda reminded me of Lilacs in an English spring.

At the Safari Sands Hotel we were directed to the less-imposing, adjacent Safari Lodge Hotel, where attentive staff welcomed us into a quiet, shaded reception area. I unpacked my belongings in spacious Room 210, and then joined Norma and Peter for a drink and a lunch of toasted sandwiches near the pool.

The sun, the food and the drink, and the relief at having arrived, brought on an overwhelming desire for sleep and I retired to my room for a kip. I was rudely awakened two hours later by 'Wilderness Safaris', who needed some document signing to say I 'had arrived and received information'. I collected my swimming things and, after correcting my name from Taylor to Tyler, signed on the dotted line.

I must have looked half asleep still, for the strapping young man in a safari suit apologised for disturbing me, explaining that the following day (Saturday) was his day off.

I joined Norma and Peter in the pool and revelled in the fresh water, which boasted something of a current from the powerful inflow and carried no sensory indication of pollution or disinfectant.

The three of us had dinner in the Welwitschia restaurant, where the superb oysters, kingclip fish, good wine, and explorative conversation as we got to know each other, made for a memorable first holiday evening.

14 January 1995

Waterhole at Etosha National Park

LA CASSE : WINDHOEK : Places with 'O' : ETOSHA

Guides/Carers

14.1.95 Saturday The following morning I packed my warm travelling clothes into a distinctive red plastic bag (courtesy of the NHS) and left them at Reception, ready for the anticipated return ten days later.

I indulged in a breakfast of exotic fruits and white toast and was joined by a Canadian businessman who was making a recce into the possibility of gathering Namibian lobsters into his 'fresh/frozen' worldwide fish company. Travelling with him was an older man who was quick to inform me that he was a gynaecologist. "My personal physician" commented the other. Norma and Peter joined us, looking safari well dressed, like the seasoned travellers they turned out to be.

We were waiting outside, on parade at 9 am as instructed, in the merciful shade of an Acacia Tree with cheery spikes of yellow flowers. At 10.30 am Peter rang Wilderness Safaris to check on the arrangements. Yes, they were on their way - from Cape Town. A Toyota minibus, "Felix Unite", drove unhurriedly over the sleeping policeman at 11.30 am and out popped Gavin, the long-haired well-muscled driver, and the smiling Andy, whose good humour never faltered during the entire trip. A client called Maurice, a well-built American, followed after them, announcing that he was going for a swim in the hotel pool. Andy looked marginally disconcerted but agreed to return and collect him later.

The rest of us were destined for Windhoek to buy camp and personal supplies. We bought drinks and fruit and Peter purchased a rather smart hat. Gavin returned with a repaired tyre to the Kodak advertisement hoarding at the pre-arranged time, we climbed in, collected Maurice, and were really on our way.

I sat on the back seat, intended for three passengers but accommodating just me and Charles, a Jewish lawyer from Johannesburg, in his thirties I imagined: so there were just five takers for this trip.

We travelled north on reasonable roads through places with wonderful names like Okahandja, Otjiwarongo, and Outjo. The people by the roadside and the cattle all looked well nourished but, since the terrain for the most part appeared so dry and desolate, I wondered how this could be. The temperature was high and even the draught through the open window was uncomfortably warm.

We arrived at Okaukuejo in the Etosha National Park, where Norma and I had a very welcome swim in one half of a goggle-shaped pool. Maurice chatted up a couple of younger women in the other half.

Later we went down to the nearby waterhole. A lone humpy Wildebeest hovered on the far side of the water and then drank. A couple of brown Hyenas skulked about and a Black-backed Jackal made a brief appearance. This was the beginning of the magic, enhanced by the team's superb savouries - such as tasty salami on crunchy bits of biscuit, and concoctions of mussels, olives and nuts. I suddenly realised in the pleasant early evening temperature, that I was very hungry. We all repaired to the nearby campsite, where we did justice to the meal prepared on an open fire.

By this time we had met Shane, our leader, a man of large rugby physique, excellent organising skills and a wicked sense of humour. As well as Gavin and Andy, there were quietly spoken Chris, and Dave, a tall slim fellow with a stronger accent, who was presently travelling the world, financing himself by working for the likes of 'Felix Unite'. These five had the unenviable task of looking after five others, mostly twice their age, who must have seemed verging on the geriatric.

We returned to the waterhole where a spotlight gave almost daylight vision. Elephants came and drank, bathed each other and generally socialized, and were altogether a delightful spectacle. One Lion came and sat for a while and then departed. Aristocratic Giraffes measured their stilted steps to the water's edge and drank long and hard.

A Black Rhinoceros came trundling down to the water with a young one: Etosha supports more than 10% of the world's population of this rare creature.

All the time we were sitting there, drinking in these viewings of large animal life, Helmeted Guinea Fowl chuntered comfortingly as they nestled down in nearby leafless trees, their dumpy outlines clear against the orange late evening sky; Rufous-cheeked Nightjars swooped, usually successfully, for large moths and other insects; an enormous noisy black insect with a heavy undercarriage was identified as a Parasitic Wasp and not to be encouraged. A large Bat was temporarily imprisoned in a thorn bush so that we were able to get a really close look at the poor thing, but it wriggled and manoeuvred itself free.

Eventually, when it had been dark for some time (of which we had lost all account), someone came down from the camp to warn us that it would be a 5.30 am call in the morning.

Norma, Peter and I sauntered back, expecting to sleep in tents, but our 'accommodation' consisted of a ground sheet, a lilo, and the sleeping bag we had each brought. Only very rarely in a hot English summer have I slept outside. In the event, it was wonderful. I lay cosily in my little space with warm air, a slight breeze and an uncluttered view of the star-studded African sky, where a shooting star and a steadily revolving satellite added to the wonder.

I remembered that I had not written my diary or ticked the bird list with which we'd been provided. I got out the torch: I knew that if I left it all until the morning there'd be so much else going on, I'd never remember. I ticked off 16 birds, particularly noting the ones which were special to me. The Helmeted Guinea Fowl fascinated me (maybe because I have some of the unhelmeted variety back home). I loved the colourful European Bee-eater, the Lilac-breasted and Purple Rollers, the smart Fork-tailed Drongo, and the collections of Sociable Weavers whose confluent communities of nests appeared to thatch the trees.

I would never have recognized half of these birds if it had not been for Charles, who was a very committed ornithologist, and Phil Hockey, the official ornithologist accompanying the expedition, whom I've failed to mention. He was co-author of the latest (Sasol) 'Birds of Southern Africa'. His enthusiasm knew no bounds nor any fatigue, but he was patient and willing to stoop to our level, an amusing raconteur and altogether very good company. He was attached to the University of Cape Town but seemed to spend much of his time in field work.

Black face : Black Mask : Black Leggings

A Rare Relationship : Namutoni

15.1.95 Sunday   The next day was a Sunday, and I couldn't believe it was only three days since I'd left home: so much had happened. Despite being awakened at 5.30 am, I surprised myself by feeling quite refreshed. We set out on the pre-breakfast drive and the pros were bemoaning the dryness, and the lateness of the rains. (I found myself hoping that they stayed away for the next ten days, when we would be sleeping in the open). We had a good view of a Black-faced Impala Ram, with its magnificent, long, graceful, lyre-shaped horns and distinctive blaze. Next there was the much larger Gemsbock, (Oryx), with its rapier horns and a black mask.

Peter spotted a bird busy 'doing something' and Gavin backed up the Toyota for us to watch a Lesser Chestnut-backed Kestrel sitting on the ground in the shrubby undergrowth, devouring what was left of a snake.

We changed and had breakfast and set off for a drive along the southern border of the lake. It was very hot and some of the smaller watering places were disappointingly dry, but with the help of the experts we identified another 14 birds. I enjoyed in particular the Secretarybird with its black leggings; the black, white and chestnut Bateleur tilting its unflapping wings from side to side, like a French tightrope walker as its name implies; and the Northern Black and Redcrested Korhaans. I was delighted to be able to buy the 'Birds of South Africa' book at the Namutoni shop the next day - and signed by Phil Hockey, of course. The illustrations were such a help that I was almost convinced I'd seen what I was supposed to have seen!

We travelled on and stopped at Halali, where I had a swim in the rectangular pool and we enjoyed a welcome fresh salad lunch prepared by the boys. Phil was going on an hour's birdwatch walk and some of us decided to accompany him. After all, it was a rare opportunity to spot rare birds with a rare birdspotter. I still felt very hot and even the swim and the cold lunch had not cooled me down completely, but I thought I'd go: mad dogs and Englishmen.

After a ten-minute walk down a red, blisteringly hot track to a dried-up waterhole, I wished I'd stayed back at camp, mumbled my exhausted apologies and ambled very slowly back, but not until I had seen a Namaqua Sandgrouse with its long pointed tail and the small Namaqua Dove, also with a long pointed tail.

I went under the shower at the swimming pool, fully (scantily) clothed and gradually cooled off.

The afternoon drive found the sun on the back of the minibus so that Charles and I were uncomfortably hot. I covered my head and neck with hat and scarf. Once again there was little water where water should have been but we had stunning views of Giraffes, Zebras old and young in abundance, families of Wildebeest, close-ups of Elephants, Black-faced Impala, elegant Springbok, hefty Gemsbok, and a pair of dusky brown, shy, large-eared Steenbok. A Cheetah ran across our path, giving us a really good, if fleeting, impression as it bounded away like an enormous greyhound.

A Bat-eared Fox presented itself, sitting quietly within easy viewing distance and a little further on, within a few hundred yards of each other, two Honey Badgers entertained us for minutes as they dug away, making clouds of dust, presumably foraging for prey. On each occasion an impressive Pale Chanting Goshawk sat waiting, as if to cash in on the meal. Phil confessed that he had been about to tell us that this apparent relationship between the Honey Badger and the Pale Chanting Goshawk was a myth and he had never seen it.

Towards the end of the afternoon we came across a waterhole still living up to its name and identified 14 more birds for the tick list: among them, the huge, unmistakable Marabou Stork with its weird combination of featherless head and neck and massive bill, the African Spoonbill, and a large raptor sitting against the sun on an overhanging branch of a dead tree near the water. There was much discussion about its identity but a majority expert opinion eventually settled for an immature Bateleur. (Echoes of that immature Lammergeyer on Mount Kilimanjaro).

We arrived at Namutoni Fort in the early evening and climbed the winding steps to the top, stopping on the first floor for a brief history lesson. The spot had been the site of an early Wambo kraal, had had the interest and blessing of Swiss botanist Hans Schinz, and had become a control post against the spread of rinderpest in 1884: the complete fort was destroyed by the Wambo in 1904, after the five German incumbents had escaped, and it was re-built after the Herero uprising. In 1907 Kaokoland and Etosha were proclaimed a game reserve but after the end of the tribal wars Namutoni lost its administrative status and was closed. In 1914 South African troops sealed off the German troops' north-eastern escape route, and they surrendered at Namutoni. It was made a national monument in 1951, and restored and opened for tourism in 1958.

Scaling more stairs and standing on the high ramparts, we watched the sunset make ever-lengthening shadows over plains that seemed to stretch for ever. Palm Swifts swooped between golden highlights of the Palm Trees and a few relaxed tourists talked quietly and drank in the approaching darkness. Suddenly I'd forgotten the heat of the day as I stood and blinked away the daylight, straining to see the fading horizon until it did the final abrupt disappearing trick.

The camping facilities were good and I needed no second bidding to have a really leisurely shower and hair wash, being advised that this was the last of such for six days.

There were another 46 bird ticks, the most for any day: the Violet Woodhoopoe, with its long red bill and not looking much like the chestnut, black and white patterned Hoopoe I'd seen before; the quietly-coloured Grey Hornbill (which made a call just like the tapping of Morse Code in long ago Girl Guide days); the Southern Yellow-billed Hornbill with red eye ring which made me feel I was being watched; the charming little Tinkling Cisticola with its bell-like call; the shiny blue-green Glossy Starlings; and the orange and black male Paradise and Shaft-tailed Whydahs.

I ate well and slept well, only vaguely aware of the Jackals rattling the slops bin, and the screeching Blacksmith Plovers.

Early start : Damara Dik-dik : Nama recycling

Baobab Church : The River and a Full Moon

16.1.95 Monday   We were scheduled for a 5.30 am start. The object of our sunrise drive, according to Phil, was to see the Black-faced Babbler: its small black patch at the base of the skull and bright yellow eye were described as 'diagnostic': it was also said to be 'furtive'. It was either very successful in the latter attributed characteristic or else it was simply absent altogether. We stayed away for two hours and, in spite of Phil's (cheating?) using recorded sound of the Babbler's birdsong, always preceded by a South African voice reciting "Blackfaced Babbler, 561" (so that other birds would know what they were listening to, suggested one cynic), answer came there none, apart from the shrill whistling of a Southern White-crowned Shrike. Phil was obviously disappointed for we were in the centre of the alleged small distribution area of this elusive bird.

We did see a diminutive Damara Dik-dik: this tiny antelope stood twitching its long mobile nose for a few seconds and then took off silently, like a disappearing shadow.

We breakfasted, changed and packed and had a wander round the well-appointed camp shop before we left.

We journeyed north west through Nama country. The Nama were the first inhabitants who migrated in prehistoric times into what was then a vast wilderness: these hunter-gatherers moved about in groups of fifty or so.

Their present-day descendants were strung all along the roadside, some groups in bright clothing, others more scantily clad, with small herds of cattle which looked well nourished, as did their owners. The land looked desperately overgrazed. Andy explained that this was subsistence farming, with government help and, usually, with one or two of the young men from each family working in nearby towns to maintain the lifestyle.

We stopped on the roadside and looked at a large kraal opposite. It consisted of a maze-like series of fences, providing spaces for the animals as well as the people.

Each chief may have several wives, and the culture and the associated way of life apparently makes for an enviable contentment.

The terrain and general landscape continued the same, but further on there were more goats, mules, and horses, as well as cattle.

The telegraph poles, which followed the road faithfully all the way, were embellished by nests of the Whitebacked Vultures, whose habitat was described as "Savanna, nests on tree tops in small colonies"!

As we entered Ondangua there were bizarre hoardings on small roadside stores: 'SWAPS COMING', 'BAR FOR SURE', 'SORRY SUPERMARKET'. Andy said that they felt there was a certain prestige in having English words displayed.

We stopped at the market and I walked round with Andy and Maurice. There was a strong emphasis on recycling. Several years on, as I write this, North Devon has probably only just caught up.

The open meat market was doing a brisk trade: a whole fillet of beef, strung up next to what looked like shin and brisket, looked really good. The spices, flours, fruit in abundance, and a fascinating collection of vegetables all held our attention. I've never seen such startlingly orange red chillies. Maurice tried on a pair of psychedelic shorts which looked dreadful: he paraded about singing loudly, to the amusement of the market men but to our embarrassment: he didn't buy them.

We continued on our way, past a bomb-proof hangar (another war legacy) to see a church in a Baobab Tree. There is a native belief that God plants only mature Baobabs, all parts of which have their uses: the young saplings hardly resemble the full-grown trees in any way, which may account for this misconception. The Baobab Tree church had a tiny altar, a cross, and copious bat droppings on the small pews. It was near an old army base, where Andy had at one time been in charge of a unit of coloured South African soldiers.

We reached a place by the river at lunchtime: a pre-arranged meeting point for us in the minibus, and for the rest of the team and the equipment in the 4WD. It was an idyllic spot and I followed a fluttering crowd of butterflies with my big camera. They latched on to low branches of trees in the shade and I tried to remember the pictures that I'd seen of this kind of behaviour: 'Monarch'?, 'Milkweed'? I didn't know and nor did anyone else.

There had obviously been some misunderstanding about the rendezvous, for we waited literally hours. It grew progressively more hot and sticky. We wandered around and then sat in the shade. There developed a well-informed seminar on English poets and novelists. I was soon out of my depth.

Some time after 5 pm the party was reunited and we all drove on to the intended camp site, which was quite breathtaking. We had a short paddle-boat instruction, with demonstration on securing the lifejacket and crash helmet, and then a brief preparatory trip on the river while there was still some daylight. I was crew with Maurice, who boasted to "have done a lot of this sort of thing", and opted to steer from behind. I was grateful, not realizing until later that I could not see him and that he was disinclined to steer or paddle!

Birdwise it had been another good day, with 24 new sightings - including a Grey Lourie with its distinctive large, ash-grey crest which put me in mind of a beehive hairdo; Greyhooded Kingfisher; Whitebrowed Robin; Plumcoloured Starlings (beautiful hue); and Redbilled Oxpecker doing exactly what its name implies. We had also had a fleeting glimpse of a Vervet Monkey with its black face, soft grey fur-like hair and powder-blue scrotum.

The sun went down and an almost full moon came up over the far side of the river. We were hungry and tired: we all cleared our plates and in spite of the heat, I slept well. I was loving this sleeping under the stars.

So *this* is WHITE WATER RAFTING!

17.1.95 Tuesday   I was aware of noisy Rosyfaced Lovebirds in full throat before dawn but I slept until 7 am.

After breakfast we had another, more intensive, session about paddling on the river, from Gavin and Shane. Shane apologized in advance for any swearing he might do in times of crisis. Lifejackets were tightened to total expiration point and crash helmets inspected: I began to feel ever so slightly nervous. I had really had no conception as to the nature of white water rafting: I'd had this picture in my mind of the African Queen, floating gently down river. This was the beginning of the proper adventure and I was in for a rude awakening.

Peter and Norma got into the first boat, and Maurice and I were installed into the second. Charles went the long way round by road that day, keen to spot birds with Phil. The river was beautiful, varying from long, wide, slow stretches to narrower, faster places of which we were given warning with "lifejackets and helmets on". No, it was not like the African Queen.

Maurice talked and sang and was quite entertaining until I became tired of paddling alone. I was quite relieved when Gavin and Chris each came up to us, separately, in their kayaks and suggested to Maurice that he should (a) paddle all the time, and (b) in time with me! Not that it made an awful lot of difference.

We stopped on the river bank for tuna and salad lunch which went down well. Most of us even dozed for twenty minutes: then we were off again and paddled on until late afternoon.

I walked into the warm water in my clothes and dried off comfortably in the evening breeze.

There was lots of bird talk. It's risky taking cameras and binoculars on the raft, and although there are sealed, tied-down containers for first aid and food, I imagined that by the time I had retrieved my camera from such, the object of my interest would have flown.

Another 20 ticks for the day including, not surprisingly, the enormous (the world's largest) Goliath Heron; the smart, big-headed black and white Pied Kingfisher; the Giant Kingfisher whose large size surprised me in spite of its name; streamlined speedy Wiretailed Swallows; and the black, white, and russet aptly-named Brubru, who could stand in for BT any time.

A full moon came up early over the hill beyond the far side of the river so that there was no real darkness as we ate our supper.

I snuggled down in my sleeping bag and hoped that my shoulders wouldn't be stiff in the morning. We'd paddled for about eight hours, I reckoned. It looked from the map as if we would cover altogether 80 - 90 miles along the river.

Shoes : Hat : Rapids and Himbas

Guides to the Rescue

18.1.95 Wednesday I slept well until 7 am, when Andy brought me a cup of tea. After breakfast we were subjected to more paddle boat drill in preparation for more turbulent waters ahead. My arms were not aching and I was feeling quite pleased with myself until one of the team questioned me about my footwear. I had on a pair of ancient, multi-coloured Van Dal slip-ons, which he vowed I would lose the first time I came off the raft. Horrors! - 'Come off?' - 'First time?'. The thought of being shoeless on those thorn-ridden banks was alarming. Where were my 'rafting shoes'? I thought quickly. "They weren't on the kit list", I volunteered. "But you knew you were white-water rafting", he came back, incredulously. I remembered my spare pairs of walking boots' laces, and took them under the shoes and laced them up round my legs so that I resembled a Roman centurion - but the footwear stayed on, in spite of all the subsequent happenings.

Another serious boob I made was somehow to leave my hat at the picnic site where we'd waited for ever on Monday. We were not obliged to wear the crash helmets on the gentle stretches of river but it was essential to cover the head from the sun. Fortunately Peter, whom I had encouraged to buy a hat in Windhoek, now had two hats and he let me use the new one. It was a bit on the large side so the other spare pair of laces came in useful for tying it on.

Thus equipped we climbed round, over uneven rocky terrain beyond the falls, to study the form beyond. While we waited for the team to portage the boats, a Monteiro's Hornbill sat obligingly on an outcrop overhead, its heavy red bill pointing down as if it was keeping us under observation.

We looked nervously at the cascade of surging water, a Grade 5 rapid, and heard how we were to keep with a line through the tongue of water to avoid going into the stopper wave. Suddenly it was realized that Maurice was not in on this essential briefing: he was summoned over the rocks, eventually appeared, and the instructions were repeated.

There were three paddle boats today: Andy was taking Charles. Charles is something of a dwarf and has a strange stumping gait with barely adequate coordination. He needed the likes of Andy. I couldn't help wishing that I had one of the professionals with me: my confidence in Maurice was diminishing by the hour.

Well somehow, more by good luck than good management, we stayed on course and it was exciting to feel the powerful swirl of water as the boat dropped successfully below the cascade. I suspect Andy tried to do something fancy and he came out but fortunately Charles stayed in.

Little cascades, stopper waves, and inhospitable rocks followed, and then a bigger rapid, through which I paddled for all I was worth, as instructed, and again we remained in the boat. We walked round a subsequent terrifying-looking rapid: Gavin came down in his kayak.

Halfway down the third rapid I leaned away from 'an obstacle' (a rock) instead of towards it and out I came. It was really not as frightening as I had imagined and I found myself clinging on to Norma and Peter's boat. 'Mine', with Maurice still sitting at the back, had raced downstream. I did my serious best to climb into Norma and Peter's boat but I just could not get far enough forward. Dear strong Shane came along in his kayak and just humped me unceremoniously over: then I transferred back with Maurice. At least the water was warm and I dried off, including the lifejacket, in no time. Sunglasses and shoes stayed in position.

The journey continued uneventfully until lunchtime, through a wider, calmer river, flanked by thorny vegetation and I got my arm gouged by one overhanging thorny branch. In view were the Zebra Mountains, striped by dark granite scree slopes, interspersed with pale, dry, winter vegetation. Olive Bee-eaters (not common in this terrain according to the 'experts') flew around everywhere, their shiny green backs catching the overhead sun.

The lunch stop was memorable not only for the food and drink but also for a pleasant encounter with a Himba family. The Himbas' forebears were Herero herders who were dispossessed by the Nama warriors during the nineteenth century and fled to the remote and inhospitable northwest: they were known as Ova-Himba which means beggars. Their presence was gentle and unobtrusive and one of their naked, well-nourished little boys collected the hard small fruits from under the wild apple tree where we sat. The women were very striking, their bodies and their hair coloured with red ochre. I had read that powdered oxides are mixed with butter fat to protect their skin from the harsh climate, but this treatment also makes them very attractive. The married lady in the group had long finely-plaited hair, mounted by a leather adornment to indicate her status. Two young girls wore toning skimpy T-shirts and skirts (fashion gets everywhere), and white belts to indicate their virginity. Another young woman nursed a toddler. The crew gave them some left-over food and received a recycled metal bracelet in return.

We were told that it would not be necessary to wear crash helmets and lifejackets in the afternoon so ours were put in the back of our boat, where Maurice said he had fastened them as instructed. We soon encountered a mini-rapid with rocks: the river was low. My steerer failed to avoid the largest of these in spite of my pleas (screeched) to keep to the right. This time I leaned towards the obstacle but I still came out while the boat remained fixed in a semi-upright position. Our boat had no rope on the side at the end I needed but I managed to get hold of the small towing loop, while a strong undercurrent tried seriously to sweep me under the offending rock.

Maurice said he'd try and free the boat (why hadn't he fallen out?) but I told him not to. I had no desire to be dragged downstream, with the boat or without it, all among the rocks without a lifejacket or helmet. Everyone seemed very far away but I saw Kevin beach his kayak and start stumbling between the rocks towards the deeper water. "Hold on" he said, and I did. As I waited, my eyes caught sight of our lifejackets and helmets floating downstream. "You were supposed to tie those in." I spluttered. He said nothing. Gavin loaded me up, pushed the boat off the rock and then got in himself. Needless to say we were reprimanded for the floating gear, which Shane retrieved. I realized that the drinks had disappeared. "They'll have sunk." said Gavin.

"You'll have to drink the river water; it's quite safe." So we did, only to discover later that the plastic containers had got safely lodged, out of sight, in the bottom of the boat.

After this excitement it was a very long, hard paddle against a brisk headwind, so it was decided that we should stop short of the intended campsite because the going was so difficult. It was nearly 6 pm and the sun was climbing down. The plan was for Shane to kayak on as far as the arranged campsite, inform the backup and bring the van to collect us.

We struggled ashore, disembarking with difficulty on the very steep muddy bank, and hauled up the boats and all the gear. It was cool and pleasant in the shade. We were all (apart from the indolent Maurice, that is, who was irritatingly chatty) totally exhausted and happy to wait quietly.

Gavin (who had actually given me a tow for the last three or four hundred yards) set about providing tea from what remained of the food: he cut up a delicious melon, found a few slices of salami and passed round small wrapped pieces of Cadbury's chocolate from the cool box. It quickly got dark and we were quite resigned to spending the night there. Resourceful Gavin lit a fire which gave light, a welcome warmth now that the air was cool and we were all in shorts, and to attract the attention of the driver, if and when he found us. I lay on one of the boats and snoozed comfortably. Gavin also walked to the side of the track along which it was imagined the back-up would arrive and stuck a paddle in the ground.

At 9 pm there was the sound of a slowly-proceeding 4WD and by 9.30 pm the vehicle had arrived on site. Andy had walked from our landing spot along the track, in case Shane had difficulties in the water. Shane had paddled on for some time until it was really dark, then left his canoe in an identified place and had run the last couple of miles along the track to the others. Andy returned with him. Then there was all the loading to do, the boats, the gear, Gavin's kayak, and finally us. This was the 4WD, not the minibus. Maurice stepped boldly forward to get in the front seat next to Shane who was driving, but Andy deflected him to the rear, and Norma and I were ushered into the plum seats.

The track was incredibly difficult to pick out and I marvelled at Shane's skill. Some sections looked positively impassable with great rocks, fine sand and steep gradients. It was an hour and a half before we saw the welcome campsite lamp hung in a tree. We gave the driver a heartfelt cheer. Norma and I had been in prime position to see the terrain and got glimpses of a Cape Fox, a Francolin, a couple of Barn Owls in flight, and noisy, aggressive farm dogs. We'd picked up Shane's kayak en route.

We were too tired to be hungry I guess, but after drinking by the fire for a while, we all did justice to the tasty rice and vegetable dish. We talked late into the night: a cosy, safe feeling to be reassembled with our competent carers.

There had not been a lot of space for looking for birds but half a dozen fresh sightings were ticked off. The handsome Whitebreasted Cormorant was unmissable, as was the comical Hammerkop and a rufous-looking Steppe Buzzard. We saw several Malachite and Woodland Kingfishers, with their eye-catching colours. A family of Chacma Baboons gave us curious stares, as well they might.

Turbulence Inside and Out

19.1.95 Thursday   I slept the sleep of the dead but woke early and resisted the urge to go for the spade and the toilet roll for as long as I could. My stomach was definitely in a state of turbulence. Foolishly I took my malaria and arthritis tablets on this unsettled caldron without breakfast and was promptly sick behind a thorn bush: I was out of sight but not out of earshot. The river looked to be fast flowing in the right direction and there was little wind, so things looked hopeful and less tiring.

I forced myself to a minimal breakfast and then the wind (internal and external) really got up, something to do with the rising temperature creating fresh air currents up river. Everyone was rearing to go and I suspect I was probably the only one who quietly welcomed the considered announcement that we would be going by road to the lunch spot, from whence we would paddle some rapids in the afternoon. By this time the wind was really strong and we would not have been able to make the required distance.

The track was even more hazardous looking in broad daylight but Shane took it steadily, with occasional instruction from Andy and Gavin in look-out position, perched on top of the vehicle. Chris and the minibus were not rejoining us until the end of the 4WD tyre tracks, along (and sometimes a long way from) the river.

The journey took two and a half hours and just before the lunch spot we saw a Himba tribesman perched on the top of a very tall Makalani (ivory nut) palm tree - Hypnaene Petersiana: I have this on authority. This huge, pale, lime-green palm with swirls of blade-like leaves formed contrasting patterned relief from the river vegetation. It was explained that he was tapping sap from the core of the palm to distil it into a potent alcoholic drink. He waved to us and we fantasised about a palm tree top bar, where it would be dangerous to stretch out to pass drinks from one to another. Several surrounding dead palms illustrated that this practice kills the trees.

Lunch and a brief rest were very welcome and I felt almost back to normal. We paddled for four and a half hours on the river, a pleasant, fairly undemanding section, with peaceful wide stretches, and occasional noisier rapids to break the monotony. We arrived at camp at sunset and were welcomed ashore with cold drinks and savouries. Shafts of golden evening light filtered through the palms and thorn trees and 'put out' the red embers of the fire on which was boiling the faithful kettle. Later, with no early moon to dim the stars, the same fire became the centre of light, warmth and conversation.

The lamb supper was tasty and substantial. I asked what variety of potato (they reminded me of Wilja that I grow at home) and what breed of sheep we were eating, and was told, with the characteristically flattened vowels, "South African". We retired early, in preparation for a 6.30 am start on the morrow.

A Grey-headed Kingfisher sang its five-note descending scale, like someone doing voice training: in spite of the constant repetition, I found it a joy to listen to. Other birds? Well, we had seen the Blackheaded, and the much smaller, Greenbacked Herons, a smart little Chestnut Weaver, and the startling Blue Waxbill, with its powder-blue head, chest and tail, as well as all the 'repeats'.

20 January 1995

The Best Bedroom

EPUPA FALLS with Rainbow

20.1.95 Friday   We paddled non-stop from 7 am until 1.30 pm. I'd stopped trying to see whether Maurice was paddling and had discovered ways of contributing to the steering from the front. He was pretty useless and didn't respond to coaxing, shouting or being sworn at by me or the team. I suspected he was not used to being told what to do. His wife had left him years ago; he told me he was looking for another and asked (within earshot of everyone else) whether I was in need of a husband: I gave the firmest "No!" I knew how, and understood some muffled laughter from the other boats!

On the credit side, well, he could quote Shakespeare and many of the English poets, and he sang tolerably well. I was surprised one day when he burst forth into Christian Mission choruses, for he was Jewish. I registered my puzzlement, to which he replied that he'd "done some work for the Salvation Army", but didn't enlarge further. Shane noticed my irritation with him on one occasion and said with a twinkle in his eye, "He's got to you, hasn't he," and I had to admit that he had, just a little.

The six-hour journey presented the usual mixture of long wide stretches with a strong headwind, and more sheltered calm stretches without white water and rapids. No-one came out of the boats today: we must be getting better at it. We had all had spills except Maurice. Norma had had a swollen knee after an unpleasant encounter with a rock, and Peter had been swept quite a distance downstream after he came off: this gave some cause for anxiety when it was discovered he could not swim and had had a heart attack two years earlier.

Rocks were still drawing our boat like magnets but usually we were so far behind that no-one noticed and we freed ourselves by a variety of manoeuvres.

Near the end of the trip, Shane stopped us and we gathered around him as he explained that the Epupa Falls, with their 200-foot drop, were just ahead. He emphasised that we were to keep into the left, out of the main stream, and beach just proximal to Gavin's kayak. Maurice looked scared and suddenly started paddling: his hat blew off into the water.

We could see the fine mist rising from the forceful water drop and it hosted a delicate rainbow in the strong sunlight: the noise of the falls was powerful and exciting and no sooner had we disembarked than we went to view the water beyond. The combination of the power of the volume of water, the glory of the spectacle and the relentless rumble, stirred the heart with wonderment and I found myself blinking back the tears. Maybe it was the relief of still being alive!

This was an organised campsite run by Germans. There was a shower rigged up in a rush hut and a flushing loo. We talked to the only other visitors, two Australian girls who were 'doing Africa' in a 4WD. There was a prominent notice requesting respect for the Himba people who are semi-nomadic and who will probably return to their apparently deserted sapling and mud huts, from which their scanty possessions were not to be removed. We had seen more of these people in the morning, in a straight-sided wooden boat, with others standing watching us from the shore. They seemed mildly curious, not at all hostile, healthy and content. They stay with their traditional ways and culture and, of course, have no educational or medical services of any kind.

Commercial ventures on the Kunene are going to increase inevitably, and one wonders how long even the Himbas can remain unspoiled by 'civilisation'. There is serious talk of building a dam in this very area in the not too distant future, when all that we could see would be flooded. (There is already the Calueque Dam higher up the river, before it becomes the Angolan/Namibian border.) There are hardly enough people to cry out in this wilderness, even if they were aware of what lay in store. Should tourism prove profitable, this may be the strongest weapon to halt the plan. The Himba environment is bound to change one way or another.

I asked the way to the shower and was directed by a dark, long-haired site helper who said, in broken English, that it would be "the most wonderful shower" I had ever had. He could be right, I thought. It was about a three-minute walk away and although in the heat it seemed more like a mile, it was truly well worth the effort.

I ruined the effect by taking a hot birdwatch with Phil, (will I never learn?) Charles, Peter, and Norma. The main object of the search was the Cinderella Waxbill (looks lovely in the book) but we had to make do with the Rufous-tailed Palm Thrush, a Longbilled Crombec (like 'our' Nuthatch, I thought), a neat little Pirit Batis, a Blackcheeked Waxbill, the drab-looking White-throated Canary, and an elegant Paradise Flycatcher. Yes, I was glad I'd gone!

After a very relaxed supper, I placed my bed where four palm trees leaned slightly towards to each other, their generous fronds separating me from a starry-domed sky, so that I felt I was in a planetarium. The noise of the falls was soothing, just punctuated by the occasional birdsong. It was the most wonderful 'bedroom' I'd ever known and I can still recall the unique ambience with nostalgia and delight.

There were crocodiles in the quieter stretches of water and the team had seen them often. Today we had been requested to 'travel quietly' in some areas as we scanned the banks for the log-like creatures, but no-one saw any.

Long Drive : Herero People

Hobatere - and a bath!

21.1.95 Saturday　　　　　　　We started out at 7 am, in preparation for the anticipated eleven-hour drive to Hobatere, on the eastern extremity of the Etosha National Park. The first part of the journey was reasonably cool but very slow. By the time we reached better roads, it had become very hot and the increased speed made a welcome draught. There was some disagreement as to whether just the front window should be open, said to produce a flow of air without getting all the dust, but by the time we embarked on the discussion we were all covered in a pinky-red film which went with the through-draught. We in no way resembled the attractive Himbas.

We stopped at what seemed like the end of the empire. In fact it was Opuwo, where we waited for the petrol station to open and, when the shop did likewise, I bought a red, white and blue striped plastic bag with a zip, to use as hand luggage for the more important things that I did not want to trust to my insecure luggage. The fastening had literally hit the dust and it was tied up with Shane's substantial tape.

I bought a cinnamon-flavoured bun at the bakery next door: it smelled and looked irresistible. Consequently I could not do justice to the team's excellent lunch. Herero women moved about under the trees and in and out of the shops. Their voluminous dresses, a legacy from the Victorian missionaries, topped with bright cloth shading hats were probably comfortable and cool, but looked incongruous next to the scantily-clad Himbas.

At Hobatere in the late afternoon, there was a bath. I languished long and luxuriously in three lots of water before I, my hair, and my clothes were clean. This was a very well-appointed campsite with hardly any visitors so we were able to hog the facilities without feeling guilty. We'd done no paddling today and yet I felt quite weary: the heat and the dust, no doubt. There was little conversation after supper and we went to bed early. A cold wind got up during the night and I wished I'd kept my trousers on.

Waterberg Plateau : Lesser Kudu, Sable Antelope
Eagles and Storks

22.1.95 Sunday   After a leisurely 9 am start we drove for three hours, and retraced our steps through Kamanjab and Outjo to the Waterberg Plateau National Park, where we devoured a good lunch. In spite of the heat I went on the Phil birdwatch, (little time left - can't afford to miss anything), saw the multi-coloured Ruppel's Parrot, and a liquid whistling Red-eyed Bulbul. More exciting was to see, on the campsite, the little Pearlspotted Owl and to hear its call, in the feather as it were, as being different from Phil's recording.

We then assembled at Reception for an even hotter afternoon game drive, in a tiered open vehicle. There were no evening drives on Sunday. I guess we were expecting a lot at the wrong time of day, and probably the wrong time of year for, like everywhere else, the Waterberg Plateau was very dry: little to see at the waterholes from elaborately constructed hides. A lone Lesser Kudu obliged: it had red ear-tags.

The striking brick-red sandstone outcrops contrasted pleasantly with all the lush green vegetation; everything seeming superior, in quality as well as height, over the surrounding African bush and savannah.

It was largely thanks to two coloured girls (who may have been Sunday drunk) that we saw anything at all. They spotted and shouted for the driver to stop so that we got views of a hunking Roan Antelope, a smaller member of its family an Impala, Gemsbok, Steenbok, curious Rock Hyrax, a Scrub Hare and, the best sighting of all, a magnificent Sable Antelope which stood quite near for a while and seemed to return our quiet stare. Black Eagles circled above the cliffs. A field of Abdim's Storks took flight while we watched on the road back to the camp. It had been a drive and a half.

22 January 1995

Sable Antelope - Waterberg Plateau

We'd been warned to cover our arms and legs for this outing, and I could still feel the sun penetrating my shirt sleeves and my cotton trousers. Maurice wore his pink pyjamas and chatted up the coloured girls relentlessly, although I don't think they had any English.

We were dropped back at Reception where I managed to fall up the steps and cut open the front of my leg, which had already been bruised on the river. I seemed to do this once every holiday. I bled all over the place and felt furious with myself for being so careless. We were taken back to camp, in the minibus, where I had a soak in the bath (again), and afterwards Gavin tidied up my leg and applied a dressing of extraordinary stinging properties, but later on it felt cared for and comfortable. Gavin was good on the first aid.

Tonight was the last supper together and I felt sad. The team was very quiet, although not for the same reason we learned. They'd taken advantage of our absence all afternoon and, after a prolonged and energetic romp in the swimming pool, they'd had a good go at the beer. Who could blame them?

One of the safari vehicles had run over a Black Mamba and it was brought to the campsite for our inspection. It was a greyish-brown colour, about nine feet long and with vicious-looking fangs - as displayed by Andy who opened the creature's mouth with his toothbrush.

The steak and the roast potatoes were first class, and they even managed to present some ice cream afterwards: goodness knows how.

I did my traditional doggerel, Andy recited his lovely little poem about the stars and, surprise, surprise, Maurice read us one of his poems. It seemed to consist mainly of 'Gloria in Excelsis Deo' several times over but had a soothing quality.

I didn't sleep well, thinking how much more exciting it is to be at the beginning of a holiday than at the end.

Back to Windhoek : Farewells : Honey Liqueur

23.1.95 Sunday   Peter was 65 today! We exchanged addresses in the optimistic assumption that some of the photos would be good enough to exchange. (I wasn't too upset that Maurice was missing.)

Dear Shane taped my bag again for the ride and gave me the rest of the roll for the plane. We proceeded south via Okahandja. It was very hot, but the unperturbed warthogs trotted about their energetic business along the way. We stopped at stalls on the roadside and I bought a soapstone Holy Family - so smooth and lovely to handle - and a balsa wood guinea fowl. I fancied a warthog but the only one I really liked was huge and very heavy. Enormous elephants and giraffes were being skilfully carved out of trunks of teak: I couldn't help wondering about the forest source.

At the Safari Sands Hotel we said our final farewells to the team, who'd been terrific. Maurice was reputed to be travelling to Cape Town with them. I went to my pleasant room, washed, organised my possessions and went to the sheltered outdoor restaurant near the swimming pool, where I sank two gins and ate two plates of toasted sandwiches in the company of Phil, Norma and Peter, who did something similar.

It had been an extraordinary trip. We talked affectionately about the team and laughed at Maurice's idiosyncrasies: more amusing in retrospect. Suddenly I saw the man himself: he'd decided to fly to Cape Town in the morning.

We read and swam in the pool in the afternoon. I spotted the sizeable Acacia Pied Barbet from my indolent position on the sunbed. We all looked weatherbeaten, in spite of being covered intermittently by helmets, sunglasses, dust, and grime, not to mention sunblock.

We celebrated Peter's birthday in the evening with good wine and an excellent meal. I couldn't resist the oysters again, and followed them up with duckling done in a cherry and peach sauce.

Phil had arranged to wait for Maurice in the bar: he never appeared, so Phil joined us for the main course. We talked until well after midnight in the bar afterwards and Phil introduced us to a very moreish Namibian honey liqueur. Then we said our goodbyes: Phil was booked on the bus shuttle service for the airport at 6 am - with Maurice.

22 January 1995

Termite mound : Waterberg Plateau

Shopping : Swimming : Sunbathing

24.1.95 Tuesday   We walked round the shops in Windhoek, and took advantage of their 'one-hour film developing service'. I bought a narrow, wool, wall-hanging tapestry, depicting stylised birds of the trip - which I could visualise alongside my grandfather clock - and a dark picture of zebras done in banana fibre (which now hangs in the loo).

We did the gins and toasted sandwiches again back at the hotel, and the swimming, and the sunbathing, and a good meal in the restaurant with honey liqueurs.

Norma and Peter talked about their son (in the family business), and their daughter, a social worker with three children, who had just started a university course. They asked about mine and about John. It was good to be able to tell them about the family, and especially about John.

Final Relaxation and Flight

25.1.95 Wednesday   I packed, taped up my sad, gaping bag, and assembled my increasing hand luggage. We took the courtesy bus into town, where we spent ages browsing in an excellent book shop. I finished up buying a very well put together anti-AIDS calendar, designed by Namibia's youth, which would be a useful supplement to the literature I use for a sex education slot.

I also fell for a book, 'The letters of Emma Sarah Hahn' (nee Hone), a missionary from England in the pioneer times of the Rhenish Missionary Society, in the first half of the nineteenth century.

We had lunch in a local restaurant and then read and swam the afternoon away. This was a splendidly relaxed way to end the energetic holiday.

We were on parade for the 6.45 pm airport bus, and a talkative group joined us in the town. A large Welshman sat next to me and talked incessantly of his party's tour of Victoria Falls and 'places around'. When I produced my twenty rands ready for the ticket, he said "Oh we don't have to buy anything for ourselves: wonderful travel company!"

Norma and Peter and I spent the last of our rands on coke at the airport, from whence we took off promptly at 9 pm. We had three seats together, me on the aisle. A smiling stewardess put my 'hand' luggage into an extra overhead compartment near the emergency exit which was just behind us. Hence we could recline our seats fully without upsetting anyone.

Even so, I slept little. I kept wriggling my ankles to try and stop them swelling but it was a losing battle on the damaged leg, which felt uncomfortable.

I longed to be home now.

Heathrow : Family : Bus and Taxi Home

26.1.95 Thursday   We refuelled at Frankfurt. Many passengers got off but no-one got on. It was raining in the UK, temperature 10°C, westerly wind. I changed into warm clothes (out of the hand luggage). Charles met me at the airport and I was more than pleased to see that he was walking tall and straight, and evidently making a good post-operative recovery after his back surgery. I introduced him to Norma and Peter and then bid them a fond farewell: they had been such good company. Charles and I had coffee, I produced my birdlist and my prints and we chatted away for a couple of hours. He left for Brunel University and I settled myself comfortably, watched the Heathrow world go by and wrote up my diary.

Half an hour before the bus was due, I trundled my trolley through the subway and into the lift, had some sandwiches at the nearby cafe and joined the untidy bus queue. It was as well I had a ticket, for the hopeful casuals did not get a seat. The world looked grey and dull and wet and I felt cold.

I started reading Emma Sarah Hahn and marvelled at her resilience in coping with a husband she hardly knew and who did not know her language, travelling in an ox-cart through the hot dusty terrain when pregnant with her first baby, and adapting to the totally alien climate, diet, population with accepting stoicism and faith and, ultimately, enjoyment. Hereroland must have been one of the most inhospitable places on earth in the mid-nineteenth century. Barnstaple, even in the rain with roadworks and no taxi at the stand, seemed quite hospitable in comparison.

I was about to hump my complicated luggage to the phone when a taxi drew in. I was home in twenty minutes, found everything in order and looked forward to having time to write up the Namibian experience and relive the adventure.

I knew I'd had a mere brush with the country but it had been enough to make me want to see more. Pictures of the prehistoric wildlife rock engravings at Twyfelfontein were very seductive, as were accounts of the Fish River Canyon, the Karakul Sheep Farm, the sands of Sossusvlei, the first missionary settlements at Bethanie and Keetmanshoop, and so on.

I think I'll be back.

Postscript:

I kept in touch with Norma and Peter, and a friend and I spent a couple of nights at their delightful house in Patterdale when we were in the area. They looked well and were so hospitable. We still correspond every Christmas.

They now spend most of the year in South Africa. And remembering, as I was writing this, that Peter had had his 65th birthday during our Kunene trip, I realised that he will recently have celebrated his 77th.

March 2007

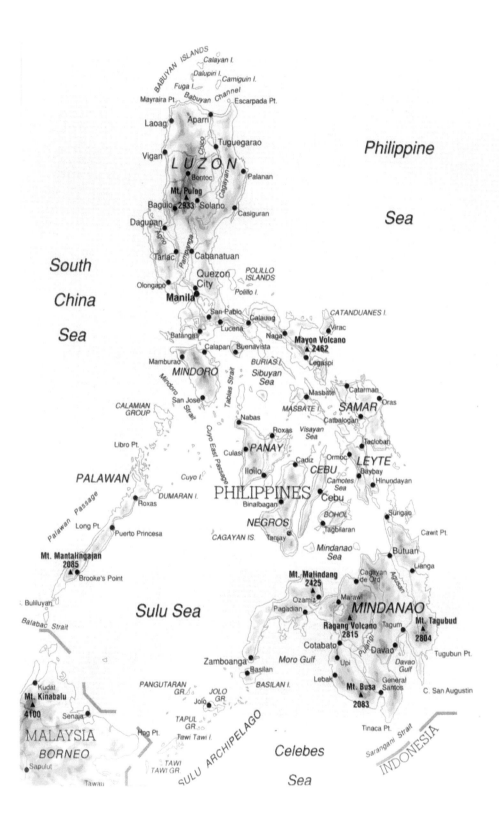

Filipino Foray   *January 1996*

THE PHILIPPINES

with **EXPLORE**

FILIPINO FORAY

I am not certain why I selected the Philippines for the 1996 experience, but I think the choice was related to a seductive page in the Explore travel magazine: it was entitled 'Island Adventure' and included plenty of travelling about by plane, jeepney, and (what attracted me most) by boat.

I have to admit that I was only vaguely aware of the geographical siting of the island complex and, when I started to read about it, I was amazed to find that there were more than 7,000 of them, and that they represented a series of half-drowned mountain ranges.

I studied the world map. There they were, separated by the South China Sea from Taiwan and faraway China to the north, and - even further away - from Vietnam to the west; then, separated by the Celebes Sea from Borneo and Sulawasi to the south, and from nowhere - for miles and miles and miles - by the Pacific Ocean to the east.

Elements of all these nationalities are said to be found in the Filipinos' appearance, their personalities, and their diet but, in contrast to their neighbours, they remain largely Catholic.

The national language is Filipino but over 70 languages and dialects reflect the population's origins - although English is spoken by many, which I found reassuring.

It sounded 'different' - and it was.

FILIPINO FORAY : 1996

Getting there!

Departure day for the Philippines adventure

6.1.96 Saturday   I seemed to be ready too early, which was worrying: there must be something I'd forgotten. Donna of R and D taxis arrived, spot on time, at 11.30 am and I stood alone at the bleak Barnstaple National Express Bus Station. It was reassuring when others joined me, stating their intention to catch the same London bus. I had made no particular secret of the fact that I was going away but neither had I broadcast it, so by the time no less than five acquaintances had driven by in their respective cars, seen me with my monster pack and waved in recognition, I guessed my departure would be well advertised before long.

The bus arrived, my luggage was stowed away in the Heathrow compartment, and I slept in my window seat all the way to Bridgwater. Here a buxom, restless, talkative lady took the seat next to me, precluding any more total relaxation. She was a government officer, probably in her early fifties, also called Jean, separated from the father of her son, about whom she was worried because she was sure he was on drugs. He was 21 and lived in an ambulance at the end of the drive to the house which she shared with her father and lots of chickens. Somehow she moved on, without any prompting, to her close association with her local 'low' church, and her keenness for women priests. She was going to Israel. Her monologue was interrupted only by the pleasant staff serving food and drink. The coach was full, arrived on time, and I lost sight of my travelling companion as I trolleyed my luggage to Terminal Three.

It was an easy check-in, with the usual fascinating airport hub. I looked round for other possible group members sporting an 'Explore' label but didn't spot any. I bought a postcard which I particularly wanted to send but the airport had run out of stamps. I even approached a Swedish couple sitting nearby who were writing and stamping cards like there was no tomorrow, but they had just the right number. Orientals appeared to be spending loads of money in the duty-free stores. A Japanese girl, with multiple purchases, was dressed like a flamboyant Mary Poppins.

The Emirates flight to Dubai left promptly at 20.40 hours and arrived apparently four hours later, but the watches had gone forward four hours, giving a very short night and I didn't sleep anyway. I was next to a charming young man from Barcelona who sold optical instruments in Russia, Sweden, and Saudi, and was longing to get home to his wife and seven-year-old daughter Abigail.

7.1.96 Sunday   During this leg of the flight we were served drinks, an evening meal and then, at 2.30 am London time, breakfast. Two whingeing Filipino women created a continuing saga of a fuss because there was no vegetarian meal for them: they'd travelled 'all over the world' and had never had to pre-order, as is required with Emirates.

There was a two-hour wait at Dubai, where we changed planes but didn't have to handle the luggage. I hoped, as I always do under these circumstances, that someone else was doing it. We lost another three hours en route for Hong Kong. This time a Chinese girl was my travelling companion. She'd been on safari in Kenya and bought a well-padded Giraffe stool, which gave the cabin staff a storage problem. Some of the so-called 'hand luggage' was amazing in size and shape. I was seated behind the same rather inconsiderate passenger as before and when he inclined his seat, suddenly without warning in the middle of yet another breakfast, mine was messily propelled in the direction of my abdomen.

Some time later there was another meal, after which I slept and then woke to find it was 6 pm, dark, and that was another day gone. We stayed on board at Hong Kong while cleaners tidied and refurbished for the new intake of passengers. I plucked up courage to ask two grey-haired gentlemen, one behind me and the other to the left, whether they were Explore's Messrs Hugh Graham and Robin Gregory, mentioned by the airline when I telephoned to check the flights. They were indeed, and had only just met, but talked incessantly of previous five-to-six-week exploits, mostly with Explore. I felt very much the novice. Hugh had us grovelling around under the seats searching for his combination lock which he later found in his pocket - this set the scene for the holiday! After take-off we had another, yes, another, light meal and were then presented with documents galore to fill in before landing.

It was an uncomplicated arrival: my luggage was the first off. It looked large and untidy beside Hugh's neat little pack. We were met by Alex, our leader, a handsome man in his late thirties, very pleasant and relaxed. Another man joined us from off the plane. I'd studied him at Dubai but there had been no sign of any Explore label. (He told me later that he purposely conceals his attachment until he's sussed out the rest of the party).

I'd thought how ill he looked, like someone in the advanced stages of cancer, his shaved head somehow adding credence to such a diagnosis. This was Reginald, the Belgian barber, heavy smoker and yet, incongruously, marathon runner extraordinary!

We were transported to the Hotel Las Palmas through the fairy-lighted streets of Manila: it was still Christmas here. Alex gave us a brief run down of immediate plans. There were eight of us in the group. I was the token woman, which meant I had a room to myself. Apart from the three people I've mentioned (Robin Gregory, Hugh Graham, and Alex), there were two Roys - one Canadian and one Cockney, a Dutchman called Jan, and a quiet, delicate-looking young lad called Matthew. We arranged to meet for breakfast at a restaurant round the back of the hotel at 8 am the following morning. I hit the hay at 11.30 pm and slept well, only vaguely aware of merry-making in the next room.

Manila and getting to Banaue

8.1.96 Monday   Alex joined us after breakfast and gave us three quarters of an hour's holiday briefing. We went to his recommended establishment to change our traveller's cheques. It was something of a dump with peeling paint, unswept floors and slovenly, uninterested staff. Hugh took ages and was christened 'Speedy'. Hugh, Robin, Reginald, and I then walked to Rizal park, where we enjoyed a light outdoor lunch of Mami chicken with egg - a substantial soup - for the equivalent of 30p. We visited the Rizal Museum where some extraordinary effects of the martyred leader of the Propaganda Movement (for Filipino equality with the Spanish) were on display: these included an eyeball (dispatched for the making of an artificial eye before his death), some vertebrae, and his sister's gloves. We took pictures of the park, the gardens and the views and then made for the Chinese cemetery. This looked quite near on the map (although admittedly off the map), but Alex had reassured us that it was only 'just off the map'. It was not. It was hot and we were tired. After conflicting directions from locals (including the police), we decided to take a cab - all except Hugh, that is, who left to do his own thing.

The cemetery was like a small town, with little streets of ornate buildings housing family tombs: some garish, some relatively simple, others quite beautiful. The wealth they implied was in such sharp contrast with some of the shanty town dwellings we had seen as we drove through Quiapo. I had wanted to visit the nearby church of the Black Nazarene but we'd all had enough pavement plodding and opted for an exciting ride on the metro, which was so overcrowded, well beyond London Underground imaginings, that I almost failed to fight my way off at the appropriate station.

It was bliss to swim in the hotel pool, with Matthew and Robin. Thus refreshed I sorted my luggage and washed my hair. We ate at Rosie's. I had garlic rice with egg ('sunny side up') and Filipino Beefsteak topping, followed by 'apple pie à la mode' with ice cream, and two glasses of dubious red wine. We migrated briefly to the bar where the music was very intrusive and precluded normal conversation. I went to bed at 11 pm.

5 am call!   This was supposed to be a holiday …

9.1.96 Tuesday   We assembled at 5.30 am to deposit surplus luggage that we were not going to need on the trek. Taxis were to take us to the bus station on the other side of town but our driver had only been driving for nine weeks and didn't know the way. Neither did Alex, but after a protracted journey we arrived in time to join the rest of the party who had become anxious, particularly as Alex was with us.

We had coffee at the bus station and bought water and biscuits for the journey. I sat near the back of the bus and everyone thought I was missing. No-one had told me that our seats were all numbered at the front. I moved to be next to Canadian Roy but the bus couldn't start because another one, parked horizontally in front of us, had broken down. We eventually left 40 minutes late, which the experienced Alex said 'wasn't too bad'.

There were multiple hold-ups en route as we went back through the city, especially around Quiapo's Black Nazarene Church. Today was the 9th January - a day when the life-sized image of the Black Nazarene was borne aloft, ahead of an all-male procession. The church and surroundings were ablaze with lights.

Once out into the more rural areas, the driving became very speedy and quite fantastic: children, chickens and dogs, plus the occasional pig, made last-minute getaways. We passed churches - Primitive Methodist, Bible Baptist, Jehovah's Witnesses, Church of Christ, and Roman Catholic; a 'Rotary' Health Clinic, a Veterinary Centre, a 'Conception' Centre (a change from contraception), all kinds of roadside stores and a Unisex Beauty Salon. Buffalo, scraggy cattle, and well-fed pigs wandered about the route. There were few birds but everywhere the most beautiful children. We stopped for breakfast around 10.30 am and, being surprised at how hungry I was, I enjoyed rice and chicken.

We journeyed on with jeepneys coming at us from all directions. The flat terrain changed into a hilly landscape with distant larger hills. I fell asleep and didn't see San Jose but Roy said I hadn't missed much. Shortly after this the bus, which had made an uncooperative, expensive noise halfway up a hill, ground to an ominous halt. We all got out, admired the view and chatted, narrowly missing complete burial under loads of fine grit, which were being tipped near the disabled bus every half hour or so. After two hours, during which time the driver and his mate made valiant efforts to repair the vehicle, which was letting off jets of steamy hot water, the word 'compression' figured in their announcement that we would all have to find alternative transport.

We collected our luggage and crossed the road to wait for any other vehicle which might take us. As luck would have it, after about fifteen minutes an ordinary service bus picked us up, so we scrambled over the luggage in the aisle and all got seats. This took us to Bayombong (I think) and from there we got a jeepney to Banaue. It had become cold and damp and very dark by now. Three other holidaymakers joined us for this last part of the journey. It started to rain heavily so we stopped, brought down the luggage from the roof and bundled it inside. I reckon we were all pretty tired by this time: early start, no lunch because of the breakdown, and now a tortuous bone-shaker of a road in cramped conditions. We reached Banaue at 6.15 pm.

The Banaue Hotel was surprisingly well appointed, unexpectedly so, when apparently at the end of nowhere. I had a lovely room, we enjoyed an excellent meal, listened to instructions from Alex for the morrow, and then watched a 'culture show' in the spacious reception area. We were encouraged to join in. Cockney Roy did so with great enthusiasm. The ladies had a less spectacular role and I was happy to be passed from one to the other. The battery in my camera packed up at the moment critique when I was about to record this colourful spectacle, but I'll never forget it. I bought postcards and a Banaue T-shirt at the in-house shop and retired to bed at 10.30 pm.

Cresta Trail

10.1.96 Wednesday   We had a civilised start at 7.30 am, with breakfast at 8 am, and were ready to leave by 9 am. We went into Banaue and bought water, and then had a one-hour jeepney journey to Banga'an. The 'roads' were dreadful - with landslides being cleared before us - and were difficult to wriggle through. There were small settlements along the way with large families, lots of dogs of indeterminate breeds, scattered chickens, and lumbering black pigs.

From Banga'an we commenced the trek along the Cresta Trail. I felt anxious about walking along the edges of rice terraces with a pack, although mine was smaller than some. It started quite well and the edging was not as difficult to walk on as I had imagined, in fact the first section was actually concrete, but this was short-lived. The paths became very narrow and consisted of mud and slippery stones. To fall to the right was to drop about eight feet on to the terrace below, to fall inwards was to join the rice and get very wet. Neither was desirable. After a small village called Nagkor, we climbed more, scrambling up steep bits of wall on to higher terraces. Wallie, a young, self-employed Frenchman who joined various groups as a helper, and organised the food supplies, gave me a hand over the worst spots. I was so thankful he was there. My knees felt like jelly. This was more demanding than I'd imagined - maybe I should have settled for that SAGA cruise. I was mightily relieved when someone said that the village in the near distance was Batad, our destination.

Once there we sat and ate our mid-afternoon packed lunch. It was a bit dry but I helped it down with plenty of water and took my malaria tablets. I washed in the primitive washplace a few yards across the mud, had a change of clothes and retired to my little curtained compartment where I lay on the comfortable bunk and wrote my diary. Matthew and Reginald went on a second trek, minus packs, to see a special waterfall. I'd have loved to have joined them but I knew my limitations: I'd been fully stretched. I'd got to save myself for the morrow.

We sat around and talked in the afternoon, and ate supper at 7 pm. The soup was hot and tasty and reinforced by some macaroni-like pasta. This was followed by some kind of chapatti, covered in tomatoes and cheese: I couldn't eat it all. We finished with delicious small bananas. A local girl came in selling wood carvings. I bought a fertility symbol, beautifully carved and with an attractive grain in the wood. More talk: getting the drop of these men! To bed at 9 pm. It rained all night. It was going to be slippery tomorrow.

11.1.96 Thursday   I awoke at 6 am and finally got up at 7 am, to re-arrange luggage and breakfast on pineapple and half a pancake. A combination of malaria tablets and anxiety about the day ahead had taken away my appetite. We started off at 9 am and had an immediate, exhausting climb, scrambling up the sides of waterfalls and rice terraces, followed by a steady downward trek, punctuated by slippery steep bits. Dear Wallie took my hand several times, seeming to know when my confidence was ebbing. We had a short stop for a drink at a panoramic viewpoint.

Then it was along the edges of the rice terraces again. When I dared to look up I was delighted to see Cambulo in the near distance. I managed to fall literally at the last fence, landing heavily on my replaced hip, catching my right knee on the way down. It hurt and I felt quite sick but I knew I hadn't broken anything. I was glad to go down to the river for a swim, when I wore my 'activity' sandals for the first time: magic footwear which stays on in the water and makes walking on the river bed so much easier and safer. I sat for some minutes in a waterfall, like a jacuzzi, quite cold but invigorating.

We stopped for our lunch at a rattan village house: delicious pineapple and melon, sad tuna salad, biscuits and tea. We all ate well but there was plenty left, which Wallie handed to the local guide for general distribution. Children, chickens, dogs, pigs, and cats hung about hopefully.

Another optional walk was taken by half the group. I chickened out again. My legs had felt like lead halfway through the morning, and I'd said aloud that I wished they were longer, which Hugh had followed with "short, stubby legs are best." Thank you, Hugh!

I sat on my bunk and wrote my diary, with background music from the children singing at the local school. I could see the yellow stone church building with its red, rusted roof, which exactly resembled the one in Batad. I watched some of the young children walking sure-footedly and swiftly over the rice terrain, which to me seemed so hazardous, and I envied their youth and agility. They were very friendly and I spoke to some of them, who asked me my name and how old I was. I took a photograph and then the kindergarten (missionary) teacher came along and I photographed her with them, and talked to her. I promised to go to her house, which was behind our accommodation, after supper.

The 6.30 pm meal started with 'hot' soup and was followed by a superb casserole of pig, duck and chicken, served with rice and banana ketchup. I'd seen Wallie buying some of the meat from the families in the houses nearby. Peter Gatting, one of the Ifugao people who are the 'Masters of the Rice Terraces', then told us something of the tribe's culture and customs. They are animist in their beliefs, and the most important feature of their lives is the family. He talked of the marriage rituals and how the only acceptable reason for divorce was when there were no children. Each one of the 'unsuccessful' partnership is allowed to look for another partner. The more children they can produce, the happier they are. As if to reinforce this philosophy, children ran in and out of the room constantly while he spoke.

I went over to see the American missionary, where I had coffee and looked at her photograph albums. She didn't seem a very happy lady as she revealed she was now unsupported by the RC church: I wondered why, but didn't ask. She was using her own capital. We exchanged addresses. I felt I ought to do something, although I wasn't sure what. I was in bed by 9 pm.

12.1.96 Friday   We left Cambulo at 8.30 am, after a breakfast of fruit and scrambled egg. I was hungry this morning, in spite of being told that today's would be the longest trek - but it started badly with stone walls and narrow dykes, and Wallie had gone ahead to prepare lunch. The first stretch was really steep and I felt anxiety returning, which just made me feel more exhausted. Once we reached the top, we walked along a high path with a kinder incline, running along the side of the valley with memorable views. I trailed behind with Hugh and Canadian Roy. Eventually we started the downward trek, when I suddenly felt as if I could walk for ever: the same sensation I'd experienced after coming down from Kilimanjaro.

A final uphill push revealed lunch all laid out before us. Wallie presented me with a bunch of the most beautiful wild flowers. These, plus the relief of completing the trek, brought a tear to my eye. He chatted for a while in perfect English, his French accent adding to his charming manner. He was obviously very happy to be married to a Filipino lady, who was expecting their second baby.

Ifugao lady : BANAUE

There was a notice in the window of the nearby little store to the effect that post was 'collected and delivered', so I produced the lonesome postcard I'd been waiting to send, and went to pass it to the lady in the hatch. Before she could take it however, her little 2-to-3-year-old daughter ran off with it, and although I followed in hot pursuit and managed to retrieve it, I decided to post it elsewhere.

The jeepney was waiting to take us back to Banaue. It got stuck precariously near the edge of a deep drop. Some of the group got out and tried to push, while the driver revved up madly. We rocked back and forth on a boulder, but eventually got free. Back at the Banaue Hotel, I dumped my luggage, had a quick wash and went off with Roy and Robin to THE viewpoint. It was well worth the trip, with the most expansive view of the terraces yet. A group of traditionally clad Ifugao people, in their colourful soft-textured clothes - a lot of red and purple - and woven headgear decorated with fabric flowers, posed for us and we took pictures and paid them for the privilege. I bought three woven purses for granddaughters, and Roy (after much deliberation) bought a traditional hat.

Then, it was back for a shower, and to wash some clothes (cold water only), to re-arrange packing again, to photograph Wallie's flowers (although I wouldn't forget him in a hurry) and to write this diary. After this house-keeping exercise, I went downstairs and had a gin. I met two young Filipinos from the university who were doing a project on tourism and the rice terraces. I answered all their questions, including my age, at which they expressed surprise: they thought I was much younger than 63 - the lights were dim! The rest of the group arrived on the scene and Matthew got cornered to do their hundredth and final questionnaire.

We walked along the hazardous streets to a town restaurant for supper. I'd been all for having a jeepney but the idea didn't catch on. The meal had been ordered earlier so we didn't have what I understand is the traditional lengthy Filipino wait. Egg soup was followed, for me anyway, by tasty pork chop suey, and then some good coffee. There was a lengthy discussion about the possibility of going to the Ati-Atihan festival in Kalibu, the day after we were scheduled to leave Panay Island. I would love to have gone but would feel anxious about leaving Alex and the group. Reginald gave a definite "No", while the two Roys were particularly keen to go. The rest of us dithered about, while Hugh declared "it shouldn't be allowed". Jan wasn't bothered but kept stirring it every time the discussion faded. I walked back with him. My legs were fine: of course I didn't need a jeepney. And so to bed at 9 pm, ready for a 5 am call. Help!

13.1.96 Saturday   I was called at 4.35 am: not good news. I had a Continental breakfast and watched the sun rise. We were in for a long, long ride to Manila. We waited for the bus and looked at all the houses built against the hillside, one on top of the other. I imagined they could all be so easily swept away in one of the typical Filipino typhoons and floods. Places had been pointed out to us on the steep cliffs on the way to Banga'an, where just such a thing had demolished small settlements: it all seemed so precarious. The seats had not been booked on this bus so we were there in plenty of time and all got places; Alex came and sat next to me and chatted about his Mum: he said how difficult she had found life since his father died. I sympathized and said I understood. She obviously had a very caring son.

We passed villages of waving children, groups of white-shirted schoolchildren of all ages, Medical Centres, 'Iglesia di Crista' - repeated in every settlement, and the usual random collections of livestock.

We stopped for a break at some time in the middle of the morning and I was tempted to sample a hot incubated duck egg (balut), much to the horror of the rest of the group: salt was provided. I found it strange but not unpleasant, rather like a hard-boiled egg with some unexpected watery fluid and a crunchy yoke. It was only afterwards when I translated these findings into biological reality that the experience became a bit distasteful. Later still, I remembered salmonella. I followed up this gastronomical experiment with a chocolate ice cream.

Come lunchtime I wasn't hungry (!?), so made do with a packet of banana crisps, but drank a bottle of coke and another of mango juice to keep up the fluids. The final leg of the drive into Manila was a nightmare of stopping and very little starting, and it reminded me of Istanbul's traffic problems and pollution. We couldn't get into the bus station as it was full - and this, primarily, because the buses couldn't get out on the other side because of the congested road. Many of the jeepneys belonged to a company called, appropriately enough, "Jam Transport"! We got off into the road, where the pollution was almost tangible, and I understood so well why many of the pedestrians covered their mouths with scarves.

Alex got a Mitsubishi taxi vehicle lined up and we crammed in. I was sandwiched between Canadian Roy, with his outsized pack spilling over on to my lap, and moaning Hugh, who was postulating plans to revolutionise the city's traffic problems. In spite of the air-conditioning we were very hot and I was uncomfortably aware of a mingling of thigh sweat. We did eventually arrive at the Las Palmas Hotel at 5.45 pm, where I washed myself, my clothes and my hair, and restructured my belongings.

At 7.20 pm, we met up to go to the Kamayan Restaurant, which looked very promising but quite expensive by Filipino standards. Hugh said it was too fancy and left, Cockney Roy had already opted out, and Alex had gone for a night on the town with some young friends - and who could blame him. The rest of us were quite euphoric after such an early start and the long day's travelling. It was almost worth getting really weary and filthy, to feel so good with cleanliness, relaxation and the prospect of food. The Kamayan was certainly upmarket, with serious-faced waiters in spotless white smocks.

I had a superb shellfish meal with the in-house (very spicy) sauce and plain rice that would melt in your mouth. It was one of the best meals I've ever had. The cost was 265 pesos - approximately £8. Some of us fancied wine, which was a mistake: all they could produce was Mateus (white) served lukewarm. We drank two bottles - those of us who were not drinking beer, that is - and they cost us more than the meal. All part of the learning curve. Reginald, our marathon runner, persuaded the management to bring him some water after a protracted wait, during which he remarked that "this place has class but no style". I really enjoyed myself.

We returned to Las Palmas Hotel where I did a final luggage arrangement for the next ten days, making it as light as possible.

White Beaches and Camping with the Mangyans

14.1.96 Sunday   Today's call was at 6.30 am. I could get used to this - perhaps. The washing was dry, and I left some surplus luggage. I carried a tightly-packed small rucksack to Rosie's for breakfast, where I drank mango juice and coffee and ate American toast. I discovered that I still had my hotel room key in my pocket: Alex gave me a black mark and took it back. We walked to the bus station and boarded the bus for Batangas. We started off on the main highway but then took lesser roads because the floods had washed away the main route. Poor Reginald got desperate with a full bladder, so we had an unscheduled stop at Lipa City, where we all took prophylactic advantage of the facilities. It was Sunday and the traffic was considerably less dense.

It was a pleasant bus with efficient air-conditioning and I sat next to Jan, the Dutchman, who gave me his interesting life history. He had been brought up in a strictly religious household where the Bible was read at every meal. Now he was an avid reader of English novels. He fell in love with a Danish girl when he was on holiday in Australia, gave up his job, married her, and has lived in Denmark ever since. He talked very lovingly of her. He described himself as "fallen Dutch Reform". I think I told him quite a lot about my life but can't really remember. He was good company and between us we put the world to rights when we were not dozing. I imagined him to be in his forties: he was built like an ox and always cradled his large pack in front of him, even on the rice terraces.

At Batangas we took a very comfortable ferry for the two-hour sail to Puerto Galera, but before we left several small boats drew up alongside selling coral. There were a few clouds about so that the temperature was pleasantly warm without being too hot. We bought sandwiches and had a light lunch on board. I sat on the top deck and read 'Culture Shock'. There were several seedy-looking young European males around up there, with a bottle of San Miguel in one hand and a Filipino girl in the other.

The approach to Puerto Galera was lovely: the quayside was alive with small shops, waiting jeepneys, and passengers getting on and off smaller vessels. The local Mangyan liaison, Willie, met us and we boarded a jeepney which took us along a very rocky road from which the dust rose so quickly that it was impossible to see where we were going. Why did I bother to wash my clothes? It was a short drive and soon we arrived at a lovely beach with pleasant accommodation. A beautiful young girl called Louella showed us to our rooms. I couldn't wait to get into the water and I swam for an hour to the next 'White Beach' bay and back. Another beautiful young girl called Edeline was selling local basket-ware and I said I'd think about buying the following day. Some of the most attractive was very large and I remembered the stuffed Giraffe stool 'hand luggage' on the plane on the way out. I got changed for supper and sat outside and read, while a couple of blond children (Swedish?) played happily on a swing.

I fancied a drink, an alcoholic drink, but they hadn't any gin. So I thought I'd have a rum and coke, which I associate with sun and sand and far-off halcyon days in Italy, so ordered same. To my amazement a bottle of coke with a straw was produced, plus a half bottle of rum. I enquired of Alex whether I was to pour my own measure but he smirked and said "That is the measure". I had no difficulty in enlisting young Matthew to share it with me, with more coke and plenty of ice. There was some dispute over the sex of the person who brought the drinks. I considered 'her' to be a flat-chested girl with a hair adornment but, in spite of my psychosexual qualification, I was wrong. Alex said he was a male, "obviously so", and that Filipino men often wore "things in their hair". Later I heard another member of staff call him Reuben.

The meal of sweet and sour pork with special rice was substantial and tasty, if delivered in slow Filipino time, but then who was in a hurry? Plenty of time to drink the rum and coke. I talked to Cockney Roy, who told how he had recently been made redundant from his job as a 'lawyer in conveyancing': "Not much movement in the property market" he said. His girlfriend had ditched him about the same time, so this holiday was a cheering-up exercise. He said it was working, and indeed he hadn't seemed miserable, but maybe that was because of his Cockney accent. I was in bed by 9.45 pm.

A welcome coconut

15.1.96 Monday　　　　　　　　A leisurely start - I got up at 7.30 am and breakfasted on bacon and egg, mango juice (I did love it) and coffee. We then got into a small boat for a 45-minute trip down the coast: cloudy, but warm and not raining. Mangyans met us, and Willie made the introductions, remembering all our names correctly, which was impressive I thought.

With them we walked through jungle land, crossing three rivers and scrambling over rocks, quite difficult and very slippery. I was most comfortable in my black one-piece bathing costume. The trees and tree ferns and flowers were quite breathtaking: so many varieties. Some were recognizable as 'house plants' at home - Shrimp Plants, Coleus, Crotons, Yucca, and so on. There were also Convolvulus-like flowers of many different colours, purple 'Mimosa', and many others which bore no resemblance to anything I'd ever seen before. We sampled the sharp fruit of the Tamarind Tree and watched a young Mangyan scale a coconut palm with consummate grace and speed, and then dispatch ripe coconuts for his fellows down below to top, so that we could drink the milk. They then scraped out the delicious lining for us to sample.

We swam in a river before eating our packed lunch, and then Alex gave another of his excellent tutorials on the Philippines. We had dumped most of our stuff at the semi-prepared camp en route, where we had also had a demonstration of matchless fire-lighting by the rubbing together of two bamboo sticks, one anchored to the ground: I gathered we would not be required to do this before supper! Some of us swam up river, clambering up waterfalls and then came back down river. I managed to knock my right knee, which swelled up rapidly, but the fact that I had to go on swimming and then master the obstacle course of a walk back was probably the best (enforced) physiotherapy. I knew once again that I hadn't done anything too awful to myself, but was a bit perturbed as to how it would be on the morrow: I really must be more careful.

Back at the now-completed camp, we had a welcome cup of tea and I lay down on the very comfortable bamboo and rush platform, our sleeping quarters. I heard a remarkable bird song but couldn't see anything. I wished someone knew something about birds. I spoke to Willie who gave me some dialect name and said there were many more birds deeper in the forest. The supper was good, all prepared from scratch, including killing the chickens. We had chicken soup, chicken and rice, fresh mango, and enjoyed a rare and lovely atmosphere at a basic bamboo-constructed table with attached 'benches'. Alex was not too well and had a temperature. He sat huddled up in his blanket and had only soup for supper. Someone suggested he had a mild attack of "his malaria". There was lots of table talk but everyone was ready for bed by 9.30 pm.

The Mangyans seemed a very quiet people: they didn't sing or chatter amongst themselves, at least not when we were around. They stared at us unblinkingly from their large brown eyes. They were neat and small and all looked very young, although Alex said that some of them, with the appearance of sixteen-year-olds, were at least twice that age and probably had families back in the forest. We, or rather I, must have seemed so physically inept and ungainly: I did wonder what they thought of us.

16.1.96 Tuesday   I slept intermittently but quite well. Surprisingly, my left knee was virtually painless and the swelling almost gone. An impressive bruise was appearing in front of and behind the joint but also spreading down to my ankle and up to my groin: it must have had quite a bleed. All my blemishes were, of course, constantly exposed in a bathing costume - plus shorts, if there was no swimming, and no imminent river crossings. I had multiple bites and scratches and the bruise from the fall on my left hip was now a rambling blotch of deepest purple.

I caught Alex frowning concernedly at the sight of my latest lesions. "Do you bruise easily?" he enquired. "No", I replied.

16 January 1996

Mangyans prepare our supper coconuts

We breakfasted on omelette, mango and pineapple. Today's trek took us across another three rivers and we stopped for a swim in a lovely pool. I was longing to dive from a high rock but hadn't the courage to trust my knee to climb up there. The Mangyans really enjoyed themselves: they seemed more relaxed today, and chatted and shouted for joy as they took their jumps and dives. Brave Hugh did an excellent dive from a pretty high rock. Later we had another stop for a drink from our water bottles, under the coconut palms and surrounded by grazing cattle with their faithful Egrets. The final stretch was a walk along a beautiful beach. It was now very hot and I knew I should stop and put on some sun shield but I didn't want to fall behind.

We stopped at a beachside shop/house where there was a positive menagerie of animals, including a large sow with thirteen suckling piglets. Matthew and I swam in the clear water and cooled off before we all devoured the Mangyans' lunch of fish soup, fish and rice, and mangos. There was then the T-shirt-giving ceremony when Explore adventurers each donate a T-shirt to one of the Mangyans. I passed over my Banaue example, which I had bought specially for this occasion. (Alex had commented, somewhat sarcastically at the time, "Ah, white, what a suitable colour"). Anyway the recipient seemed pleased enough. I also off-loaded several drug firm free biros, which produced great delight. (I realized later that some were stamped 'Viagra!'). There were 10 Mangyans. A young girl at the house was anxious to exchange addresses and I promised to send her a Valentine card, which was what she wanted. Then it was farewell to the Mangyans and back into the banca.

We had a much rougher crossing back to Tamaraw Beach than on the way out. I swam round to the 'White Beach' again, where Edeline and another young vendor spotted me and walked back and forth along the shoreline until I emerged from the water. I bought a small tray from Edeline and a basket with lid from her friend. Common sense was telling me how difficult these things would be to pack but the girls were charming and the goods very attractive. I dripped into my room to get the money. I felt quite tired. The swim to the 'White Beach' had taken me 40 minutes against a strong current (which I could have anticipated if I'd thought about the banca ride) and then only 20 minutes to swim back to Tamaraw.

I changed and fancied a drink but there was no rum left, so I had to settle for virgin coke. Fish, fried vegetables, and rice made a welcome supper. And then to bed by 9 pm, ready for a 5.45 am call.

Jeepney, banca, ferry, jeepney, flight, banca to Boracay

17.1.96 Wednesday   I slept well but was aware of heavy rain falling most of the night. I wondered what the roads would be like in the morning. After pineapple pancake and coffee for breakfast at 6.45 am, I settled the bill, gave in the key, and then a wonderful driver steered us to Puerto Galera by jeepney, on very muddy, skiddy roads. Willie met us there and announced that the ferry had broken down. So we continued in the jeepney to Sabang, where we paddled to climb into a banca which took us to a waiting ferry. I sat upstairs with Cockney Roy, who made me laugh with groups of jokes and witty definitions, followed by periods of silence while he refuelled. One of the morning's offerings was "definition of frustration: Hugh with laryngitis." It was pleasant to sit at the back of the ferry. The sun shone intermittently and we reached Batangas at 11.45 am, where we took a quick walk from the ferry to the ordinary service bus, which was pretty full. I was accommodated on the back seat, warmly sandwiched between Matthew and Hugh. The journey was very slow initially but gradually improved. The driver was asked (and bribed a little) to drop us off at an unofficial stop near the airport.

We took a five-minute life-in-your-hands walk through heavy traffic and across highways in blazing sun to the jeepney station. There, Alex organised a vehicle to carry us a short distance, whence we had another hot, short walk to the airport, RAF Manila. We were put on stand-by for the 1.20 pm flight but there was no room, so we settled for the booked 3.30 pm flight. We needn't have hurried. It was a pleasant air-conditioned airport; I ate a hot dog of all things and had a Sprite. The place was teeming with people: a good number of mixed marriage couples with babies. A comfortable three quarters of an hour flight to Kalibu (on Panay Island) was followed by a 2-hour jeepney ride to Caticlan, where we boarded a banca/ferry to Boracay. It was now very dark and we landed on the beach with much splashing, where it was difficult to manoeuvre the narrow boarding panel with luggage and little light. Then, it was just a final short walk to Summer Place, which was really beautiful. My bamboo cottage was No.11 and I was so busy looking up for the number that I fell over a tree stump, landing directly on my long-suffering right knee - the blow being reinforced seconds later by my pack falling over my head. I was thankful to be opposite my door and scrambled inside.

My knee looked awful. It had swollen up instantly again and this time was much more painful. The sensible thing I knew would be to decline supper and go to bed, but I decided against this, so had a long, hot shower, donned long trousers to hide the swelling, took two Migreleve tablets and went and enjoyed an excellent meal of garlic and prawns. A few gins gave reasonable analgesia, and I spent a happy couple of hours dancing at the disco. Bed was at 2 am and I didn't dare think about the morning. The leg was by this time swollen all the way down to the ankle.

Island-hopping and Relaxation

18.1.96 Thursday I had breakfast (coffee only) at 9 am, after a really good sleep. The leg looked more 'stubby' than usual but less swollen than last night. I went out snorkelling from the boat with Matthew, Robin, Reginald and Jan. The coral was not particularly exceptional but there was great variety of shape and shade, and some wonderfully colourful small fish. My knee made getting back into the boat with flippers very difficult, so I stayed on board at one of the sites and talked to the two young crew who looked like teenagers. It transpired they were both in their thirties and had seven children between them. They asked me about my family and my age, and then announced that most Filipinos are dead before they are sixty-three - so I'm on borrowed time already.

Halfway through the day we had lunch at Bare Rock: garlic soup and mango juice for me. Back on shore I was glad to find some shampoo. My hair was thick with salt and dry with the sun, and I'd left my own shampoo in Manila. I washed my hair, showered and changed, and went out, looking at all the attractive little shops along the shoreline. This place is really commercial but not unattractively so. I tried on a lovely black and white sarong-like garment with straps and a skirt which buttoned at the front, but it was too small, or rather I was too big. The kind lady insisted that it was the garment which was too small. She invited me to look at the fabrics behind the shop, where I selected a different black and white patterned length: she measured me and said it would be ready tomorrow. I paid the full 300 pesos so she would know that I was in earnest.

I met the group at a local Thai restaurant at 7 pm as arranged, where Alex, Matthew and Reginald joined us, somewhat belatedly. Matthew was slightly the worse for an excess of coco loco, a local knock-out drink of several spirits and fruit juices which tastes innocuous and is served up in a coconut. The restaurant was very quiet and the meal of fish soup (with ginger), oyster beef and sticky rice was one to remember. Matthew recovered well with food and wanted to go to the disco: no-one else had the interest or the motivation except me so I joined him. It was far too early and nothing had got going. We sat around for a while and had a coke but then Matthew decided he had a headache and his sunburn was troubling him so we walked back along the beach. We'd just about reached Summer Place when we met Alex and Reginald, all spruced up and changed and proceeding in the opposite direction: they were coming to join us. Too late! We stood and talked for a while under a coconut palm, which suddenly shed a large heavy part of itself, narrowly missing Alex as it hurtled past his ear.

I was happy to climb into bed at 11 pm.

19 January 1996   Boracay Bay at sunset

19.1.96 Friday   After a banana shake for breakfast I settled my room bill for the meal, breakfast and drinks - 290 pesos, which I thought was very good value. I then felt a griping pain in my abdomen, with the usual consequences, so decided on a quiet day: got my things together and made for the beach. The sky was a welcome grey so that it was not too hot to sit outside and write my diary. I indulged in a bit of doggerel about the group and watched several Japanese families on the beach: some of the adults looked prosperously overweight. They had some difficulty getting into the bancas and there were shrieks of dampness and delight.

I had a light lunch at Summer Place, joined by Jan and Cockney Roy. Then Alex came. During the afternoon, I swam and walked along the beach. It was relaxing and idyllic. Later, I showered and dressed and went to collect my garment, which fitted well. I also bought a Boracay T-shirt and then walked back in the pouring rain. We visited the bar called Coco Loco, where I indulged in a drink of that name, and shared it around. It did taste very good and warmed parts that other drinks don't reach as quickly. We moved on to 'Alice in Wonderland', where my meal revolved round Lapu Lapu (Red Snapper).

Afterwards we went next door to listen to two good guitar players. I left at 11.15 pm. It was to be one of those 5.30 am calls tomorrow.

Panay to Palawan

20.1.96 Saturday I amazed myself by waking at 4.30 am, so was well conscious for the 5.30 am call. I packed, with the luggage getting heavier and more unwieldy with each purchase. We walked to the banca in the dark through big waves, but the boarding plank was luxuriously wide. It took us to Caticlan, where a comfortable air-conditioned Mitsubishi vehicle was waiting to take us on the long drive to the south of the island of Panay. As we went through Banga and Mambusao we saw some of the costumed groups getting ready for the Ati-Atihan festival at Kalibo. They were certainly spectacular and I felt a touch of envy for the two Roys who had left our group to attend this celebration. We were now unlikely to see them until the last day of the trip.

We continued through Dao and Dumarao, and I think it was somewhere near Passi that we went over a larger than average bump in the road and someone shouted that the spare wheel had come off. It took some time to fix it back on. We stopped in Passi for a coffee, a doughy roll and the loo, and then continued to Iloilo airport. The TV was blazing forth and an insect had very inconsiderately bitten my right upper eyelid during the night so I moved on to the pre-departure lounge, shut my eyes and reflected on the wonderful flora we'd passed all the way down. There were lots of holidaying Filipinos about but very few Europeans.

The 45-minute flight to Puerto Princesa (Palawan Island) was comfortable and, after collecting our luggage, we walked the short distance to the airport hotel. I went through the ritual shower, changing and washing of clothes, and then took a motorcycle rickshaw along Rizal Avenue to the cathedral. I watched a wedding where all the guests were in cream, like the bride. It was a very relaxed ceremony, with an overhead display of the words of the hymns. I sat and enjoyed the peace, the cool and the celebratory atmosphere.

It was an excellent meal at the Kahaua restaurant in the evening: fish dish, mango and fruit juice for less than £5. The group was a bit whingey: tired I think. We had seen and done a great deal in the last 2 weeks. My leg was still swollen, the foot now black! I was in bed by 9.45 pm.

More island-hopping and going across Palawan

21.1.96 Sunday I got up at 6.45 am - I amazed myself - and selected Continental breakfast, which included fruit, but there wasn't any. This hotel is not as good as it looks. I sat with Jan and Robin, and Hugh who - for the n'th time - went on about the wonders of the Yemen, where it seems he spent his most memorable holiday ever. The day was very grey, a bit like the group. Matthew was not feeling too well. Alex seemed keen to send us on our jeepney way to Honda Bay. We transferred to a very basic banca without a ladder, so that I swung round on my bottom.

The weather gradually improved, as did the mood. We had a three-quarters-of-an-hour trip past idyllic little islands, surrounded by Mangrove swamps. We walked on Snake Island first, where Matthew and I went exploring the Mangroves and the marine biology. Weird and quite sinister sea slugs mooned about like near-moribund lumps of protoplasm. We watched a sea snake gliding through the shallow water, exotic in white and amber, with twin white flags at the sides, just behind its head. Crabs of all sizes and colours scuttled between the Mangrove roots, and we studied holes in the sand surrounded by shells and debris: these suggested some sort of under-sand tunnel system but we didn't see anything going in or out, despite lingering there for some time. We had a glimpse of an unattractive black head with searching eyes and a big mouth, which someone suggested could have been a Moray eel. There were small waders of various kinds, little finchy birds in the Mangroves which reminded me of Darwin's finches in the Galapagos Islands, and some kind of whimbrel. Once again I longed for an ornithologist.

The snorkelling and swimming were great, and we sat and ate our packed lunch (purchased en route to Honda Bay) whilst just soaking up the sun and the scenery. We stayed on the island for about an hour and a half and then, under the now clear blue sky, left for Starfish Island, where the boatman advised about paying the small landing fee and a 'shed fee' but we were quite happy to sit in some natural shade. We swam and snorkelled again, and then had the special trip back to Honda Bay, with ever-changing views of more islands and a glimpse of Cathedral Mountain as we went. Alex was waiting for us with the jeepney.

We had a two-and-a-half-hour ride to Sabang, further up across on the west coast, with all that glorious botany again en route, views of white-faced cliffs said to be marble, 'Three Pyramids' rocks across a bay, and children waving everywhere. Matthew and I rode on top for the last half hour - suggested by Alex who then said he hadn't spoken. (Illegal and not covered by Explore insurance). It was quite comfortable among the luggage, and the feeling of glorious freedom, the cooling movement of the air and the breathtaking views, made me feel quite heady. We ducked for overhanging trees every now and then. On one occasion three parrots flew out of branches above our heads, protesting noisily.

We gave a young German couple a lift a couple of miles before Sabang. They were involved for 6 months in some fertilizer project in the national park. Sabang looked very inviting: a long stretch of beach, dotted with a few children and a lot of shells. We stopped for a drink of coke and then walked the ten-minute stretch along the beach to our accommodation. We were all ready for the evening meal. I plumped for the pork chop(ped), rice, and chop-suey, followed by papaya.

I found red ants swarming over a packet of biscuits when I returned to my cottage but managed to disperse them all before the lights went out at 10 'o clock.

Some time in the middle of the night, when I ventured outside the mosquito net to go to the loo, an enormous black-and-white moth followed the light of my torch. I watched it for some time: fascinating.

Bats in the Cave and the Monkey Trail

22.1.96 Monday Breakfast was at 7.30 am, after an excellent night's sleep. The water was very rough so the boatmen carried our packs to the waiting banca, which was a better-than-average model with comfortable 'park' seats on either side. We stopped at a beach further up the coast where opportunist monkeys stole some of the packed lunch sliced bread while we had an invigorating swim in the surf.

St Paul's cave and the subterranean Cabayugan River was our next port of call. We donned lifejackets and hard hats before climbing into narrow boats, 4 apiece, for the journey into the eerie darkness. Reginald was provided with the torch at the front of our boat and he flashed it about continuously as if we were at a disco. I studied the caves in the light of the slower-moving illumination from the other boat. There were stalactites and stalagmites of all shapes and sizes, some joined together to form columns, some appropriately called 'mushrooms', 'jellyfish', 'cathedral', 'Holy Family' and so on. Thousands of bats hung from the ceilings and walls, a few occasionally swooping above our heads as they moved position. There are said to be 18 different kinds of bats in the cave, the 'Flower Bat' being the smallest. Swifts also roost and breed in the cave but they eat outside. It took about 40 minutes to do the U-trip and by the time we came back into the daylight we were quite chilled. This was a good excuse for another swim, trying to ride the waves, and then we had our picnic lunch under the trees and the watchful eyes of the monkeys. A couple of Monitor Lizards humped nonchalantly around.

We packed up and followed the monkey trail, going up many, many steps to be above the luscious vegetation, some of the steps having an apology for a handrail, but most of them being 'naked'. We stopped at another small beach, swam and had a rest. I dozed off and thought I was in the Galapagos: too much travelling can lead to confusion. We walked the last leg of the monkey trail back to St Mary's, where I lay in a soothing hammock for half an hour, listening to the waves and suddenly feeling a bit sad that John was not there to enjoy all this with me.

In the evening we took the 10-minute walk into 'town' along the beach in the moonlight. My leg was a bit uncomfortable again: too much physio today. We had a good meal. My 'Prawn Gambas' was out of this world: what do they put in the sauce? I shared half a bottle of rum (plus the coke) with Hugh - and others. We strolled back to Mary's Place. It was a lovely spot, with a well-tended garden of flowers that vaguely resembled European Clarkia, Convolvulus, and Red Lobelia. Some exotic lilies had strange, fruiting bodies and attracted slim, yellow Humming Birds. Swifts swooped about everywhere, as they have done in most of the places we have visited.

More of Palawan's west coast islands

23.1.96 Tuesday A slight headache today. The washing was not dry so I packed it wet. I'm definitely getting more casual and less efficient with the packing. There was a superb fruit salad of papaya, pineapple and coconut for breakfast. The same comfortable banca arrived to take us to Port Barton, further up the west coast of Palawan. It was a wonderfully clear day, with blue sky and constantly changing coastline views as we sailed between the islands. We stopped after two hours, swam from another amazing beach (I'm running out of adjectives) where the sea was teeming with wildlife, and then ate lunch in the welcome shade on board. The four crew members were all pleasant and helpful. One had the most wonderful muscles!

We continued in the banca for another hour or so and then it poured with rain as we approached Port Barton - the heavy, tropical variety. We were booked in at 'Swissipini', comparatively upmarket cottage accommodation, owned and run by a Swiss gentleman and his Filipino wife. After the usual ablutions we had the evening meal on the premises, and I went for the exotic pork with rice, with fruit salad to follow.The group was no longer tired, but now very relaxed and somewhat wound up. We played cards and drank rum till late.

A noisy American, domiciled nearby for most of the year, came and talked to some of us while we were sitting under an archway outside, I can't remember exactly when. He moaned about his hard life, making sure the generator was working, going fishing, getting the food he needed, etc. It didn't sound all that bad to me. He always returned to the States for a couple of months during the rainy season, when he'd known it to rain for 18 days without stopping. "The beach here just disappears," he said. I asked him what had brought him here in the first place but he wasn't very forthcoming, and then he volunteered "Most of us have a pocket of shit", and admitted he'd been a fugitive some years earlier.

Trekking, Snorkelling, and Trespassing

24.1.96 Wednesday   I think the rain had continued most of the night but the morning sky was clear and the air felt fresh and free of dust. We breakfasted at 8.15 am and then walked for two hours along tracks to a waterfall, led by a local guide for the last section of the trek. I had worn my bathing costume from the start so that I wouldn't be bothered about getting wet when crossing rivers on all fours (which I sometimes found easiest) and I had nothing to carry. I hadn't even taken a towel. We swam in the pool below the falls for ages. The sun was hot on the way back. I thought I saw some Drongos and Woodpeckers. We had a late lunch at Swissipini, where I had the Wild West beans which went down very well. It clouded over again and Hugh, Robin, Matthew and I wondered about the wisdom of our booked banca trip to explore the local islands. It drizzled miserably on the way out in the open boat but gradually improved. The small banca was called 'Animar'.

Exotic Island was the first stop, where we enjoyed the best snorkelling yet: good coral, deep shelves, and lots of fish, many on the black-and-white theme but with dashes of other colours. While we were there, a Swiss couple came ashore and talked to us. They were probably in their thirties, and we'd seen their attractive blue and oh-so-silver vessel anchored in the bay. They'd been sailing round the world for four years and planned to take another two years before returning home. My mind boggled at the undertaking for such a timescale. They were alone and well informed on all the wildlife they had seen and were likely to see. They'd dived about five miles out and swum with the whales, having all the required diving equipment on board. I was impressed, very interested, and just a little envious - but then, there I was, already thinking that three weeks was a long time to be away from home.

Paradise Island was next. Here, an abandoned cottage was haunted by a very thin, very plaintive ginger kitten. Matthew persuaded one of the boatmen to give it one of the small fish he had caught. It devoured it viciously and voraciously. Beautiful shells lay all around: impressive coral again. Hugh said he was going to swim to the island opposite and set off without delay. The boatmen saw him and were very concerned: the island was privately owned by a German married to a Filipino who used it once a year, and it was always patrolled by a warden. We shouted to Hugh but of course he couldn't hear us. It wasn't long before we spotted two men, in what looked like black track suits, emerging from the bushes beyond the shore. They followed Hugh, who had by now gone ashore, along the beach until he took to the water and swam back to us in remarkably quick time.

It started to cloud over again and we banca'd back to Swissipini. Lights came on at 5.50 pm, by which time it was almost dark. I devoured crab-burger and chips for supper. Then it was rum, rum, and cards again. A lot of fun was had by Alex, Reginald, Matthew, and me. The others were not into cards: nor am I in my 'normal' life, but I did enjoy the game and the company.

Routeing for Home

25.1.96 Thursday   I packed (again) and then had fruit salad for breakfast. It was farewell to Port Barton.

We rode in the comfortable banca (Nancy) back to Sabang. It was a lovely trip, flying fish, breathless views, blue sea and sky all the way. Some of the group read at every available opportunity. I'd forgotten to bring my book but I couldn't take my eyes off the surroundings anyway. The yellow peril ('our' jeepney) was awaiting our arrival and we put our packs inside and went for a swim in the very rough sea. The picnic lunch was on left-overs. Jan and Reginald refused to eat the 'four-days-old stale bread'. Actually it was only three days old and was fine. The bread is white and sweet and seems to keep remarkably well, in spite of the climate.

We piled into the jeepney again, Matthew and I choosing to ride on top: no-one wanted to join us so we spread ourselves comfortably about - but not for long. It started to rain heavily and they stopped and let us back inside: with some smirking from those indoors. However, when the weather brightened we went on top again but it was not so comfortable now because the mattress of luggage had been taken inside from the rain. I sat on a spare wheel. Children at the roadside, and those in other vehicles we overtook (and we did a lot of that), waved and smiled. We came off the roof on the outskirts of Puerto Princesa when the dust got unbearable. I felt very dirty and dishevelled for the Airport Hotel and couldn't wait to get a shower and clean up. The water supply was unreliable and when it did drip through, it was stone cold. My room was called 'Camia' and looked wonderful, but the fan didn't work, nor did the air-conditioning, and the water stayed cold.

I collected the extra luggage and went through another packing exercise, then had a cold, weak, unsatisfactory shower. I lay on the bed and dozed. For the first time, I felt as though I'd had more sun than was good for me. My face and my forearms were burning. I guessed that it was probably caused by sitting on the top of that jeepney, with the direct sun and a dehydrating wind.

We went for a meal to the Kahaua again and had the 'special' - soup, lobster and other shellfish, and a sweet. Mine, plus 2 cokes, cost the equivalent of £6.50.

I presented my doggerel, which was generally well received. Hugh got up and went to the loo just before 'his' verse, but then he always does the same to Alex, when he's briefing us for the day. Finally to bed, at 11 pm.

This was the end of the holiday: I felt sad but couldn't wait to get home.

Manilan Experiences

26.1.96 Friday   I slept fitfully, very hot; and awoke with a cold sore, and a swollen face. I had fruit-less 'Continental breakfast' again and sat with Reginald, Hugh and Robin. Robin, a retired bank manager, was much-travelled and very fit – he's into long, demanding walks and climbing. He was telling us, in his quietly-spoken way, about one of his experiences when Hugh cut him short with his Yemen talk - again. We then heard that there was snow in the UK.

We walked over to the busy Puerto Princesa airport at 10.30 am, ready for the 11.30 am flight. We were in the air for one and a half hours, during which we were served with a piece of heavy cake and strange coffee. The jeepney waiting at Manila took us to the Las Palmas Hotel, where we reclaimed our luggage, which was all complete. I washed and changed and got a taxi to the Church of the Black Nazarene in Quiapo. Alex had suggested I took the metro but remembering how difficult it had been to get off the metro at the required stop, I chickened out. The driver was an elderly man, very polite, and with a dreadful chest which necessitated his opening his window and having a good spit every now and then: hardly surprising with the dreadful pollution. He'd been driving a taxi for thirty years. The trip was very slow and he dropped me off on the opposite side of the road to save the protracted journey through the one-way system. He indicated the underground pass and charged me 40 pesos.

The pass was like a rabbit warren, littered with small stalls, many of them selling gold. I was fascinated but held on to my pockets, as advised by Alex when anywhere in the Quiapo quarter. I came up once on the wrong side of the street but was more successful at the second attempt. The church was absolutely packed with people, standing room only. The familiar Sung Eucharist commenced, words spoken alternately by a male priest and a female assistant. I stayed quite a while, moved by being part of such a large and enthusiastic congregation. The Black Nazarene, a life-sized Christ, knelt on a platform there, and bore a huge cross on his shoulder.

It was pouring with tropical rain when I emerged, and I sheltered under the awning of a stall selling tacky, religious souvenirs: puppet-like Black Nazarenes, ornate candles and tinselled pictures. The rain seemed relentless and I became embarrassed by my opportunist use of the stall shelter without making any purchases, so I decided it was worth getting wet in an attempt to summon a taxi back to Las Palmas.

A red vehicle was dropping someone off: there was an argument about the fare. I should have got the vibes. The disagreement was resolved one way or another and I asked the driver if he could take me to the Las Palmas Hotel. He wanted 100 pesos up front. I wasn't sure about this, and said I'd paid less than half that for the outward trip. He said the traffic was much heavier now. I was getting wetter and wetter and succumbed, passing over 100 pesos. He then said he didn't know where the hotel was. I groped in my pocket for the card which dear Robin had passed to me in case I lost my way on this lone expedition. He nodded, burped loudly, and turned up the music to a deafening level. The route bore no resemblance to the outward trip and as we bumped across building sites, derelict, litter-strewn wastes and through tiny back streets at an incredible speed, I became anxious. I was mightily relieved when 'Las Palmas' appeared. I got out and thanked him but as I closed the door, I couldn't resist a "twice the fare for half the time". Relief had made me bold. After all, it was only £2.50 but dear by Filipino standards.

I had a swim in the hotel pool where three young Indians were having a moan at its smallness, but two of them did not seem able to swim. I packed for the last time, had a shower in hot water and at 6.45 pm we met for a meal at the Kamayan, where I was not disappointed with the succulent shellfish and the clever sauce. We were serenaded by three blind guitarists, playing lovely soft melodies. Reginald was casually dressed in a black vest, evidently too casual for the Kamayan, for they provided him with a purple robe which he soon let slip from his shoulders because he was too hot. I wore a black embroidered top I'd bought at a local handcraft shop in the afternoon. Reginald said it was sex discrimination again when I was allowed to show bare arms. Hugh was not with us but we were joined by the two Roys, returned from their separate sojourn, rather full of San Miguel. We discussed tips for Alex, who had been very competent, tolerant and sociable.

We queued up at the cash desk to pay our separate bills and each of us was presented with a small colourful packet with seagulls flying across the cover and the word "Trust" in one corner. I imagined they were tissues but Jan whispered to me quietly that they were condoms! I exclaimed mildly, whereupon Canadian Roy volunteered "I'll take them off your hands ". I came back with "No, I use these in my work ", and then, when I saw his shocked expression, felt obliged to explain that I was involved in Family Planning - other people's!

We joined Alex at Rosie's at 9.30 pm. The music was very loud, so hardly inspiring. Earlier, when Cockney Roy had worn, for just a few minutes, his eye-catching white, red and gold Ati-Atihan costume, Canadian Roy had been regaling us with his 'king of the disco' talent, so I got him on to the dance floor: he didn't last long. I was not impressed. I said an early farewell to Jan and Matthew, who were not on our flight, and just remembered to retrieve my air ticket from Matthew's safe box. He handed me a half bottle of the delicious local lime gin, a sort of professional fee I think - he had not been too well on a number of occasions and had discussed with me his Irritable Bowel Syndrome. Tonight it was bed at 10 pm, to await a 2.30 am call.

Really going Home

27.1.96 Saturday   The call came at 2.20 am. I had more or less packed the night before; nearly left out the wash things and the wet bathing costume. In Reception I met with Hugh, Reginald, Robin and Alex. I handed over the tips envelope to Alex and he gave me a kiss, which took me by surprise as he'd been friendly but pretty formal and 'separate'.

The jeepney took us to the airport where there was a slow, slow check-in (newly computerised). The baggage search was unexpectedly thorough, and a solemn-faced Filipino lady shook the contents from my handbag whereupon, and embarrassingly, the seagull condoms fell to the floor. She gave me a quizzical look, as did some Americans in the queue behind. I bought coffee and dried mangos with the very last of the pesos after I had handed over the airport tax of 500 pesos.

It was an uneventful flight from Manila to Hong Kong, where there was a one-hour wait while the cleaning was done. Then on to Dubai, constantly putting back the clocks and being presented with an abundance of local papers. I visited the Dubai duty-free but bought only an Elton John CD. I studied the jewellery but the gold ear-rings seemed very expensive, duty free or not. I had a seat in the middle, near the front and next to Robin, which was nice. Hugh was in front of us and Reginald was somewhere at the back in the smoking area. There were the usual hand-outs of blankets, toilet bags and hot face cloths.

An Arabian girl, sitting at the next seat but one, was battling with a restless, unhappy baby and eventually another seat was found for the pair, where there was more room. I have noticed that the Emirates Airline is very accommodating to the needs of young families. The man on my right had been travelling the east, touting for students for Plymouth University as it has now become. Plymouth would be receiving over 1400 foreign students during the next academic year, the courses ranging from one semester to three years. He reckoned there'd be a Medical School there within the next decade.

I dozed a bit between the meals which kept coming, culminating in afternoon tea not long before we landed at Heathrow. I changed into my long wool skirt and sweater which I'd had in my hand luggage, anticipating the English January climate. I didn't have to wait very long for my luggage, said goodbye to Robin, a real gent, and to mad marathon Reginald, who was off to see his passion of four years, a lady who produced for the BBC and lived in a flat in London. Hugh had wandered off somewhere as usual.

I pushed the trolley through the Customs and round the corner, and there was dear Alison, with Freddie who shouted "Granny" much to my delight. He continued to identify me loudly in the lift and into the car in the car park: it was lovely. Charles had done a splendid roast chicken meal, and Helen and Mark joined us. Coming home was all right.

I excused myself at 10.30 pm when I could hardly keep my eyes open, and slept well in their spare room.

Charles had had disappointing news about his back problem while I'd been away: it seemed unlikely that anything further could be done surgically. Coupled with this were the shorter-term problems of a ceiling-shattering burst in their own home while they'd been with me at Heronslake at Christmas. In spite of all this they made me very welcome and once again I felt so grateful for family.

28.1.96 Sunday I got up at 9.15 am after a good night's sleep, apart from several sorties to the loo. I think my metabolism was out of sync: I hardly went at all on the homeward journey. Freddie was immersed in the placing of his prehistoric animals on the number blocks on his clock: he is a delight. We chatted, had an early sandwich lunch and then Alison, with Freddie, took me to Heathrow Bus Station. The bus came almost immediately and I had a comfortable journey home. As far as Taunton I was next to a South African lady who had been to Johannesburg with her husband for a two-month holiday. They'd enjoyed the experience but were glad to be now living in the UK.

R and D taxis were on parade and I found Heronslake all in order - warm, with the heating on. Calls to the carers, Edna and Ann, confirmed that there had been no problems. I'd got away with it again!

I doubt I shall ever go to the Philippines again: there are so many other places I want to visit and, at one trip a year, I have not the years left to go to them all, even once. It had been a wonderful experience: the first week was more strenuous than I'd anticipated but I guess it's good to be stretched - in retrospect anyway. I have lasting memories of images of the 'Cresta Trail' over the rice terraces, the Mangyans, Snake Island, the Church of the Black Nazarene, to mention but a few. And then there was the group, all very interesting and individual characters: I warmed to Alex, Matthew, Jan, and Robin more than the others and didn't really miss female company. One definite advantage of being the only one of my sex was to have had accommodation all to myself.

I shall watch the political situation in the Philippines with renewed interest, although it seems that the legacy of the Marcos era will hold a continuing power and will have a corrupting influence for many a long year.

Legs, especially the right one, were very stubby after the long flight but were expected to improve rapidly with freezing temperatures and Tubigrip!

Caring people   -   Memorable lodges

January 1997

ZIMBABWE

with **AFRICA EXCLUSIVE**

ZIMBABWE 1997

Why Zimbabwe?

I had originally booked my two-week January excursion through Jules Verne, having been attracted by a visit to Victoria Falls and to four days on Lake Kariba, which were both included in this holiday in Zimbabwe and Zambia. Within a week of paying for my holiday in full, the Kariba cruise was cancelled, the departure date was changed, the tour was shortened, and other minor alterations were made, so that there was little left to resemble the original advertisement.

I got a full refund and rang Africa Exclusive, who had arranged my Kilimanjaro trip after another let-down, four years earlier. John Burdett was instantly helpful and a tour in Zimbabwe, staying at four different lodges plus a night at the Victoria Falls Hotel, was arranged and booked within the next ten days.

The weather between Christmas and New Year got progressively colder and I looked forward to some warmth. I was not particularly anxious about the house because my elder daughter Wendy, with husband Trevor and friends, were to stay for the first week of my absence. (The pipes did indeed freeze up, so it was good that they were there).

The protracted bus journey to Gatwick was quite soothing and I had time to collect my thoughts and read about Zimbabwe. At the airport I signed my passport as asked (!), got some Zimbabwe dollars, phoned Wendy and ate a Danish pastry. I love this 'in limbo' interval of anticipation.

The holiday lived up to expectations - from the delightful lodges which varied from glorified tents to well-built stone and thatch dwellings, to the infinite variety of game, including very close encounters with lions (on foot), and to the sighting of over 140 different species of birds (these may not have been up to my sons' expectations but were enough for me). The plant and insect life was incredible, all revitalised after the recent rains.

The company was good but it did seem that I cleared each lodge on arrival, which meant that I had the advantage of a professional guide all to myself on more than one occasion - but more fellow guests invariably arrived for company the following day.

The guides were without exception well informed, full of interest in every aspect of plant and animal life, in rock paintings, and in local communities and, above all, in the future of their beloved Zimbabwe. The Land Designation Act was a source of anxiety because it meant that many well-run projects initiated by the white man might be taken over by coloured men who had not the experience, or the will, to continue them in the same vein. One guide gave me quite a jolt when he said he wanted to leave Africa to get away from the black man. He'd been a professional hunter/guide for over eighteen years and loved the work, but had given up trying to change attitudes. "There are lots of good black guys" he said, "but there are also many who don't care about the long-term future of this country. They show no interest in their poorer fellows - and as for their cruelty to animals ......"

All the guides had detailed knowledge of weapons and were real Mr Fix-its when it came to looking after vehicles. The girls who worked at the lodges also had to be able to turn their hands to anything. They had to be pleasant hostesses when each new traveller arrived, to supervise the food, to liaise well with the staff, to have good natural history knowledge (most of them had their Guide's licence) and, in the case of Ursula at Malalangwe, to feed the rescued Tsessebe, Bushbuck and Warthog. They drove whatever vehicle was available to take guests game-viewing, and to go to and from the airport.

All the transport was interesting: a variety of open vehicles, some giving a smoother ride than others, although they'd be hard put to find a smooth ride on some of the unmade roads. The little cruise ships at Masango for Lake Kariba were mighty speedy and took us to farther shores to walk. The canoes were more leisurely, the two-man variety: I was reminded of my white water rafting experience on the Kunene, which incidentally stood me in good stead.

The seaplane was terrific, giving such wonderful bird's eye views of the water, the islands, and the big game. The return trip on the plane was almost too exciting, as the pilot endeavoured to make up for his hour-late arrival - a delay which could have meant my missing my international flight. I'll never forget the look of relief on his face when I said my watch was three minutes fast!

It was altogether an unforgettable holiday and I understood once again how people become hooked on Africa. It really is addictive.

But … it is always good to return to base. As the plane started its descent at Gatwick, I felt, as I always do, quite emotional. I think it's something to do with having gone all those miles and having had all those adventures and yet arriving home safely in one piece - well almost!

ZIMBABWE ZEST

The beginning

30.12.96 Monday   It seemed a far cry from Christmas as the weather became progressively colder, and I stood shivering at Barnstaple's uncovered London bus stop. By the time we reached Gatwick it was snowing heavily and I couldn't imagine ever being warm again. I had the company on the plane of a young Zimbabwean girl, Lily, who was returning from her catering course in England to be bridesmaid at her sister's wedding. I didn't sleep in spite of being tired and the kind attention of the staff. Both international Air Zimbabwe flights were excellent. The country's domestic flights are another story.

Elaine : David Gower : New Year's Eve

31.12.96 Tuesday   I was met at Harare by Elaine bearing a board reading 'Jean Taylor' - a board which appeared on every waiting courier's notice for the rest of the holiday. I was always so relieved to find anyone there, that I almost got to like the name! Elaine drove me the hour and a half to Wild Geese Lodge, which is as lovely as it sounds. It was still only 8.50 am. After unpacking and a nap I lunched with David Gower and his family - which included a dear little infant. I found David as charming a man as he seems on the TV.

I walked all afternoon (after the gate in the electric fence had been opened for me), rejoicing in the glorious wild flowers and the warm sun, and enjoying occasional glimpses of Kudu, Zebra and Impala. This was New Year's Eve, when I had planned to have an early night but was told firmly that such was out of the question.

In fact I had a memorable evening with Elaine's relatives, a bunch of young, well-heeled Zimbabwean farmers who were intent on keeping everyone's glass full of red wine, the widow of David Carney in whose memory this lodge had been created, and Catherine, a mathematics teacher from Chipping Norton and recently separated from her Reverend husband. She had opted to come to Africa for Christmas and New Year to see her son bungy-jumping at Victoria Falls. The meal was a veritable feast, which was completed just in time to let in the New Year with bagpipes, played by a handsome black Zimbabwean. My early night was an early morning - 3 am.

The real thing : Hwange : Hide Safari Lodge
Coincidence

1.1.97 Wednesday   I was awakened with tea and toast at 7 am, to be ready for the drive back to the airport where the internal flight took me, via Kariba, to Hwange. Simon met me and, after the casual collection of the luggage, we drove off in an open vehicle, scattering a variety of Ducks, noisy Helmeted Guinea Fowl and a lovely Hoopoe. Sable, Steenbock, Giraffes, and Elephants showed themselves en route through the Hwange National Park, together with a host of (as yet) unnamed birds.

Jane greeted me at the Hide Safari Lodge, where a waterhole just sixty or so yards from the thatched dining area made a promising sight. Among the other guests were Eileen and David, who were finishing a three-year contract in Harare before starting work at the Cotton Exchange in Liverpool - just one of the touching points in our lives, the most remarkable being that David was a relative of the Turner family who own the 'Big Sheep', an excellent educational and entertainment farm diversification (especially for grandchildren), less than ten miles from my home.

While we ate, a family of daring Warthogs munched their way between the neighbouring walk-in tents, which were our accommodation. A quiet kip and then we drove deeper into the park and walked, under the supervision of Andy our pony-tailed guide, for nearly three hours, viewing exotic plants, insects, varieties of Shrikes, Hornbills, Francolins, Oxpeppers, and Weavers, together with an abundance of Antelopes and Leopard Tortoises.

It was dark when we got back and there was hardly time for a shower before supper, when we were introduced to Brian and Tracey, the other two guides who were 'an item' and about to be married.

The day was not over yet. At 10 pm we were whisked off on a night drive, during which we saw a Bat-eared Fox with her young, Spring Hares ('Boings-boings'), Scrub Hares, Mongoose and Civet - as well as larger game, all against a background of powerful lightning, and to the intermittent penetrating sound of Bullfrogs, presumably anticipating the rain.

The Big One! All day

2.1.97 Thursday   I had to remind myself of the day and just where I was when the morning started with a 5 am 'knock-knock' and a cup of tea. I went for a drive and a walk with an American lady who was doing some botany research - following up the effects of several years of comparative drought; a young South African teenager called Megan; and Brian the guide. We saw Wildebeest (I still like to call them Gnu), a great herd of Buffalo, young Honey Badgers, a Duiker and a group of Giraffes - including one very young member which just stood and stared at us after all the others had moved on.

Swallows, Kites, Whydahs, Rollers, Hawks, and a clutch of Ostrich were added to the bird list, and lolloping Baboons, plus a huge Dung Beetle manipulating a mechanically disadvantageous small football of his favourite fodder, kept us amused on our return drive. Brian stopped to talk to the Painted Hunting Dog research team (previously known as Wild Dog). They were not having much success in locating their collared animals and seemed very down in the dumps.

I enjoyed the full breakfast which awaited us on our return - but we didn't spend long over it. At 9.40 am I went with Eileen and David, and a senior chap called Danny (who resembled Mr Meldrew from 'One foot in the grave'), in the open vehicle driven by Tracey. She drove us to a different area of the park and we spent nearly an hour just watching an Elephant clear a large patch of ground of some creeping weed, which he then manoeuvred and swirled around with his trunk as if he were eating spaghetti.

Lots of Milkweed butterflies were disturbed by his feeding but a circle of Egrets welcomed his presence and moved along with him. Bee-eaters and Waxbills were 'ticked'. An enchanting Vervet Monkey clutched her young baby: it was difficult not to be anthropomorphic.

During lunch there was the most violent clap of thunder that any of us had ever heard - which was followed by discussion among the staff about some alarming figures of people killed by lightning in this part of the world. Shortly afterwards the storm broke, with sheets of heavy rain being interspersed with lashings of the biggest hailstones that I have ever seen. I wondered for the first time about the weather at home.

It was too wet to walk in the afternoon so Andy took Mr Meldrew, Eileen, David, and me through multiple deep, muddy puddles in his robust vehicle. He helped another guide get his vehicle going and got well splashed for his efforts. We saw an impressive Tawny Eagle, a Rufus-necked Lark and a Golden-breasted Bunting, and then had an exciting few seconds' view of a Lioness. She walked out of the bush and then returned to the cover almost as quickly.

We sat and watched an incredible sunset under the unsettled sky and drank a bottle of champagne provided by Eileen and David, whose 9th wedding anniversary it was. We ate lamb for dinner, followed by a slice of heavy cake, a special offering by the cook for Andy's 24th birthday: a day of celebrations.

Simon took the night drive, which started quietly with the odd Jackal and Bat-eared Fox, numerous 'Boing-boings', and the constant, high-pitched tones of thousands of anaemic-looking frogs which crowded every newly-arrived puddle. "Their noise says 'I want sex!'" said Simon, his large white teeth being the only visible feature of his face in the pitch black.

Then suddenly we saw them! No less than seven Lions came into view, all running in a line, the leading male with half a young Zebra hanging from its jaws. Simon drove the vehicle round to the other side of the bush into which they had run and there, sitting in the middle of the road and not moving, was a very young Lioness, looking as if stunned by the lights. Near her sat an equally stationary Nightjar. We watched them for several minutes, until the Lioness strolled away and the Nightjar fluttered off. Quite a night: quite a day!

The Queen: a close view

3.1.97 Friday   Here we were, at Friday already, and I awoke before the 5 am call. We walked for three hours with Andy and stood within sixty yards of six of the Lions as they crossed the railway lines. Having seen them off the premises, as it were, temporarily anyway, he led us back into the bush where we lay in a sandy copse and listened to the three Lion cubs (of which he already had inside knowledge) suckling their mother. We couldn't see the whole scene because of the thickness of the bush, but every now and then, when there was movement, we'd get a glimpse of a bit of Lioness body through the disturbed undergrowth. I was frightened to move and I could feel my heart pounding.

Andy instructed that should the Lioness become aware of us and suddenly emerge with aggression, we should climb up the nearest tree ... I think he was serious. We stayed for what seemed like ages and then withdrew, very slowly and quietly.

Walking back through the bush, we admired some beautiful white day-lilies brought forth by the rains, which had also enhanced the scent of the basil which was all around. Deeper in the bush, we came across the carcass of a large Zebra, which was about half eaten. The Lions must have gone for larger game after we'd seen them last night, and now possibly we'd disturbed them before they'd finished feasting: they'd be back. There was much Lion talk at breakfast and I wasn't surprised when Brian said we were returning to the site of the Zebra carcass, but this time in the vehicle: I wasn't sorry. I got the impression that he considered Andy to have been somewhat foolhardy in subjecting us to such a close encounter with the suckling Lioness.

We alighted at the morning's sighting area to find the carcass had been moved several feet and was now almost completely devoured. A couple of Spotted Hyenas skulked away as we approached, but some Cape Vultures and a single Lappet-faced Vulture were more reluctant to leave. How quickly that carcass had been cleaned.

Kingfishers, Quail and Black Cuckoo were added to the bird list. We had good views of Zebras, which neighed like Donkeys; of a single Elephant; Sable; Impala; Giraffe; Wildebeest; and Waterbuck. They all seemed nervous and restless after the Lion's activities: they were not the only ones! The roadside was dotted with orange pimpernels, lemon-yellow ground hibiscus, and a lovely scented white pea.

At lunch I met Lorraine, the widow of the builder of the Hide Safari Lodge. She was standing in for Jane, as Jane's husband was ill and Jane, who was three months pregnant, was 'a bit under the weather'.

Simon took the afternoon drive and we sat and watched cattle and Elephants moving to the pan for their evening drink, against a re-assuring calm sunset. Four kinds of Stork joined the ensemble and a foursome of Ostrich danced a dervish at one end of the water. Lion talk persisted through supper but the night drive did not reveal any more of these kings and queens. We did see a Slender Mongoose and a Spotted Genet, as well as Foxes and Springhares moving for all the world like Kangaroos. Nocturnal Dikkops hung about in the headlights, which also caught three tiny birds huddled together in the small fork of a tree.

Onward - by bus - to the Falls

4.1.97 Saturday   It had rained incessantly all through the night. I didn't fancy a walk in the mud, so I opted for the drive. Tracey took me and Linda (who was working in South Africa but came from Manchester) and Alete, who I thought was Dutch South African: these two girls arrived yesterday. A Spotted Hyena stopped right in front of us in the light of the sunrise and I clicked my camera. An immature Black Stork, with greenish legs and bill, provided a temporary identification problem but lingered long enough. The sky was clear and the heavy clouds had rolled away.

I was leaving later in the day so, after breakfast, I packed, updated my tick list, and had half an hour's kip to compensate for the dawn start. These things I did to the constant rhythm of a sun-hatted black guy who was cutting the grass with something resembling a hockey stick: very labour-intensive but the result looked perfect.

I was sorry to be going after lunch but this was the pre-arranged tour. Young Dutch and Belgian couples had just arrived and seemed very pleasant. Brian drove Linda and Alete and me in the open vehicle. We started off in lovely sunshine but it wasn't long before storm clouds gathered with amazing speed, and heavy rain drenched us all to the skin in spite of a generous provision of waterproofs and blankets. We dropped off Linda and Alete where they had parked their new BMW car at the entrance lodge to the park. It would not start in spite of Brian's efforts and he told them he'd be back after he'd dropped me at the airport. En route we saw a side-striped Jackal, probably flushed out by the rain, several Giraffes, and two splendid Elephants.

On arrival at Hwange, I felt like a drowned rat: one glance in the clouded washroom mirror told me I looked even worse. Tracey was at the airport, awaiting a flight from Victoria Falls which had never arrived. I soon learned that my 3.15 pm flight to the Falls was a non-event, and that eventually a bus would be put on instead. Tracey and Brian left to jump-lead Linda's car, and then returned to meet their belated arrivals and see me on to the bus. It was going to be dark by the time I got there, and there'd be no seeing the Falls tonight. The bus ride was quite interesting, the bonus being that I was able to view the very green landscape.

I was met by a middle-aged black driver with short-cropped white hair, and was the only passenger in the minibus. At the hotel I was led (through the Stanley Room, which opens on to a large outdoor eating area and from which there is a breathtaking view of the bridge), to Room 79, which was hot and sticky and had just a ceiling fixture where the fan should have been, but I soon sussed out the air-conditioning, which was very efficient. It was at this juncture that I discovered my hold-all was not waterproof. Thank goodness I was something of a plastic bag lady, but not all my luggage was thus protected.

I unpacked everything and turned my room into a Chinese laundry, with clothes draped all around. I tidied myself quickly and went and had a meal outside: klipfish, followed by fruit salad, washed down with a gin and ginger ale. I sat for a while and contemplated the view of the bridge, until it was overtaken by a balmy darkness and subsequently rain. I then had a long, indulgent bath, washed some clothes, and was in bed by 9.30 pm.

The Falls - briefly
Bulawayo history : Malalangwe Lodge : Rock paintings

5.1.97 Sunday   I slept till 6.45 am, when I got up, packed my dried clothes, and made for the Falls, leaving everything except the required ZS 20 in the personal safe. I was horrified to find that the entrance fee had gone up from ZS 20 to ZS 100, not because I considered the price prohibitive but because I then had to do the twenty-minute walk three times - in the rain. It was all worth it. I paid homage to Livingstone, took the steep steps down to the cataract view, took lots of pictures there, and of other views on the return walk, and then had breakfast outside because the rain had stopped. The same driver was awaiting me at 10.15 am after I'd checked out. He was surprised that I'd not done the sundowner cruise on the river: well, I might have done if I'd had the scheduled flight!

There was the usual laissez-faire atmosphere at the airport but the plane took off promptly. I was met by Tara and Troy with the inevitable 'Taylor' on their board. We went through Bulawayo town at the beginning of the two-hour journey. It had a feeling of space and order about it, with wide roads originally built to accommodate cattle, eighteen abreast. Tara provided this information: an ancestor had been a surveyor under the direction of Cecil Rhodes when the town was being built. The Jacaranda Trees were laden with their lilac-coloured blossoms: Bulawayo is also known as Jacaranda City.

Tara liked to talk and I listened with interest as she told me about the family farm where the ten black local employees earn ZS 360 per month. "We cannot afford to pay them more even though we'd like to. If we doubled their wages we could pay only five of them. They do get free accommodation and electricity, plus vegetables from the garden, and we pass on all our clothes to them: but I wouldn't like to live on ZS 360 a month".

We saw elegant Eland and Reedbuck on the way to Malalangwe Lodge which, together with the surrounding stone-and-thatch cottages, was set into the hillside with views of insecure-looking kopjes and gentle grassland all around. It was stunning; (John Burdett knew where to send his clients!). I was greeted by Ursula, a very slim, smiling girl with crinkled blond hair. We had lunch almost immediately: savoury pancakes and salad, followed by fruit jelly and cream. My fellow diners were a retired GP and his lady, Ray and Kay who were into dragonflies in a big way and sported appropriate badges on their safari waistcoats, a younger couple - both lawyers - who were about to return to the UK, and Rodney, a very quiet guide.

Bookey Peek who, with her husband Richard, owned and ran Malalangwe, appeared later with their charming seven-year-old son David. Bookey showed me to my room up lots of stone steps, with turn-offs and corners, from which I had a fantastic view of the Matopos Hills. I had an instinctive reaction that this was going to be great: I felt it was less frenetic than the hide. I unpacked and sat on the balcony with my bird list.

Later I went for a drive with Rodney (who was not so quiet after all), and Zizzy and Justin, the lawyers. We had close-ups of Sable, Eland, Reedbuck and the gentle Kudu, Giraffes, Impala, Gnu (as Rodney called it), and Zebra. Rufus-naped Lark and Flappet Lark obliged, as did the Yellow-fronted Tinker Barbet whose call put me in mind of a bicycle pump being used with haste. This Barbet evidently disperses the seeds of a mistletoe-like parasite.

We left the vehicle and walked up one of the kopjes to see some extraordinary rock paintings, done by bushmen thousands of years ago. They were 'replaced' by the Kukulu over two thousand years ago, who had probably superimposed their larger, less skilful images. They were full of movement and detail: Giraffes walking through the bush, one upside down - presumably dead; witch doctors with bizarre head-dresses and alarmingly painted faces; a Steenbock being hunted from behind a tree by a bushman with a detailed quiver of arrows. It was somehow humbling and moving to see how these recognisable painted masterpieces had survived.

Zizzy and Justin left for home in London. Richard Peek came to say goodbye to them, a cheery, bearded man bearing a bright 'new' green beetle of some sort. Later I went for a long walk with Rodney between kopjes: the terrain was just breathtaking. Afterwards I came back and used the luxurious corner bath and really soaked. In the evening I had dinner with Bookey, Ray, and Kay who, with Richard, were all leaving at 4.30 am for the Eastern Highlands. Pity! They seemed such good company.

Rewarding walk and ride with Rodney : Unrest : Tsessebes

6.1.97 Monday   I've been away a whole week! Today it was a 6 am call. Rodney and I walked for three hours at a steady pace, under a cloudy sky and with a slight breeze: my sort of weather. We saw Canaries; Sparrows; Barbets; Bee-eaters; Larks and Swallows; a Wattled Plover; Fantailed Cisticola; Spotted Flycatcher; and an impressive Wahlberg's Eagle with its T-square tail.

Startling black-and-yellow immature Locusts, Praying Mantis, Leopard Butterflies and lots of Damsel Flies added constant delight. More rock paintings held our interest for over an hour: I kept seeing new features. Rodney is very knowledgeable and I felt very privileged to have a 'private' guide. He talked at length about the Land Designation Act, which gave the government power to take property from the whites and 'return' it to the black community. He cited an example of a farm he knew before designation, which had been making a profit and supporting over 3000 employees and their families working there. Now it supported just 800 at subsistence level, the land was not being properly managed and the soil was getting poorer by the year. This Act came into being when Richard and Bookey were halfway through their Malalangwe project and they were aware that they could lose the whole enterprise. Richard made his money in the family taxidermy firm.

On the walk Rodney showed me the poached-egg-like seed case of the Pterocarpus Angelinus tree, and the crunchy Helichrysum-like version of the Proteus Angelinus. A large male Eland walked close to us and a couple of Rock Hyrax, those diminutive relatives of the elephant, skittered over the side of a kopje. Over breakfast Smith's Red Rock Rabbit ran over the stones outside the window and then we were called to look at a distressed baby Bar-throated Apalis sitting in a cactus in the courtyard, its poor mother even more distressed a few yards away. It appeared that their nest had been dislodged from the nearby thatch, probably by Monkeys or Red-winged Starlings.

I enjoyed a breakfast of poached eggs and then accompanied Ursula to see a young Tsessebe called Tess (what else?) who had been ripped from the womb of her shot mother and was being hand-reared with difficulty. Also in her patient care were two young, orphaned Bushbuck, with lovely side stripes, which reminded me of the Kudu. Pumba was her fourth charge, a weird and wonderful young Warthog whose mother had also been shot. Her hope was to be able to reintroduce them all back into the wild. Pumba was at present being encouraged to abandon the wooden box which served as a bed in the utility room, and to use a burrow which had been dug under the lawn.

At 10 am (yes, it was still only 10 am!) Rodney took me for a ride and we sat and watched a baby Tsessebe as it walked away from its mother, joined the Impala, and then had the arrogance to be quite aggressive towards them! They evidently made allowance for its youth and ignored it completely, so that it gave up and strolled back to its mother. Shortly afterwards, a six-week-old Giraffe had a go at kicking a full-grown Zebra: there must be something in the air this morning. The birds we saw included a Capped Wheatear; Jameson's Firefinch; Orange-breasted Waxbills; Rock and Golden-breasted Buntings; three lovely Crowned Shrikes chortling and fidgeting in a tree, Willow Warbler, and two magnificent Black Eagles. I was feeling a bit burnt by lunchtime and re-applied the creams.

Clouds gathered in the afternoon and heavy rain set in for hours so there was no evening excursion. I looked at some of the books in the little library and really enjoyed a well-illustrated work with rock paintings and accompanying poetry, in particular "And now the beautiful trail of old age."

We had an early dinner and Rodney put on Richard's slide show which started with sunrise over Malalangwe, went through the day with birds and animals, waking, feeding and sleeping, until the sunset, after which there were great shots of the Spotted Eagle Owl, and the Leopard. On the way back to my room, an Elephant Rock Shrew scampered ahead of me, turning every now and then, presumably to see whether I was still there.

7 January 1997   Sunrise over Malalangwe

Sunrise : Matopos Hills : Graves : Sunset

7.1.97 Tuesday   I awoke spontaneously at 5.30 am and took a picture of the sunrise outside my room. As I pressed the shutter, a quick-moving Klipspringer took off from behind me. I went back to bed and slept till 7 am. Then I took pictures of Ursula's pets before breakfast and, later, Rodney and I took off in an air-conditioned nine-seater minibus for a day in the Matopos Hills.

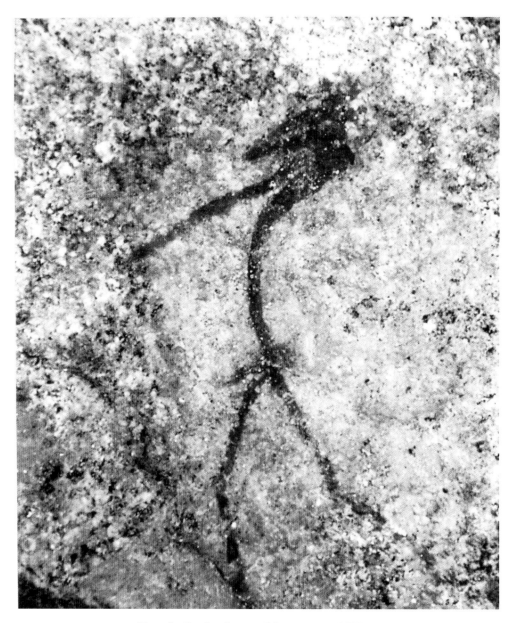

Rock Painting : Matopos Hills

It was a pleasant ride to the Matobo National Park where we were met by ever more astounding views of kopjes topped with enormous, and apparently precariously balanced, boulders - which according to Rodney "never fall off!"

We walked up the hillside to Cecil Rhodes' grave, which was like being on top of the world, with magnificent panoramic views in all directions: no wonder this was his chosen place. Dr (Sir Leander Starr) Jameson, British Colonial Statesman and close colleague of Cecil Rhodes, is buried nearby, and a less attractive but conspicuous memorial is dedicated to Major Wilson and his men.

The 'lizard man' did his hourly party trick and fed many of the brightly-coloured creatures who responded to his whistling call: a host of American tourists squealed with delight. We lunched by a small dam and watched Black Eagles, Egyptian Geese, Dabchicks and a Pied Crow. Later we saw a Chinspot Batis, and heard its three-blind-mice call, well mimicked by Rodney; and had good views of the Malachite, Brown-headed and Striped Kingfishers.

At the entrance to the park there was something of an argument going on between the uniformed official and a taxi driver with an American passenger. Evidently only certain vehicles with permits (who had paid for the privilege) were allowed in. The American was spotted later in the park, striding near a Secretary Bird, so presumably he'd got a lift with a licensed vehicle.

We followed white Rhinoceros as they trooped about and took frequent mud baths: a very young one made us both smile as he played, kept rolling over and walked backwards away from his mother. We climbed up into a hide where a couple of Germans told us to "shush" before we'd said a word: the nearest excitement was a group of Giraffes, all of 300 yards away.

We walked back to the vehicle and had some tea. The light was still good and we went quite a trek to view a vast collection of rock paintings. We sat quietly and studied them for half an hour: as before, the longer I looked the more I could see: they were wonderful. The light was fading by now and we made a steep climb to the nearest neighbouring hill where we sat and watched the sunset over the Matopos: an unforgettable experience. We stumbled down in the near dark and back to the minibus, and Rodney rang Ursula to say we were just leaving. On the return journey the headlights picked out a Jackal, a Spotted Eagle Owl, two farm cats, and straying domestic cattle.

It was gone 8.30 pm by the time we got back. So, it was a quick wash, a drink and an appreciated supper with Ursula, Rodney and a couple called Robin and Lyle who were staying the night. It had been a wonderful day and I needed no rocking.

Rodney had been excellent company. As well as being able to answer almost everything I asked and being sufficiently honest to say when he didn't know, he told great tales of his experiences as a fully-qualified hunter with a variety of clients: of the rules of the game and how proper hunting is all about conservation. He carried a sadness about the changing Africa and doubted very much whether there would be as much to enjoy for the next generation. He'd like to go freelance as a hunter/guide and had recently bought a Toyota pick-up of his own. He'd invested in good weapons and was saving for a decent camera. He was a very serious young man, only 22, but seemed older. However he did make me laugh as well. There were three sounds he dreaded to hear: 1) the sound of slipping trainers on sheer rock face; 2) falling boulders (so some of them do 'fall off'!); and 3) the sound of camera/binocular lenses crashing against hard rock.

Rescued Bushbuck

Farewell to Malalangwe : Musango : Lake Kariba

8.1.97 Wednesday   I needed the 5 am alarm call to wake me this morning; I managed a banana and a cup of tea and took a final picture of Pumba being fed by Ursula. I said goodbye to dear Rodney, and Ursula drove me to the airport. Having experienced cancelled flight, I had asked Ursula to check today's flights. It had been just as well, for they had said that the flights to Harare and Kariba had been cancelled because I "hadn't taken the Hwange to Victoria Falls flight" - which of course had never happened.

The plane took off on time and the connection worked. I devoured two small breakfasts on the two short flights, neither of which was full. Tawanka, a young coloured man, met me at Kariba with the 'Taylor' board. The truck battery for the luggage was dead so we had to wait while they found another. I was then driven to the office, where I left most of my luggage in my holdall, extracting bare essentials as requested and putting them in a flimsy red, white and blue angular zipped bag which I had bought in Namibia when the zip went on my main luggage. I was then driven to meet John, the pilot, and we climbed into the small seaplane for the flight to Musango. I admired some beautiful mauve flower spikes on the edge of the water as we got in and Tawanka picked me a bloom. I suspect John had never even noticed them before! A Goliath Heron stood on the other bank a few yards away.

It was an exciting short flight with wonderful views of the southern shore of Lake Kariba and numerous small islands. Elephants and Wildebeest, Waterbucks and Impala grazed and moved across the separate landscape. John pointed out things of interest: conversation was impossible because of the engine noise.

I was met by Jeannie and her husband Mark at the small landing stage and we walked up the steps to the lodge. I downed a large glass of ginger beer thankfully and was shown to my room. This was a pleasant affair of canvas under thatch, with mosquito net zipped in as windows. I had a wash and rinsed out my safari suit, and had 'brunch' (I'd already had two and a half breakfasts).

I sat next to Steve who built and owned the lodge. Later he showed us a collection of dinosaur bones and fossils found in the location, bemoaning the fact that some school teacher had removed the best - along with the annotation he'd picked up from the Natural History Museum - after they'd studied the specimens. There was an odd-looking piece which he handed round for identification. I plumped for fossilised faeces, which created quite an impression because I was right. I heard a whisper of "She's a doctor", although I didn't feel this was particularly relevant: it was the fresh kind I'd needed to study from time to time!

Then came siesta time. It had been a long day already, hot and humid, but I slept a little, and then watched a Reed Cormorant on one of the dead, half- submerged trees. When the drum was sounded for tea upstairs, it was a very comforting sound.

Mark took us off on a cruise in a motor boat, 'us' being me, plus Judy and Brian of similar vintage to myself, from Beer in East Devon, where they ran a holiday complex. It was a complete change of environment to be both near, and on, water. African Jacana, White-crowned Plovers, three Grey Herons in a tree, a great swirl of Open-billed Storks on a thermal, Wood Sandpipers, and Red-winged Starlings - not to mention snorting Hippos, Crocodiles gliding noiselessly from the shore as we approached, and swimming Waterbuck - making it an interest-packed outing. The long head and neck of a Monitor Lizard looked like my idea of the Loch Ness Monster. Elephants came down to drink and both Fish Eagles and Ospreys flew overhead.

Mark reckoned that there would be a storm very soon and we started to speed back to the camp. The clouds were indeed very dark and heavy and had gathered so quickly. In no time there were lightning flashes all around. We'd hardly commenced our return when there was a deep shudder, closer than thunder, as the boat rose out of the water and then splashed down again. Mark turned off the motor and went to investigate. The propeller was badly damaged. He was visibly upset and very puzzled. He'd been using the recognized 'safe' channel but it seemed we'd hit a tree stump, a legacy from the making of the lake thirty years earlier, when the Zambezi had been dammed. The hardwood trees were still very much in fossilized evidence above the water, easy to see and providing ideal perches and roosts for many of the birds, but the submerged variety were another story. There had been a comparative drought for five years, which didn't help, and Mark had already pointed out earlier the much higher water mark, where the level used to be. Some of the smaller islands were now actually linked to the main island. Coupled with this, more water was nowadays being taken from the dam than had originally been intended.

For the immediate present the result was that we had to chug extremely slowly in the dark (no more shore lights to be seen) and it took over an hour to limp back to camp. Mark had his Global Position apparatus with him, for which we were all very grateful. This did not assist in the avoidance of trees, now barely visible in the dark, or with stumps - which were totally invisible in light or dark - but he calmly got us back, without any problems or show of anxiety.

It was after 8.30 pm but a splendid barbecue was awaiting us and the rain did not really get going until much later. The passion fruit mousse sweet was particularly good, as was the red wine. Not surprisingly the table talk was of tree stumps, the falling level of the water and the lightning strikes. I'd forgotten to bring my torch with me from my room, so when bedtime came I was glad to have Judy direct me there, as my accommodation was as far away as anyone's. The grounds were not well lit.

Seductive sounds : a fast meal

9.1.97 Thursday   I had a civilized call - at 7 am. We went out in the canoes: Judy and Brian in the green one, Mark and me in the blue one. There were Crowned and Blacksmith's Plovers; Cape Turtle Doves; Darter; White-breasted Cormorants; Great and Cattle Egrets; Common Sandpiper; Bearded Woodpecker; White-throated and Wiretailed Swallows; Water Dikkops (known locally as the 'Kariba battery bird' because of the winding down quality of its call); and African Jacanas ('Lily-trotters'), who picked their way over Water Hyacinths, not Lilies.

We stopped for a drink up a narrow creek and watched an immature Fish Eagle (it looked like an Osprey to me). We got back just before more rain and sat upstairs, reading up on the birds.

Brunch was welcome and the meat balls, tomatoes, poached egg and spaghetti went down a treat, with fresh fruit to follow. Steve, his brother Martin (a doctor on holiday), and Mark talked about pilots who'd crashed their seaplanes - possibly because John had just arrived to collect Judy and Brian for the first stage of their trip home: they looked a bit anxious. (Here I am, clearing the place again …).

I didn't try to sleep in the afternoon: there was too much to see and listen for, and the start had not been that early. I'd been puzzled by a noise the previous night and had thought in turn that it could be someone trying out a boat engine, then possibly Buffalo, behind the rooms. Now I could see it was Hippopotamuses, heaving and snorting in their territory at the edge of the little bay below. The Tropical Boubou kept up its weird call from another planet all afternoon.

During tea upstairs we watched a herd of Elephants with three very young ones coming down to drink, and then there was a gunshot which sounded uncomfortably near. Mark had shot a six-foot-long hissing Cobra in Graham's room!

The services of Happy, a gaunt young black man with enormous specs, plus another boat were hired for the evening cruise: just Mark, Happy, and me. We went to the Shunga River and watched Buffalo, Impala, Waterbuck and Elephants, surrounded by a ring of Cattle Egrets. Two cabin cruisers and a houseboat appeared, the first time I'd seen any other craft on the lake. We went further away and then sat and had a sundowner. A Crocodile stalked an Egyptian Goose as it stood sunning itself, and got very close, but the Goose got some last-minute warning from outer space and made a noisy take-off. Ten minutes later the Crocodile had to settle for a lesser meal of a Blacksmith's Plover, which it took with lightning speed. Its grieving mate lamented loudly for minutes, its situation not helped by a pair of Common Sandpipers mating in front of its very bill. She flew off in disgust.

The skies were grey but it was calm and peaceful, with a strange yellow light. Hundreds of Cattle Egrets roosted in the dead trees, and the odd Hippo staked out its territory. We came back in time for a shower and change before dinner. In the course of the pre-dinner chat Martin told me about his chequered career in medicine. At present he was doing house jobs again to regain his Zimbabwe citizenship, which he had forfeited by being out of the country for too long. He thought he might go to the UK to do a Master's degree in Community Health, a qualification much needed in Zimbabwe.

There was chicken for dinner, and lots of technical talk about firearms disasters, and snoring. We were visited by a Rhino Beetle, and went out to look at the noisy Reed Frogs in the swimming pool.

National Park : "Education" : Butterflies and Birds

10.1.97 Friday We went aboard the cruiser to Heron Island (I have seen more Herons at Heronslake, my home in England), and then to the park, where we walked for four hours, following steaming dung of Buffalo and Elephant to which we got really close. We heard a Hyena's high-pitched call and saw Bushbuck, Waterbuck and Impala. We stopped at the park premises to see a two-year-old Black Rhino, a 'rescue job', called 'Cheeky', and talked to his keeper.

At the National Park Station we saw Sgt Shoko, who was drying Catfish for food for his staff. A small school was being built and I couldn't help but smile at the inscription on the T-shirt of one of the labourers - "Sex instructor: first lesson free!" On the walk back to the boat we found a Rhino's midden, with fresh additions; the scattered members of an Elephant skeleton; and a dead tree made delicate and mysterious by hundreds of beetle holes.

I was getting very warm and the wise Egrets were sitting in the shade, as was a Trumpeter Hornbill and a Goliath Heron. We cruised back for brunch. I had a swim and washed my hair.

I'd seen some beautiful butterflies for the first time and I borrowed Mark's book to try and identify some of them. Like the alien plants, some of them resembled species I knew, but weren't 'quite right'. I'd recognised the ubiquitous Milkweed, but others I decided were the Dusky-veined Acraea, the White-barred Charaxes (very smart), the Foxy Charaxes (lovely rich foxy colour), Black Charaxes, Diadem (a bit like a Milkweed), Lemon Traveller (resembles the Orange Tip), Green-banded and White-banded Swallowtails, Yellow and Blue Pansies (which really do resemble the flowers), and Spiller's Canary Yellow.

I sat behind my room and watched the birds come to a small bird bath filled by the recent rain: a White-browed Robin, an Acacia Pied Barbet, a Black-collared Barbet (is there no end to the variety of Barbets?), a Greyheaded Sparrow, a Lesser Masked Weaver, and a pair of busy little Blue Waxbills, which really made my day. After all this excitement I slept for an hour and a half.

The evening canoe trip was under overcast skies, with Mark and two new arrivals, a young Swedish couple, Mike and Jennie. We got out of the canoes for a walk and then had drinks and snacks on the shore, listening to approaching Elephants, and hearing a Leopard. I managed to slip on the red earth and spill half of the savouries! The canoe was manoeuvred between lots of hefty Hippos, and whilst canoeing back in the dusk we saw and heard Pied Wagtail, Kittlitz Plover, and Three-banded Plover.

Supper was good, with a bream starter, a juicy steak, and a fruit salad.

Community projects : CAMPFIRE : Predatory Lions

11.1.97 Saturday It was supposed to be a 7 am start but we waited more than half an hour for the Swedes, who had not realized the significance of the 'knock-knock'. We went off in the land cruiser to Mola village, where we visited, first of all, the primary school which copes with 700 children, which has a ratio of one teacher to forty pupils and which is free. A young male teacher was eager to answer all our questions but his young female colleague, Florena, was quiet and shy. She'd only just arrived, she explained. There were fees for secondary school education and not many could afford to go on to further education, and, "even if they do," he said sadly, "it often leads nowhere because of the shortage of local jobs."

Next we visited the 'designer home' of a local eccentric, where walls had been built round the garden and niches created in the dry stone for plants and small shrubs. His own carvings occupied nooks and crannies, and a collection of carved walking sticks hung on the gate. Jennie and Mike bought a large life-like carving of a snake for ZS 350, which seemed cheap considering the hours of skilled work it must have entailed.

Then we saw a local farm, where ground nuts and spinach were grown, as well as cereals. I remarked on the apparent good health of the cattle, and was told "This is a good time of year". An extraordinary collection of healthy-looking poultry ran about free range: Hens and Chickens of all hues and sizes, and Guinea Fowl doing their own noisy thing above the rest, presumably domesticated. They were all shut up at night, the farmer explained, and sure enough there was a collection of makeshift Heath-Robinson contraptions of coops.

116

The local clinic had our attentions next. I was impressed with the Family Planning poster, which included the up-to-date and currently fashionable 'Norplant' contraceptive implant, but on speaking to the lovely nurse, I wasn't surprised to learn that it was not available - far too expensive I suspect. The 'pill' and condoms are freely available and "fine" she said, "so long as they remember to use them!" There were currently only four in-patient beds but the number was about to be increased to ten.

Finally, we were taken to the premises of 'CAMPFIRE' – Community And Management Project For Indigenous Resources Enterprise, which raises money for storing seed and fertilizer, and for buying farming equipment: lodges such as Masango contribute to this fund.

On the way back to brunch, we met a couple of National Park men on the edge of the village. Lions had killed thirty-six goats the previous night and they were awaiting instructions and reinforcements about hunting down the animals, darting them and transporting them elsewhere. The batteries in their handsets were flat, so Mark lent them his to get a message through.

During the outing we'd seen, amongst other birds, a male Paradise Whydah with an Impressive harem; Jacobin Cuckoo; Namaqua and Green-spotted Doves; and a Steel Blue Widow Finch. The road had been very rickety and I was sure Mike and Jenny had been shaken about on top. They'd put the old woman inside and I wasn't sorry! I had a swim in the pool before brunch, and a kip afterwards. This is the life.

At teatime a Crested Barbet and a Firefinch came to the bird table. It was a beautiful evening with a clear blue sky and a warm wind. We cruised east along the lake and then watched Elephants, Zebras, Waterbuck and Impala coming down to drink. And, of course, more birds: Black Egret; Glossy Ibis; Grey-headed Gull; Ruff; and Squacco Heron; (I love that name).

12 January 1997   Crocodile : Lake Kariba

It was dark when we got back: to a sweet and sour pork supper, and a lemon pudding. A honeymoon couple had arrived, Jean (male) and Liselle from London, but they were South African and had come 'home' to be married.

There was lots of Elephant talk tonight. Mark was in good form and kept us all entertained, especially Graham who was a hunter-guide apprentice, with wide eyes and blond hair (I don't think I've mentioned him before). There was also Colin, who had been working as a guide in Masango. He'd been freelance and had now finished his 'locum', but was staying on for a while whilst deciding what to do next.

Local language was discussed: it was Tonga. Mark, who spoke fluent Shona, nevertheless seemed to understand the locals very well.

Calm Kariba : Fraught Leaving : Personal Damage

12.1.97 Sunday This really is my last day. The rain poured down from 5 am, so the early morning walk for the four young ones was off. I'd decided not to go, anyway, because it would be a long thirty-six hours before I got home. They walked later, and I opted for the canoe after breakfast (yes, we had breakfast this morning). Colin took me and we canoed a good distance along the west of the lake. It was now a beautiful morning, with a feeling of freshness after all that rain. This was how I wanted to remember Lake Kariba. I took pictures of a young Crocodile, Fish Eagle, Kingfishers and Goliath Heron. Colin was good company and I heard a slice of his life history. Some South African author had named him as being involved in the illegal trafficking of Rhino horn and he was trying to clear his name and claim damages, but the lawyer's fees were crippling him. It seemed that his brother was similarly cited and had 'committed suicide', although Colin was convinced he was murdered.

Colin had someone whom he described as "a sort of girlfriend" who lived in Scotland, on what sounded like a rather splendid country estate. She was an artist, painted thoroughbred horses, and had been to and stayed at Masango, but she had parents who declared that they would never let her live in Africa: I thought Colin was still hoping. A Red-winged Pratincole interrupted our conversation and then we beached the canoe and walked, barefoot, on the soft, rain-washed red soil.

I was then given a lengthy dissertation on the Termite mound. Colin said it was an example, par excellence, of successful community living. He removed a small piece of the wall on the west side and, within seconds, the little workers were there to make it good. The vegetation everywhere was fresh and gloriously green, and I was glad that I'd come in the rainy season.

We got back about 12.30 pm and I had a long drink of ginger beer. Jenny (Mark's wife) was on the bar and we chatted. She told me the sad saga of her parents not approving of Mark, and of how they had got married in secret, eighteen months ago, and then told them afterwards. Her father had not spoken to Mark since. (It's time I went home – everyone is confiding their troubles!) In the short time I'd known him, Mark seemed a sterling chap to me: steady, conscientious, well informed, kind, and quite disciplined. I was not surprised to learn that he had been brought up as a Quaker.

After lunch I finished packing and went and sat upstairs, to wait for the little seaplane which was scheduled for 3.30 pm. I waited and waited and waited. Jenny tried to get a line on the air-to-land but with no success. Eventually she got John's office, where the girl just said he'd been delayed and that she'd ring back as soon as she had any news. At 4.10 pm the message came that he would arrive in ten minutes. My take-off time from Kariba was 4.55 pm, and I had the rest of my luggage to collect from the office and a journey by road from the seaplane to the airport. If I missed the Kariba flight I'd miss my international connection from Harare. I tried not to look over-anxious as there was absolutely nothing anyone could do about it.

John arrived just before 4.30 pm and off-loaded a blonde lady (an Australian botanist, whom I had heard was coming), with numerous potted plants, live fish in plastic bags and multiple files. My African bag was flung in and I flung myself in as quickly as I could. We banged the landing stage as we took off and John looked at his watch and said "Not bad, a six-minute turn-around".

I took a last look around at the scene below, making sure that I had an indelible picture in my mind and, for a few seconds, I forgot the time. I was brought down to earth in every respect when I climbed out of the plane and into the Landrover. The helper had very thoughtfully collected my more orthodox bag and he rode shotgun to watch the crossroads - where we didn't make the obligatory stops if he reported the way was clear. I prayed he had both good eyesight, and the ability to assess the speed of traffic which was travelling at right angles to us.

We didn't stop once until we got to the airport, where John ran on to the tarmac while my ticket was studied at what seemed unnecessary length, my handbag emptied, and my pocket-less dress scrutinized manually. I had permission to board and I bounded across the tarmac like a Klipspringer, congratulating myself on my fitness, and thankful for the absence of arthritic symptoms in the lovely climate. I attempted to continue this easy style up the narrow steel aircraft steps, but stumbled halfway, then regained my balance. John was standing at the top of the steps with two members of the crew and I thanked them all profusely - the crew for holding up the plane for five minutes following John's call en route, and John for getting me there. He did admit that he had made a mistake, having recorded the plane's take-off time of 4.55 pm as his pick-up time! There were disapproving glares from a couple of passengers as I flung myself into my seat.

It was only after we were airborne that I felt warm fluid running down the front of my leg. In no time my safari boot was full of blood and I could see that I'd seriously skinned my left shin. I was aware then that it would take ages to heal, and that I wouldn't be able to swim for weeks while I was having the necessary daily dressings but, together with the late pick-up, it made an exciting end to the holiday and kept up the 'fall' tradition.

An unsmiling 'Africa Exclusive' lady met me at Harare. Her board just said 'Africa Exclusive'. I missed the 'Taylor'! I amalgamated my two lots of luggage just in time, for the Africa bag was splitting seriously, and we went to the International Terminal where I paid my Airport tax, filled in the immigration form, the lady left, and I repaired to the washroom to clean and dress my bloody leg.

I slept intermittently on the homeward flight, quite well really, next to a very tired French youth who had done the long flight from Mauritius, and was now to stay in London for a few nights before going off to travel the world.

We had just an hour's stop at Frankfurt, where lots of Germans got off but hardly anyone got on. I took advantage of this time to go to the loo and change into warm clothes, anticipating freezing temperatures after the Captain's announcement that it was minus 10 in London. In fact, it was nearer plus 10 when we eventually arrived, and he apologised for his mistake: it was minus 10 in Frankfurt!

I caught up with Ray and Kay while we waited for the baggage. Our plane had been held up for fifteen minutes in Harare awaiting 'their' flight from Bulawayo, which was scheduled to make the connection ten minutes after take-off, so they had been two of the four passengers for whom we had waited. I wasn't the only one holding up planes! Kay noticed my blood-soaked sock and said "You will get that seen to as soon as you get back, won't you?"

I had a return bus ticket but there was no bus until 1.30 pm, so I got the Shuttle to the South Terminal at Gatwick and bought a rail ticket to Exeter. My train took me to Reading first, which had a reasonably close connection to Exeter, but an uncomfortably close connection to Barnstaple, where I had to rush over the bridge, with luggage, to buy a ticket. From there I had a very pleasant taxi ride home, with a driver who remembered collecting me once before, after another of my January excursions.

Heronslake looked lovely in winter sunshine, with afternoon shadows across the lawn. It had been another fabulous trip but, oh, it was so good to be back!

12 January 1997

Colin   Jenni   me   Mark   and   Steve

Ludhiana family and Twitchers

January 1998

PASSAGE to INDIA

and NEPAL

with **FAMILY** *and* **NATURETREK**

PASSAGE TO INDIA - AND NEPAL   1998

After Christmas 1997

29.12.97 Monday   I eventually finished clearing up after a wonderful family Christmas when most of the family had been home, the only absentees being the Indian contingent whom I was about to visit. I'd done most of the packing, even written the return luggage labels, moved the sheep to the northern compound where there should be just enough grass to keep them ticking over till my return, and taken Hollie the dog to her holiday digs.

I felt exhausted by 6 pm and after a lingering bath and a serious cutting of the toenails, I snuggled down in the electric-blanket-warmed bed, with the radio. I was surprised not to be able to sleep and decided I'd probably drunk too much coffee.

Wendy rang about 8 pm to wish me a happy trip and then the Shuttle Service (taxi) rang to confirm the directions to Heronslake. I eventually dropped off to sleep around 10.30 pm, only vaguely aware of the radio, and was startled when the wake-up call came at 2.20 am, my least favourite time of day.

Travel : Small plane : Big plane : Hand luggage

30.12.97 Tuesday   I had left just enough time to get myself together before Mr Ludgate arrived, a pleasant man, probably in his late forties. En route for the airport I remembered I'd left the plastic container of half-cream milk on the table instead of in the freezer. Too late. The weather was wet and mild, the roads wonderfully clear. We arrived at Bristol airport in such good time that nothing was open. It was very quiet and had an air of subsidiary importance about it, putting me in mind of early departures from Tiverton railway station. One weary-looking man leaned on his luggage trolley. Staff gradually shuffled in and within minutes reappeared in their smart uniforms, the females clip-clopping over the shiny tiled floor in apparently regulation high heels.

Eventually the desk opened and one of the afore-mentioned chic ladies in the blue KLM uniform attended first to the weary man, then to an agitated young man who was travelling home to Turkey with what he admitted was very heavy luggage, and then to me. I was relieved that the paper work for Amsterdam and the onward flight to Bombay was all done in one fell swoop, and that I would not have to handle my luggage until I reached the Indian subcontinent. I sent up a silent prayer that, unlike my only other experience of travelling to India twenty years earlier, my luggage and I would arrive together.

I was feeling hungry and indulged in a cup of coffee and a croissant in the departure lounge. The plane had about thirty seats. My two pieces of hand luggage, one containing belated family Christmas presents for Mark and Helen and their expected baby - and which I was determined to keep with me - and the other, a survival kit in case my main luggage did go astray again, were frowned upon. The former was the heaviest, and was unceremoniously removed and placed in the hold. I fretted about this all through the one-and-a-half-hour-flight to Amsterdam, fearing that it might continue its way, unaccompanied, to somewhere other than Bombay.

Breakfast was served and I was just dozing off when we started to descend over regimented, irrigated fields, lit by the early morning light. My precious hand luggage was nestling comfortably with others at the bottom of the steps.

The walk to Gate 3 seemed to go on for ever and I was glad to arrive and find a seat, even though I had only the hand luggage. A young security lady gave me a lengthy and very detailed grilling about my luggage, including the usual "Who packed it?", "Where's it been since?", "Do you have any parcels packed by anyone else?" - to all of which I replied honestly at the time. It was only later that I remembered the presents from other members of the family and friends, which I certainly had not packed, and I had no idea of their contents.

The morning was bright and fine, and it was quite soothing to sit in the light, airy waiting area, with panoramic views and live potted plants. I'd got this far! We took off on time and I was in 11A again, by the window. It seemed for a while that I might have an empty seat next to me but by the time we started up the runway the plane was full to bursting and a last-minute arrival for 12B had ousted a restless little Indian from that seat; he studied his boarding pass and discovered he should have been in 11B, next to me. He was loath to move and became quite aggressive. He said he lived "around Hyderabad". He spent most of the journey with the regulation blanket over his head, snorting and groaning. I was amazed at the number of pieces of his hand luggage, some of which were removed by the stewardess and put in locker 29, with my bag of presents.

There were several Indian babies on board, one only a month old and surprisingly called 'Melvin'. He and his parents were just in front of me. Melvin was a dear little chap, done from top to toe in a blue babygrow, sucking a matching dummy, and topped with an extraordinary blue crinkled hat which made him look like a miniature chef.

A grumpy grandpa on the opposite side of the aisle improved after he'd been airsick a couple of times. Thereafter he nursed and amused his grandchild, a little girl of about eighteen months in a frilly pink dress. I wished I was sitting nearer a couple from Atlanta, with whom I'd had just enough conversation to discover that he was an orthopaedic surgeon who was on his way to a hospital in Bombay to help with hip replacements for five weeks. His wife was an elegant woman who had read everything on India she could lay her hands on and intended to make the very best of her stay.

My restless Indian sneaked to the back of the plane to retrieve his faraway luggage when we were just ten minutes from Bombay, and deposited it by his feet. An immediate reprimand from the KLM/NW steward sent him grumbling and scurrying back to replace it. "You do not give people very good welcome!" he shouted. He actually dared to rise again during the compulsory seatbelt pre-landing limbo and was balled at by a now very angry steward. As they stood and confronted each other, eyeball to eyeball, it looked for an anxious moment as if they might come to blows.

The lights of Bombay seemed quite without any order: they were like large, random Christmas stars, joined by strands of straggling tinsel. It had been a good flight apart from the Indian neighbour, who I decided was probably bordering on the unstable. The meals had been tolerable, not too spicy, and plenty of fluid had been offered. There had been wonderful views of snow-capped mountains until the blinds had been pulled down so that the passengers could see the indifferent film on the screen, about some everlasting volcano: my clue for a snooze.

I marvelled at the patience of the stewards and stewardesses. It was the Indians who seemed to show the least consideration, getting in the way when they went walkabouts, taking for ever to decide whether they'd have vegetarian or not, and constantly exploring their overhead luggage. I had planned to take frequent walkabouts myself after reading an article on 'economy class thrombosis', to which women on hormone replacement therapy might be more prone. I had taken aspirin and worn support tights but really couldn't face disturbing the Indian and his blanket more than twice.

I was the last to get off the plane because my hand luggage was so far away and there was no way I could struggle against the tide of the madding crowd. It didn't make any difference: we still had to wait for the vagaries of the luggage carousel. Bombay airport was hot and crowded, just as I remembered it, but I didn't recall having to go by coach to the domestic terminal for the internal flight to Hyderabad twenty years earlier, but twenty years is a long time and maybe I'd forgotten. While I awaited the 'free bus', keeping some part of my anatomy in contact with every piece of my luggage, young Indians did their best to persuade me to book into a hotel for a short night, but I was anxious to remain with the other domestic terminal travellers, and was relieved to clamber into the crowded vehicle with them.

ARRIVAL : INDIAN AWAKENING

31.12.97 Wednesday   The domestic terminal was deserted and had that middle-of-the-night air about it. I bagged a trolley and plonked myself in one of the few seats: the heat was oppressive. I removed my walking boots in which I'd travelled, took off my heavy sweater, surreptitiously removed my sweltering support tights and long underslip, and located my sandals in the main luggage: bliss!

The desk opened about an hour later and we checked in. A young Indian insisted on helping me and then asked for his reward. I hadn't had a chance to change any money I explained: "English paper money will do" he volunteered. £5 seemed somewhat excessive and I discovered I had only £10 notes, which was definitely too much when all he had done was to nudge me out of the way so that he could push the trolley. He grumbled as I placed two £1 coins into his outstretched hand.

I went and had a wash and re-did my hair. The two attendants lay fast asleep on pieces of cardboard on the floor, their bright saris pulled over their heads. One awoke and nodded approval at my efforts to put up my hair. Hers was enviably thick, dark and lustrous. Exchange bureau next. I changed £100 of traveller's cheques - 64 rupees to the £ - after someone else had managed to rouse the attendant. Well, it was the very middle of the night, 2.30 am. The flight was at 6.30 am. I talked to a young German couple working in Pondicherry. They carried two precious mountain bike tyres as hand luggage. Two other young Germans were off to some "fantastic" Ashram party in Bangalore.

It got to 4 am: still another two hours to go. Some waiting passengers lay asleep in strange positions. The restless Indian turned up. He was overseeing a young Indian girl whose boyfriend was teaching her to play pontoon: all three looked miserable. This was a long night in spite of India being six hours ahead of the UK. At last it was time to board for the Hyderabad flight. As we walked across the tarmac, a young Indian lady in a gorgeous emerald green sari took hold of my arm and asked whether I liked India. I replied honestly that I had been only once before and that was twenty years earlier, when I'd found it all quite fascinating. "But you do like it?" she insisted. We were on the plane by this time, me in 8F and she somewhere near the back. No-one ever did come and sit by me; in fact I had a whole row to myself. I revelled in the unaccustomed space, sorted through the contents of my overcrowded handbag and spread out the free Times of India. This was the last day of the old year and a page of 'the year in pictures' put Princess Diana first and Mother Teresa third.

Another vegetarian breakfast and by the time everything was cleared away we were getting ready to land. Suddenly I felt wide awake and excited. I lumbered up the steps of the airport bus with my hand luggage and thence to the baggage hall where I spotted Mark and Helen and ran over and gave them a big hug. My bag was first off - for only the second time in my life - so we were off together in no time at all. Helen was blossoming with a seven months' pregnancy and Mark was sporting the beginnings of a distinctly gingerish beard. We were beset by a group of positively charming young Indian children, one of whom looked marginally undernourished.

We took a taxi to the Operation Mobilisation premises where the Interserve conference was being held. Interserve is a Christian missionary foundation which seconds people to work with international institutions in Medicine, Education, and Development, as well as non-Governmental Organisations. At first it looked as if we would not be going anywhere when the vehicle took some time to start. This was India! Ten minutes later we were looking at the gates and someone came to undo the padlock. I joined Mark and Helen in Block B3 where poor Mark was to sleep in the corridor and I was in the official bedroom with Helen. We talked for a while: it was so good to see them. I washed and changed and lay on the bed and, in spite of various interruptions such as Mark returning for some piece of equipment, screeching parakeets, and a recalcitrant crowing cockerel, I more or less slept until Helen came for me, three hours later, for lunch. In the dining room I was introduced to a whole host of welcoming people. One such was a Doctor Matthews who, with his wife, ran Child Development Clinics in Vellore and Madras, where they had known Anne and Murdoch, my sister and her husband, when they were working there.

The delegates had an important meeting in the afternoon, so I had a chance to wander around the grounds and enjoy the exotic insects, blooms and butterflies, some of them so photogenic, but my small camera wouldn't work. The New Year's Eve meal was very special: beautifully laid out and including the relative luxury of meat, the edges of all the plates decorated with slices of mango. Mango was one of my mouth-watering memories of India and I wasn't disappointed. Ice cream followed, a real treat and enjoyed especially by the children, of whom there were many of varying shades, shapes and sizes. They excelled themselves later in the evening, the younger ones (with their carers, who were looking after them while their parents were busy at the week's conference), entertaining with songs, actions, and lighted candles, and the older ones with sketches. Jeremy did some professional juggling with facial expressions to match the act, and Duncan and Tracy conducted a team version of 'TheTwelve Days of Christmas'. Rob did a clever monologue on mnemonics, well-recognised by the Interserve delegates who had attended the afternoon meeting. Mark had done a good job training up a few sets for Scottish dancing on the lawn and, when it came to the actual performance in the lights from the conference hall, many more got the gist, and danced away to such tunes as the Gay Gordons, the music ringing out strangely into the Indian night. Special refreshments were served during recovery time, during which I talked to Dixon, a vet working with Interserve in Allahabad.

The Watchnight Service was preceded by prayers, meditation and choruses, (with the words on an overhead screen for the uninitiated like me), and then the ex-Principal of All Nations Bible College gave a brief address on one of the psalms. It was good to hear his words related totally to the section of scripture in front of him, but I longed for the King James' version. New Year dawned and we all wished each other a happy one, including another couple who had known Anne and Murdoch in Madras. Who needs letters of introduction?

Postscript: The camera just needed a new battery.

FRIENDS AND GOLCONDA FORT

1.1.98 Thursday I got to bed about 1 am and slept immediately, staying asleep until Helen turned off the fan, when I awoke with a start and had difficulty getting off again, but then slumbered on until 10 am. I couldn't believe I'd arrived only twenty-four hours earlier. I walked round the grounds again watching for Parakeets, Mynas, Barbets, and Bulbuls. The rest appeared for chai (very sweet and milky) after their meeting had overrun. It was warm and bright, like an ideal English summer day.

We all assembled in the auditorium for singing led by Kevin and Tracy, before saying farewell to a Swiss family, Vreni and Rolf and their three boys, including the lively little Benjamin, who were returning to their own country after working for several years in India.

At lunchtime I talked to Chemene and David: an Australian couple working at a boys' school. She nursed their third 'surprise' baby, conceived unexpectedly after her husband's vasectomy!

Lunch over, we waited for a bus to take us to the station where we intended getting a taxi to take us to the Golconda Fort. No bus came but we got a lift with a friend of a friend of one of the delegates. Oh, the driving! The place was teeming with Ambassador cars, cycle rickshaws, auto-rickshaws, motorbikes, pushbikes, and motor-scooters carrying whole families, not to mention ambling pedestrians who seemed to believe they were immortal, and the odd animal. This was New Year's Day and all the world was going somewhere.

There was some bargaining with the taxicab driver. Mark had been advised that four hundred rupees was a reasonable fare for the half-hour drive to the Fort, waiting the three hours it was envisaged we might spend there, and then driving us back to Hyderabad. This sum was eventually agreed. The entrance fee was a mere two rupees. We walked gently in what was now the considerable heat and followed the tour as shown on the map provided.

The Fort was built by Qutub Shahis, possibly on the site of an earlier structure of the Hindu period, when the Yadavas, and later the Kakatiyas, ruled this part of India. Sultan Quli Qutub Shah made Golconda his capital in 1512, and thus it remained until 1590, when Hyderabad became the capital. During the seventeenth century the last of the Qutub Shahi kings, Abul Hasan, held out for seven months against Aurangzeb's Moghul army, but following Aurangzeb's death, Golconda was abandoned. The gates were punctuated at frequent intervals by magnificent giant studs to keep out the elephants. The huge battlements seemed to wind up the hill on which it is built and were surrounded by crenellated ramparts. There is still evidence of the complicated water system, not to mention the advanced acoustics, so that a hand clap in the entrance can be heard right up in the citadel. We wandered around the remains of palaces, assembly halls, all spaciously appointed, and the sun shone on some of the old stone, creating shadows in more sheltered areas. It wasn't hard to imagine life in such a grand setting.

The topmost building was deemed to be unsafe, so that was out of bounds. Twenty years earlier I had visited it, with my sister's friends. There had been a large canon in the grounds then, on which we had photographed the children.

We took the taxi again to the Qutub Shahi tombs, impressive buildings in spacious gardens. It was something of a bank holiday equivalent I suppose, and there were large families enjoying the lovely grounds and taking each other's photographs, although it was made very clear on the way in, that photographs were forbidden. The young girls wore saris of some wonderful colours, rivalled only by all the magnificent shades of the Bougainvillea. The taxi took us back to Hyderabad station where we climbed the stairs to the restaurant of the Alpha Hotel. The driver haggled over the four hundred rupees - we had been longer than three hours - and I felt like giving him the other hundred for which he was asking, but knew I must keep out of it. He hung about for a while, arguing his point in Hindi with Mark and Helen who responded impressively but stuck to their guns.

The chicken with masala sauce which we all ordered was quite the hottest creation I've ever tasted and none of us coped with the whole portion, in spite of washing it down with large glasses of lime and soda, and modifying the intensity with extra nam bread. "More spicy in the south", said Helen as the fire continued to burn in our throats. The place was hardly overstretched when we arrived but was filling up when we left, at about 8.30 pm. There was plenty of staff, from a young lad anxious to collect the glasses before we had finished, another young man in a check shirt who took the order, to yet another young man in a yellow shirt who was called to discuss it further. Several other young men of varying ages and shirts walked about and stood in a central countered area: there were no girls or women on the staff.

We sat next to the open window, separated from the traffic-filled view and all its associated lights, noises, and fumes, by a narrow open balcony, faced with patterns of thousands of coloured fairy lights, some of them twinkling in an intermittemt on/off programme. The whole scene reminded me of Manila. The meal was only 261 rupees. After another bargaining exercise with a taxi-man, we had (for Hyderabad) a good run 'home', where we had much-needed showers. I was getting used to the stand-up loo and the dodgy water system.

MECCA MASJID at Ramadan : CHARMINAR : BIRLA TEMPLE

2.1.98 Friday   I slept late but reasonably well, despite the pillows being a bit hard, and the mosquito bites itching. A coughing fit had developed between 6 am and 7 am but Mark and Helen didn't seem to notice. I thought I'd just lost my voice from excitement and fatigue but I had to admit I'd got a cold.

It became very frustrating when I couldn't sing, or make conversation with all these new people, without coughing. We breakfasted on snacks which Helen had bought before we left the restaurant last night. Mark did some washing, and then we said goodbye to an Indian family working in Bhutan.

We caught a bus (standing initially) to Hyderabad station, and then took a long auto-rickshaw drive - longer than it had seemed from the map - and fraught with characteristic near misses on all sides. Various notices and placards caught my eye as we drove jerkily along: 'Spoken English', 'Dental Care', 'Sex Clinic (for men and women)' and so on. Eventually we arrived at the Mecca Masjid, one of the largest mosques in the world, built in the seventeenth century during the reign of Muhammad Quli Qutb Shah. It was the beginning of Ramadan, so positive armies of skull-capped men were approaching and gathering inside. We took off our shoes as instructed and peered through the doorway. The building was spacious and plain in Islamic style, the facade being somewhat marred by great chicken wire meshes, put up to discourage the pigeons - hundreds of which were being fed encouragingly in front of the building. The masterful colonnades and door arches were made of single blocks of granite, said to have been quarried eleven kilometres away and dragged to the site by fourteen hundred bullocks.

Mark went on a little exploration with Helen while I watched the men of all ages, sizes, and shapes, in attire varying from formal snow white to multi-coloured casual, stoop and wash themselves in the rectangular pool and then proceed to the temple. We were something of an oddity. There were very few women about and no other Europeans. A group of young boys found us fascinating and Helen practised her Hindi.

We made for the Charminar next. This high triumphal arch was also built by Muhammad Quli Qutb Shah, in 1591, to commemorate the end of a plague in Hyderabad. I had memories of this place from 1977 when, with Anne and Murdoch, I had climbed up the narrow staircase, cushioned on all sides by bat droppings, to enjoy magnificent views of the city from the elegant balconies and the top of the minarets. I was therefore looking forward to a repeat experience. Unfortunately such an excursion was no longer permitted since, in 1986, several people had committed suicide by leaping from the top.

Mark had photocopied what he considered to be the relevant pages from the Lonely Planet guide and we took an auto-rickshaw to find a restaurant recommended therein. It appeared to be off Hyderabad's Mahatma Gandhi Road. The driver said he knew the way, as they always do but, after a prolonged and increasingly expensive search, he started across the bridge to Secunderabad. (No doubt there's a Mahatma Gandhi Road in every city). Mark stopped him, paid him off and, after consultations with other drivers at the entrance to the bridge (where we seemed to be holding up the traffic) we found one who seemed to have some idea: he collected a helper which was encouraging. They located the district but the restaurant was no longer in existence. We settled for soup and pizza in an upstairs, artificially-lit emporium, 'Pick and Move', where a number of attractive young locals were enjoying their holiday. The intrusive modern pop music crescendoed to an unbearable pitch every time the door opened, but the food was good and we stayed just long enough to eat it.

The rickshaw had no trouble with our next destination, the Birla Temple, a stunning white marble building built on a high rocky hill in 1976. It was dedicated to Lord Venkateshwara and afforded panoramic views over the city. Holy men were accommodated in various nooks and crannies where their devotees presented them with money and other gifts.

We were hot and sweaty by the time we'd walked up to and down from the temple, for the weather had continued very warm. We bought an ice cream just below the temple area and sat near a charming Indian family: I couldn't resist taking their picture. The young girl came over all shy and covered her face. Helen bought food for the morrow, and I fell for a few bangles for the grandchildren as we walked back to the main road.

We took a taxi back to Operation Mobilisation conference centre and organised luggage ready for the morning. We ate supper in the dining room and Mr Dass, the administrator came to talk to us. We went back to his flat, which was below ours, for tea and cake, where his lovely wife and daughter Esther were very hospitable. He talked about his 'cluster of talents' but not in a boastful way. The Christmas decorations were, quite reasonably, still up: it all seemed such a long time ago. Books crammed the shelves along one of the walls. There was a lot of frenzied activity and flapping of curtains in the kitchen doorway before the appreciated home-made goodies and tea were actually put before us.

We took our leave at about 9.30 pm, anticipating an early start the following day. I had a touch of colonic spasm in the night: Birla ice cream and, or, Dass cookies?

TRAVEL : INDIAN STYLE

3.1.98 Saturday   It was a 5.30 am start, and very dark. We lugged all our goods, Mark doing a noble job with the heaviest of my bags. The night watchman roused himself and unlocked the gates and we waited for a No.229 bus, which came along relatively quickly. We got on, with our excessive amount of luggage, and took over the entire long back seat, which was fortuitously vacant. Once the bus got going I realised why: it was definitely the most uncomfortably mobile part of the vehicle. We arrived at a location called 'Paradisa', and the men sitting nearby (there were no women, apart from Helen and me) told us in chorus that this bus does not go to the station. So we piled off and got two auto-rickshaws to complete the journey: Helen and me and some of the luggage in one, and Mark and the rest in the other. I had imagined that it might be easier (and safer) to travel at this time of day with less traffic, but our driver was a speed maniac and beat Mark's driver by thirty seconds!

We were in plenty of time and ploughed our way steadily through the anxious-to-please red-clad coolies, whose services were refused by macho Mark, and who plodded on, regardless, with the heaviest of the gear. We were in the S12 - 13 - 14 three-tier bunk system, the middle one folding away during the day. Mark rapidly stowed and secured the luggage under the bottom bunk, with the expertise of one who has done it all before.

Beverley, an associate of Helen's, known not unreasonably but affectionately as 'big Bev', joined us during the early part of the journey from further down the train, where she was in AC class. This I discovered later stands for 'air-conditioning', which sounded attractive but with it went no outlook on to the passing landscape, which I would have sorely missed.

We played cards - some Swiss game with animal-faced cards - and ate our lunch as we rushed through little stations, stopping occasionally. At Burkhedi, cattle, goats and pigs wandered by the side of the track, and vendors displayed their wares with a sense of urgency outside and in the carriages. After Butbouri we stopped at Magpur, aware of our approach to something larger at the sight of, first, poor-looking tents; then, inferior lean-to's; followed by rough-tiled shacks, and finally tenements. Between Godani and Narkher, the shy photograph girl from the Birla ice cream stall, plus her father and brother, passed along the corridor. The father spotted me and laughed, as did his daughter when she saw I was not grasping a camera. There was a lovely sunset over a rural scene of occasional bullock carts, cattle herds and a few brightly-clad working women in an otherwise deserted landscape. What a contrast to the overcrowded streets of Hyderabad.

It was time to settle down for the night. It was decided I should sleep in the top bunk, where I would be warmer (I hadn't got a sleeping bag) and less disturbed by ambulant nightwalkers. I made a special point of drinking little, and having a prophylactic bladder-emptying session before climbing up over, as it were, taking to my bunk at the extraordinarily early hour of 8.45 pm. I deposited my shoes on top of the fan cage just an arm's length away, donned a pair of thermal socks given to me by daughter Wendy for one of my previous expeditions, plus my long travelling skirt and thick jumper, and slept soundly until 10.30 pm when a certain sensation suggested I should take a trip down the corridor. I repositioned for a while, telling myself it was all a matter of self-control, but it wasn't: it was a matter of imminent overflow! My shoes, retrieved from the fan cage, would not go on over the thick socks, which I was forced to remove, banging my head on the ceiling in the process, having forgotten about the limited space between me and it. From this lofty situation, therefore, I put on shoes and climbed clumsily down the scanty ladder. It was probably as well that the middle incumbent, Mark I think, was sleeping with head towards the window, as otherwise he may have sustained head injuries.

People were strewn all over the place and, when I eventually reached the loo, surprise surprise, it was occupied and I had to wait and study the surrounding unconscious population: all ages, in all apparel and all positions. Still, it was an improvement on twenty years earlier, when the bunks had had only wooden slats and there had definitely been so many bodies between me and my destination that I'd actually stumbled over a couple.

Thus relieved, I slept until 6.30 am, occasionally half-waking at some stop in a characteristically noisy station.

DELHI : HUMAYUN'S TOMB : HOSPITALITY

4.1.98 Sunday   It seemed strange, as it always does on a Sunday when I'm not at my home church, Torrington's St Michael and All Angels - not that I'd have been much use in the choir, by now having no voice at all. It had been much colder in the night and I'd added my fleece for another layer of insulation. Everyone started stirring just before 7 am, packing up, (some of the Indians' bedrolls were unbelievably unwieldy) and making for the loo queue. As they went to and from their ablutions, they crossed the paths of various vendors selling coffee, chai, bootlaces, squeaking dogs, and a muezzin tika'd and turbaned, crying out the prayer time, and offering fresh flower petals to put on his picture of a god, in exchange for money.

We were nearly into Delhi and got off at Nizamuddin, where we met up with Bev. After the ritual bargaining, we all took a taxi to her house in New Delhi. Here we enjoyed a welcome breakfast and a shower. Then we went by auto-rickshaw to Humayun's tomb, built in the sixteenth century by Haji Begum, senior wife of Humayun. It was a lovely warm day and the sunlight accentuated the contrasting colours of the red and white sandstone, and the black and yellow marble, beautifully integrated into the building. The high-arched entrances admitted plenty of light and a bulbous dome topped the tomb, the whole complex being surrounded by formal gardens. Less well-preserved tombs of Isa Khan and Humayun's barber stood in the grounds.

We drank in the peaceful setting of this place, which gave humbling views of the surrounding countryside. Inside there were bees and bats: outside, Hoopoes, Striped Squirrels, and Parakeets, one nestling - possibly nesting - in a crevice in the dome. There was not a single inscription to be seen.

We then visited Duncan and Tracy (whom I'd already met at Hyderabad) who lived in a very attractive house in an upmarket area of the city. (Duncan worked for an insurance company which was trying to get a foothold in India.) The area director of Interserve, Richard Clark, and his wife Janice, who were visiting various Interserve Partners in India and Nepal for three weeks, were also guests for lunch. We ate delicious chicken, talked, and had a conducted tour of the house, which was very spacious with lots of marble. This may well have accounted for the slightly chilly feel to the place but offered, no doubt, a pleasant relief when the weather outside was unbearably hot. We chatted over the washing-up and Tracy touched on the necessary security: I thought I'd find that difficult.

Back at Bev's we drank tea and indulged in various reminiscences of India and elsewhere. I read my bird and butterfly books and almost fell asleep. At 7 pm Bev drove us to the Haus Khas restaurant in the district of the same name, where we did a little shopping first, in the nearby craft complex. I bought a wall-hanging for 950 rupees, with the intention of hanging it at the top of the stairs at Heronslake.

We had an excellent meal in pleasant, if draughty surroundings, with lots of talk, and entertainment by a Rajasthan music group, dressed in bright pink and playing strange instruments. The meal was 1030 rupees - about £17 for the four of us, so I hardly broke the bank by treating everybody!

MAN IN WHITE : MESH : GANDHI SMITRI

5.1.98 Monday   I slept well in a single bed next to Helen's, in spite of coughing which evidently did not disturb her as she only commented on the alleged snoring. I had been only vaguely aware of the arrival of Kathy, who had come in by plane from Germany in the middle of the night and lay asleep in the third single bed. Kathy was Australian and had been doing some work in medical statistics in a hospital near Missouri, where Helen and Mark did their language study.

During breakfast, I was fascinated by a man in white who lived at the substantial house opposite, as he gave out money and bananas to an orderly queue of needy people, who were succeeded by an equally well-disciplined line of people in wheelchairs. Evidently this is a Monday morning ritual. I asked Bev about the man. She said, "'He goes to the temple' people say, so he's probably a Hindu, otherwise they'd say 'He goes to the Buddhist temple' ". I found it quite moving.

We went off in Bev's car to a shop with goods made by, and sold in aid of, MESH, Maximum Employment for Socially Handicapped. Here worked Jackie, who had just been awarded an MBE for her work in the Indian community. The five of us sang the National Anthem to bring her down from upstairs where she was stock-taking, and then curtsied to the blushing lady. The local employees looked bemused by the whole performance. There was plenty of good quality stock and I bought some napkins to replace my ancient homemade seersucker apologies, and a purse, and a bag, with children's birthdays in mind again.

We continued to Fabina's, at the N Block in the market (this is a shop which could be compared with the UK Marks and Spencer, but on a smaller scale), where Helen and Mark bought a carpet and a waistcoat, amongst other things. I collected a clothbound book (in which I hoped to write my best poems), a sea-green silk Kurta (which will become an A-line dress), and a pair of white cotton salwar (trousers). We lunched on white rolls and salad in an un-Indian restaurant, with Engelbert Humperdinck coming over the air. We had a brief look at the cheap books and clothes in the tinselled Khan market, and then left the commercial world by taxi, for Indira Gandhi's house which had been made into a museum.

Unfortunately it was closed on a Monday so we went instead to the Gandhi Smitri, where Mahatma Gandhi used to visit. A series of scenic models gave his life history and there was a wealth of documents and photographs. The grounds were pleasant and quiet, apart from little crowds of Mynahs telling their tale. I sat by a small pool where the purple water lilies were closing as the sun went down.

Bev was busy on the computer when we got back, catching up with her work for the Emmanual Hospital Association, and Kathy was asleep in 'our' room, so we made tea in the living room. Later, we all had a game of Kunhandel (the Swiss game with the animal cards) followed by a very English chicken dinner with mashed potato, and retired to bed just after 10 pm.

MORE INDIAN TRAVEL to LUDHIANA HOME

6.1.98 Tuesday   The day started with a 5 am alarm. We took a taxi to the Ajmeri Gate of the railway station. We then had a long walk over the bridge towards Platform 1, only to discover that the train was going from what had been nearby Platform 10, so it was back again, with the luggage. (I shall definitely have a coolie when I am on my own.) The train left late, and then lost more time on a subsidiary route because (it transpired later) the main line was blocked.

On arrival at Ludhiana we took two (which seemed to me, very shallow) rickshaws to Mark and Helen's accommodation in the Christian Medical College compound: an unprepossessing tenement-like building from the outside, but roomy and airy inside, with a balcony overlooking a large garden at the back. We unpacked and had toasted sandwiches and coffee, followed by a wash and change. I took a walk round the nearer part of the compound and saw Rose-ringed Parakeets, Indian Robin, Indian and Pied Mynahs, and Blue Rock Pigeons.

Nick, (who had been Best Man at Helen's wedding), his Indian wife Jane, and their young daughter Natasha came for supper, which Helen somehow managed to provide with so little time. We ate stir-fry, potato and cauliflower cheese, followed by apple pie and ice cream. Natasha was a dear little girl. Nick hadn't changed: he had much the same somewhat ponderous speech and was very likeable. They left on the family vehicle (the motor scooter) just after 10 pm. We left the dishes for Lali, who comes in tomorrow morning.

LUDHIANA LIFE : CMC HOSPITAL

7.1.98 Wednesday   Unusually, I slept until 9.30 am. After breakfast I went shopping with Helen in Ludhiana, where she bought blankets in a store with the largest and most varied stock of blankets that I've ever seen. No bargaining here: a 'fixed price' policy. The streets were crowded with the Indian mixture of bullock carts, motor-scooters, rickshaws of all kinds, cycles and pedestrians. One man carried a huge collection of green bananas on his bicycle; a stationary buffalo cart held up everyone else while its driver appeared to have a chat with a long-lost friend. Bright saris adorned the front of many of the roadside stores, gathering dust visibly. Shop assistants, who welcomed our presence even as we passed, all seemed to be male except in a narrow side street store where women were serving other women with an hypnotic selection of silks and trimmings. I bought some golden tasselled trim for a lamp.

We had a soup lunch, and then I was given a conducted tour round the CMC hospital. All the infrastructure was there but there was a distinct element of neglect about the whole place: rubbish collected in odd corners as if no-one had the time or energy to throw it out. I felt I'd like to take a scrubbing brush and large buckets of hot soapy water and clean everywhere. There was undoubtedly a lot of good work being done there regardless, and the staff members were delighted to see Mark and Helen back from their break. I stood by in wonderment as they conversed in Hindi.

The hospital was founded by one Edith Brown (later Dame) 1864-1956 who, like so many other pioneering medical women, had qualified at London's Royal Free. Dr Betty Cowan, now in her eighties but still spending half the year at the hospital, came and had tea with us and then she showed us the hospital archives under the library. Here she had put together boards of documents and photographs illustrating the hospital's history since its foundation in 1894.

We walked back to Mark and Helen's 8 Honeycomb Terrace, and ate paneer (cheesy chunks) for supper. It was our intention to go to Amritsar on the morrow and, during our hospital visit, we had discussed the business of getting a taxi there with 'Honey', a medical social worker. He had been very chatty and helpful and said that he'd get back to Mark.

He called to tell us that the particular taxi he had in mind was not available but that he had arranged that someone else, a person who was associated with a disabled hospital employee, should take us. Mark had been anxious to make a very early start but Honey discouraged him, saying it would be better to wait until the fog had cleared. A starting time of 8 am was agreed upon.

TAXI TRAVEL : THE GOLDEN TEMPLE

JALLIANWALA BAGH

8.1.98 Thursday   The taxi did not come until 9.45 am and the fog was still pretty thick. It persisted all the way to Amritsar, where it suddenly lifted as if by magic.

The sun shone and it was really warm as our skilful driver found a parking place in the apparently full car park. We walked to the Golden Temple and came to the shoe-shedding point, where everyone was removing their socks as well, and proceeding in bare feet. I was wearing thick, dark brown support tights under my trousers. I removed my shoes hopefully but an accusing finger was pointed in my direction by one of the stewards dressed in yellow, with a blue turban. (Only the Queen had been permitted to advance in socks - and they were white. She wouldn't get verrucas.) Helen suggested I cut out the feet but I was loath to ruin them and finished up going to a nearby washroom, where the whole process created a lot of interest. Thus properly dressed, or undressed, I was allowed on to the hallowed ground and was immediately struck by the large numbers of people of all ages walking round the great pool where the temple is built. Amritsar means 'pool of nectar'. They were abasing themselves on bended knees with hands together at every available opportunity. Many men and children immersed themselves in the water, but a large notice read 'No Swimming', although large shoals of sizeable fish were getting away with it.

7 January 1998   A Shop-keeper in Ludhiana

It was a calm and peaceful scene with everyone, apart from three hyper-kinetic youths, behaving in an orderly, respectful manner. It was easy to forget that this was the site of much bloodshed during the traumatic partition of India in 1948, and again in 1984 when occupying Sikh extremists were evicted by the Indian army.

The Golden Temple (also known as Hari Mandir) is the holiest shrine of the Sikh religion. We walked steadily round the Parikrama, the marble walkway which surrounded the sacred pool, taking photographs, just drinking in the exotic ambiance and viewing the Golden Temple from all sides. It was a two-storey building of marble and was reached by the Gurus' Bridge. Pietra dura work, symbolising birds and animals, decorated the lower walls. The golden dome, said to be gilded with one hundred kilograms of pure gold, represented an inverted Lotus flower; the architecture was a blend of Hindu and Muslim styles. When we eventually got to the point of entering the temple, many of the pilgrims were offering what looked like lumps of brown fudge between large leaves: some were accepted and some returned. I read later that this was sweet doughy prasaad.

Priests sat in various cubby-holes in the temple and read aloud from the Granth Sahib, the Sikhs' holy book, and the original copy lay in a place of honour under a pink shroud. We filed through slowly, in the stream of people, and I felt something of a fraud, being there mainly out of interest and curiosity, rather than as a true pilgrim. Ours were the only white faces in the temple and prompted a great deal of unabashed staring and some mirth. Queues formed for the free food on offer on the opposite side of the walkway, but we finished our tour, retrieved our shoes, and opted for a refreshing cup of chai in a nearby stall in the old town.

8 January 1998

Helen and me : The Golden Temple at Amritsar

138

We followed this up with a visit to Jallianwala Bagh, or Assassination Garden, where two thousand Indians were shot indiscriminately by the British during India's struggle for independence. We looked down the vast well where many attempted to escape but died from drowning instead, and the Martyrs' Gallery, telling the story of the dreadful massacre. It's a wonder the Sikhs are so civil to the British.

We visited another temple, like a smaller more garish version of the Golden Temple and walked about in the surrounding area of the old city. By 5 pm the sun had taken on an attractive distant glow as it started to set, and it reminded me of the same time of day over the Bosphorus, where there is also much pollution, and which is said to account for such special effects. The associated fog or smog was coming in and it was time to leave. Our driver had smiled patiently all day and seemed pleased to be off. The first hour and a half was reasonable as regards visibility, but then, as it got really dark, the fog was like a grey impenetrable wall. Yet everyone (including our driver) kept on driving as if they could see for ever, overtaking on either side, whether cycle, some form of rickshaw, huge lorry, family scooter, bus or car, many of them without lights. Tractor vehicles carried enormous loads of cereals, contained in huge pendulous sacks which drooped over the sides, and dark little bullock carts limped along on the nearside verge, quite invisible until within a couple of yards.

In one place a new bridge, plus the road before and beyond, were being re-constructed and carved out of the high ground on either side. The traffic was single lane but there was no direction and each vehicle fought to move forward. Camels pulled cartloads of cement. Driving was competitive in the extreme. I suspect that our driver hardly ever dipped his lights, for every oncoming vehicle which possessed lights flashed repeatedly. We stopped at India's answer to a transport café, where the water jugs were chained to the tables, and had a snack and a cup of chai.

After another two hours' terrifying drive in the fog we arrived, alive, at Honeycomb Terrace, where the driver was paid the agreed eight hundred rupees fare, plus a generous and well-earned tip. He'd given me a rush of adrenaline that I hadn't experienced since Namibia's Kunene River experience. It seemed an aeon since we'd got into the vehicle, when Mark had remarked quietly, "There are no seatbelts!"

It was 9.30 pm and the drive home had taken four hours to cover what looks to be about sixty miles on the map. After a late supper, we sank thankfully into bed. So that was the Golden Temple.

DENTAL HOSPITAL and SHOPPING : DOMESTICITY

LONE TRAVEL to BEV'S

9.1.98 Friday   Unsurprisingly I slept until 10 am, and afterwards, whilst having a shower and washing my hair, I somehow managed to flood the adjacent loo.

We then went with Mark to see the Dental Hospital, an impressive, comparatively new building which appeared clean and well-organised, although Mark said it could be chaotic when all the students were there in term time. A few of the final year students were around, treating patients, and getting the required number of cases. They and the staff all seemed very positive, and pleased to see Mark who took a couple of slides. We went to a nearby street to buy fruit and vegetables and then to collect a film from a shop which had displayed an enlargement of one of Mark's photographs of Scotland. The whole area was teeming with life, as usual.

I sat in the garden. The day was comfortably warm, and recently-planted annuals were thriving. A lawn was to be laid in March. A lemon tree, and another bearing guavas, added interest, as did two larger, shading trees which I couldn't name. Ground Squirrels, Mynas, Hooded Crows, Indian Robins, Magpie Robins, and the ubiquitous Parakeets came and went around the place.

Mark talked about my proposed trip to Kathmandu, and how I should make time to visit Bhaktapur, the most mediaeval town of the Kathmandu Valley, and see its Durbar Square and its temples. I made a note in the diary. We ate a late lunch after dear Helen had been removing some of the ever-present dust from the living room.

We walked around the compound in the afternoon, but didn't see any new birds, and then it was time to have a cup of tea, before leaving for my train to Delhi, which was supposed to leave at 6.50 pm (this had been confirmed after having been given conflicting information from next door). Two cycle rickshaws were needed for the three of us, plus my luggage. Just before we alighted I passed Mark my camera to take a shot of Helen and me in the rickshaw, but the battery had dropped out and I couldn't face searching the luggage for another.

We advanced to the appropriate platform, Mark doing his usual coolie act. The station was alive with all kinds and conditions of men and women and, throughout the long wait for the late train, I was fascinated just to sit and stare. Helen said that she and Mark usually gave only to the occasional female beggar, but tonight they broke their rule and gave to an aged very frail-looking man with barely enough clothes to cover his body. Mark pointed out a trio of male transvestites.

I bade farewell from the train after I'd found my booked seat and dear Mark had lifted my heavy bag up on high and deposited it in the overhead accommodation. I was seated by a window and next to a Sikh of mature years who quickly fell asleep. The train travelled very slowly and became uncomfortably hot. I needed to remove my sweater and visit the loo, but didn't like to disturb my sleeping neighbour. He stirred, so I quickly took advantage and did both.

I enjoyed the Indian 'non-vegetarian' meal and the Sikh seemed surprised I had eaten it all. He put down his Reader's Digest and started to chat. He asked the usual questions - What was I doing in India? What did I do for a living? Where in the UK had I been born? He had been in the UK with REME, and his father had been a doctor in the RAMC. He was delighted to hear that my father had been an engineer. The train pulled into Ajmeri Gate, Delhi, two and a half hours late. I had expected that coolies would come on to the train and take my luggage, but no such luck. My Sikh took down the heavy bag, so that was a start. A skinny little Indian in black leather got on and offered to take my things. By this time nearly everyone had got off the train but one middle-aged businessman was still gathering his papers together and I asked him whether this would be wise, having been told not to give charge of my luggage to anyone except red-clad coolies. He talked to the young man and said he seemed OK but, "Be careful!" he warned.

We walked to the bottom of the stairs which led down from the middle bridge as I had been instructed by Bev, but she was nowhere to be seen. I was uncertain what to do but decided to wait for a while. The usual rash of taxi-men and rickshaw drivers came rushing over to offer their services. I said I was waiting for someone. The undersized black-leathered man insisted on waiting with me, although I had already paid him the recommended ten rupees. He looked ill and, as I'd watched him struggle over the bridge with my luggage, which was comparatively light for a proper coolie, and had seen that he had, every now and then, to drag it along the ground instead of carrying it on his head, I knew he could not possibly be a coolie, but there was no-one else and I couldn't have coped on my own.

One of the taxi drivers suggested that I ring my friend and this didn't seem such a bad idea. I had Bev's particulars in the back of my diary and, putting a two rupee piece in a nearby machine I dialled the number several times, only to get a strange buzzing sound, so I gave that up. I was going to have to get there under my own steam, which was just what I had dreaded.

The driver who had shown me the phone watched me changing my mind, and I gave him Bev's address. He carried my luggage to his vehicle in the car park: it was an auto-rickshaw! I'd really fancied a taxi at this time of the night (early morning). We travelled a short distance and then he said he was stopping at the office because he didn't know where Birbal Road was. I was called in to study the map. The man behind the counter said it was forty kilometres away but I knew it was nowhere near as far as that. I looked at the map and suddenly, more by good luck than local knowledge, I spotted what I had thought to be the telephone number, but which was actually the district code! No wonder I hadn't got through on the phone. But this was good news, because it located Birbal Road immediately and we started off forthwith.

The rickshaw was in good order and cleaner than average but it was just a rickshaw all the same, and the cold draught of the early hours, plus a certain weariness, not to mention anxiety, made me shiver. There was little traffic about, which was a bonus, and we arrived in the Birbal district quite soon. Here I recognised nothing. My driver stopped to ask the way at some all-night factory, but didn't put the brake on, and I thought the rickshaw and I were going off on our own!

At last we were there. The agreed fare had been two hundred and fifty rupees. I'd had little option and it had hardly seemed a good moment to start bargaining. I paid up, very relieved to have arrived. Later I compared this fare, for a twenty-minute ride in an auto-rickshaw, with the all-day excursion to Amritsar in a taxi for eight hundred rupees! The security man was awake so I didn't have to rattle the gate. Poor pyjama'd big Bev had been told that the train was one and a half hours late, had gone to meet me in her car, only to be told when she arrived that it had been and gone earlier. She'd returned home hoping to find me there, so was delighted that I had ultimately arrived. We chatted briefly. She asked whether the rickshaw man had used his meter. I said shamefacedly that I had asked but that he had replied "The meter's the cheater and anyway it's after midnight and the charges are different." I was glad she didn't ask the fare.

I had intended to rearrange my luggage and incorporate the things I'd left at Bev's (even heavier tomorrow - help!) but I just hit the hay and set Bev's alarm for 7 am (help again).

DELAYED FLIGHT - what's new? - to NATURETREK, NEPAL

MEETING 'MY' GROUP

10.1.98 Saturday .... which came all too soon. I did the luggage bit, labelled it, had a porridge breakfast, and a good chat with Bev. She'd been a real pal to me, and to Helen and Mark. I'd liked her from the moment she came to stay at Heronslake with Helen and another friend, years ago.

The taxi-man quizzed me in a very strong accent on the way to the airport and I had difficulty in understanding him in my weary state. "Any boys? Your age? Husband? You like India?" etc. The fare was two hundred and twenty rupees, a proper taxi with meter, this time. Once there I grabbed a trolley, of which there seemed to be a dearth, and walked into a very confused airport. Everything was late because of the fog. I queued for my boarding pass, my ticket creating some confusion because it stated a later flight, but the alteration to a morning flight had been confirmed. I queued again for the luggage, security, and, finally, for multiple stamps from immigration.

My flight, RA 206, did not even appear on the screen. I sat between some smiling Nepali people and was reassured to read my flight number on their luggage. One of them offered me what I thought was a piece of fudge, which was on a string with others. They were so pressing that I pulled off the end piece and popped it into my mouth with a grateful smile. Seconds later I wondered whether I'd done the right thing, for it was as hard as stone and had no flavour that I could detect, but I noticed they were sucking away at their pieces. It never did grow smaller or more flavourful and finally I removed it discreetly and put it in my handkerchief.

Some time later an 'RA 206 delayed' notice flashed up on the board, as if we didn't know. Everyone was looking fed up, even the cheerful Nepalis. A persistently chirping sparrow viewing us from one of the roof lights was the only living thing unaffected by the general gloom. I needed the loo and signalled to my Nepali neighbours to keep an eye on my hand luggage. They nodded and smiled. I couldn't have been away more than five minutes, but during my brief absence 'RA 206 new time' had flashed up and my friends were looking agitated, as we were being asked to proceed to the departure lounge.

We went through security with the hand luggage, including the handbag which was opened and searched. The departure lounge for Gate 1 was down a flight of stairs, pleasant and airy and not as crowded. A large overweight Brit stamped up and down, shouting angrily and getting pinker by the minute. I prayed he wouldn't have a heart attack which would be dreadful for him, make me feel obliged to do something, and delay the flight even longer. He was accompanied by an uneasy-looking young woman, probably his daughter, and he eventually took her advice and lay down on the cool floor.

At 12.30 pm there was still no sign of boarding. I wrote my diary, and ran to earth the spare camera battery, inserted it and sealed it with elastoplast from my first aid kit. We took off at 1.15 pm, only four hours late .... The late lunch was mildly spiced and more than palatable: it was a long time since the porridge breakfast. My luggage arrived complete at Kathmandu, where I could not see the promised guide and made enquiries at the desk, fending off the taxi-men. Then I spotted an insignificant 'Naturetrek' notice, handwritten on a small piece of cardboard and held up by a diminutive young man. As I approached him joyfully, another slightly older man appeared, announcing he was Tika, the guide, and giving me a warm handshake. His name means 'a blessing', the same word for the Hindu forehead mark, and more than a blessing he proved to be in the coming week.

I had expected the UK contingent to be there before me but they had also been delayed and were due in half an hour. It was obvious that I was not going to have the time to take Mark's suggested excursion to Bhaktapur, which was a shame. The Greenwich Village Hotel was on the outskirts of the town and by the time I'd checked in, changed and had a wash, the UK group had just arrived and we were all briefed together in the rather sepulchral lounge. I was treated with an unaccustomed deference by the four men, and I wasn't sure whether this was because of my age, my sex, or both. It was only later I discovered that they had thought I was a joint group leader, this idea having arisen because my name was asterisked, along with Tika's, in the helpful holiday notes we had received before departure. In fact it indicated only that we were both joining in Nepal. My elder son had expressed the view that the trip was "too advanced" for me anyway and the idea that I could be mistaken for a leader was hilarious. It soon became obvious that I knew less than anyone else.

I studied the assembled group, who were to be my companions for the next week: John and Steve both had glorious Gloucestershire accents. John was a big man, well over six foot, with a lived-in face like the late Sid James and with a warm, gruff timbre to his voice which may have had something to do with his liking for whisky and cigarettes. He spent his holidays bird-watching, and ringing birds in the Gambia, and had worked in printing in Bath, from whence came such things as the Readers Digest. Since the Maxwell era he had not been not too enamoured with his job but, at fifty-seven, knew he must soldier on. Dippers were his special interest.

His workmate and fellow ornithologist, Steve, was a younger man with sandy hair, balding from the front but with flowing locks from the back view: rather like a depressed Hoopoe. He was a very pleasant and well-mannered gentleman, who had a thing about Harriers: he was very generous with his scope.

Paul was a large, lumbering chap from Sheffield, positively obsessed about birds of prey, of which he had a very wide knowledge. He'd recently lost his job and, more recently, his sleeping tablets, which may have accounted for his use of vodka as an alternative therapy. He seemed a bit unstable and I had to admit to feeling uneasy about his state of mind.

Alistair was a young, polished, rosy-cheeked bachelor lawyer from London, specialising in conveyance of computers. He was a very speedy spotter of the LBJs (little brown jobs) as they partially exposed themselves behind one leaf after another and flitted at ninety miles per hour in between. His analytical mind made him a very good conversationalist, when I suspect he sometimes played the devil's advocate just to wind us up.

Tika gave us a brief resumé of the week ahead, starting with a visit to the Bhojan Griha restaurant that evening, and what a great beginning it was. We were greeted and 'Tika'd' at the entrance, given an excellent meal seated on cushions at low tables, and treated to traditional entertainment by dancers, comics, and a fire-eating doctor, all accompanied by a group of musicians, with strange instruments, in the far corner of the room. There were very few people taking advantage of the place which, according to Tika, had opened only recently.

Refurbishment of the building was still going on and an impressive courtyard, viewed from the upper floors of the restaurant, had been cleared in preparation for restoration. The open archways lit by candles, and the ritual washing of the hands and removing of the shoes before entering, all added to the special atmosphere and subsequent memories of the place.

We returned to the Greenwich Village Hotel and had a nightcap, but didn't linger long because it was to be a 6 am call. (I hoped I was going to survive.)

PHULCHOWKI SLOPES : BOTANICAL GARDENS

BIRDS in ABUNDANCE

11.1.98 Sunday   I responded sluggishly to the early morning call. Breakast was in the dining room, but I couldn't face anything cooked so helped myself to an enormous helping of muesli and yoghurt.

We were driven part way up the slopes of Phulchowki, the frozen snow preventing the drive all the way to the top, which had been the intention. It was cool on the forested slopes in the early morning but the sight of a couple of elegant Kalij Pheasants on the drive up, just walking across the track, warmed us up. Common Buzzard and Black Kite flew high overhead. An inconspicuous, undemonstrative Ashy Wood Pigeon was pointed out to me by Steve, as I struggled to locate it through the binoculars of which I was not an habitué. A Little Swift, and a Red-rumped Swallow, were more in my line, my attention caught more by their flight than by anything else.

The steady walk down the hillside was fresh and invigorating, with magnificent views of the Great Himalaya, snow clad and sparkling in the early morning sun. The others were so bird orientated that I felt they were missing the literally wider views. We saw a Great Himalayan Barbet, sluggish in flight as if it had to make a real effort, and with an eye-catching red vent; its head was dark and heavy, and the yellow bill proportionately large. White-breasted Kingfisher, White-cheeked Bulbul, and a bold little White-browed Scimitar Babbler were not difficult to spot, similarly the White-collared Blackbird, which was for all the world like a vicar in full flight.

Conspicuous House Crow, Jungle Crow, Common Mynah, House Sparrow, Tree Sparrow, the colourful Eurasian Jay, Green Magpie, and Red-billed Blue Magpie presented little identification problems, and neither did the (Dark-breasted) Rose Finch, the male of the species conveniently hopping on to the path a fair way ahead. This was where the scopes came into their own and I shall never forget the contrasting dark red and crimson of that bird's nape and forehead. Thank you, Steve. We stopped for our picnic lunch of a piece of chicken in some cold batter or other, tasty and well spiced, stale bread cheese sandwiches, and fruit - and I ate the lot. I was really hungry, which I suppose came from not indulging in a fried breakfast. We sat on a low wall from which we could see the marble quarrying on an adjacent slope. This was sadly affecting the character of the area, deforesting as it went. We were not allowed to linger over the meal (a hallmark of the whole week) and I quickly learned not to waste time talking, otherwise everyone else was finished and ready to go before me.

The Woodpeckers in the forest created much interest and I liked them because they were large enough to see relatively easily, although spotting the differences between Fulvous-breasted Pied (red and black crown), Brown-fronted Pied (brown forehead) and the Rufous-bellied Pied varieties required expert assistance. The small birds, half-concealed behind large leaves and continuously changing perch, were really difficult to get into view for long enough to be certain. I believed Tika, who said that examples of such were Olive-backed Pipits, even though I couldn't find them in the 'Birds of Nepal' (now out of print, much sought after, and loaned to me by Mark and Helen.) In the same book I looked for the Black Bulbul, Hypsipetes Madagascariensis, only to discover it was also called Grey Bulbul: it is a funereal looking bird anyway, not having the gloss of some black birds. We had good views of three different Redstarts, an attractive male Hodgson's Redstart with its blue-grey back, white forehead and reddish underbelly - rather like 'ours'; an impressive male Blue-fronted Redstart; and a lovely Plumbeous Redstart, which played about near to us, flashing its maroonish tail to everyone's satisfaction.

A flash of shining gold was said to be a Golden Bush Robin: Tika recognised it from its high-pitched call. Someone else spotted a Red-flanked Bluetail which I didn't see and could not even find in the book. A Blue Whistling Thrush looked black until it was caught in the sunlight, when it became a rich navy blue. Later, when we had descended to the Godawari Botanical Gardens, we saw a couple of Black-throated Thrushes flicking up their tails like outsize Robins. Warblers were distinctly elusive but worth concentration, for the sighting could be rewarding. The bright yellow underparts of the Grey-headed Warbler were far more impressive than the feature which has given it the name; the Chestnut-crowned Warbler was as its name, and more striking than the insignificant little Pallas's Leaf Warbler. The Orange-barred Leaf Warbler sported two orange wing bars, the anterior one a mere echo in colour intensity of the other. I had a really good view of this bird through Steve's scope, and still have the image of its petite perfection in my mind's eye.

On our official list were two Niltavas, the Small Niltava, Niltava Macgrigoriae, and the Rufous-bellied Niltava, Niltava Sundara; but in the esteemed "Birds of Nepal", they became Muscicapa Macrigoriae, and Muscicapa Sundara, and joined the rest of the flycatchers. The small one was dark and neat and seen in the Botanical gardens near the stream: the rufous-bellied variety was larger and, as its name suggests, the blue of the back and head contrasted strikingly with the warm colour underneath. The small Red-breasted Flycatcher graced us with a fleeting visit although, it not being the breeding season, the 'red' was an insignificant pale orange. The active Yellow-bellied Fantail Flycatcher was spotted by Tika much higher up Phulchowki.

The rash of Laughing Thrushes (Latin Garrulax - I like that) included the White-throated, the Chestnut-crowned, the Striated and the Streaked (spot the difference), all very Babbler-like. A bird to remember, for me anyway, was the Cutia of which, thanks again to Steve, I had a super view, making out the conspicuous bars on the pale flanks, highlighted by the darker rufous back.

There followed sightings of a whole variety of birds which, to my tired eyes and diminishing concentration, mostly resembled Babblers, such as the Hoary Barwing, with a floppy crest; the smaller Chestnut-tailed (bar-throated) Minia; the White-browed Tit Babbler (Fulvetta), in a state of permanent surprise; the Chestnut-headed Tit Babbler (Fulvetta as well, I think) and lots of the large Black-capped Sibias which suddenly seemed to be everywhere.

Then there were the Yuhinas: the Whiskered (Yellow-naped); the Stripe-throated Rufous-vented; and the smaller White-bellied; all crested. The Tit tick list also did pretty well with Great Black-throated; Yellow-cheeked; Yellow-browed; and Black-lored (Red-headed would be a better name). Bright spots of the day were the Green-tailed (Nepal) Sunbird, with its truly iridescent tail colour; the Brown-throated (Nepal) Treecreeper (I love the way they move); the Buff-bellied (Fire-breasted - as is the male) Flowerpecker; Oriental White-eye, whose eye ring on its greenish head made it look wide-eyed and afraid, which it may well have been with all of us around; and, finally, and probably my favourite of the day, the Chestnut-bellied Nuthatch, which looked very much like our own Eurasian form and made me feel comfortably at home.

My legs were aching by the time we'd walked round the Botanical gardens at the end of the day, my eyes felt as though they were on permanent searchlight duty, and my neck was set in a fully-extended position. Back at the Greenwich Village Hotel, it was good to have a shower and change, and, after a concentrated session of undivided attention to the ritual tick list (which now I am so glad I had had), we ate an excellent meal in the hotel. We sat and talked afterwards - about birds of course - but many other things as well. They were a pleasant bunch and I liked their company. We sat in the bar where they'd run out of gin, so I drank vodka instead. It was good to relax but I didn't hang about too long, leaving them for bed about 11.30 pm in preparation for another 6 am start.

Postscript: We also saw Muntjac, Spotted Deer, Barking Deer, and Rhesus Monkey.

TRISULI RIVER : more and more Birds

CHITWAN JUNGLE LODGE

12.1.98 Monday Today, after a very early breakfast, we were to travel south east along the Trisuli River. The fog was thick when we started off (although not as bad as on the Amritsar journey) and we travelled slowly, with time to observe all the colourful lorries and read the inscriptions between the garish portrayals of gods, goddesses, and eastern motifs. We read "LOVE IS LIFE, HORN PLEASE", and Tika translated from the local language "Come slowly, there is no place in heaven".

Later, when the fog had lifted, we had impressive views of the tight terracing (worked thus as the forests had been steadily cleared), which reminded me of the rice terraces of the Philippines. Along the edge of the Trisuli River we looked for the Ibisbill, whose decurved bill is adapted for digging under stones in the riverbed. Unfortunately for this bird the locals were now harvesting all the stones, pounding some of them and using them for building sturdy houses, which would be more likely to resist the periodic floods that swept away the wood and thatch variety. Tika related his own experience of arriving back at his village on the edge of Chitwan National Park to find it under water, and his wife and two sons, the younger only twenty-two days old, sitting in the top of a tree. He had, with other villagers rescued them, and other families, on to the bare backs of elephants: he admitted he now had a stone house, while regretting the serious decline of the Ibisbill in the area. It was like a collection of cottage industries punctuating the length of the river bank, small encampments with shelters, fires, heaps of stones of different sizes, and of grey, cement-coloured coarse powder. The Ibisbill wasn't easy to see, its grey body outline broken by the black forehead and face, and well camouflaged among the remaining stones lying in the shallows of the river.

This watery area provided sightings of such birds as Cormorants, Red-naped Ibis, Ruddy Shelduck, White (Pied) and White-tailed Wagtails, the latter a larger bird and called Large Pied Wagtail in some books. We stopped on a bridge and got out to look for the Wall-creeper and the Brown Dipper, and saw both, the Wall-creeper skimming up and around a boulder by the edge of the water, and the Brown Dipper bobbing up and down on wet rocks. The large lorries rolled by, vibrating the bridge to an alarming extent. A White-capped River Chat sat and fanned its tail on the damp boulders. We saw Common Stonechat (Collared Bush Chat) and (to me very similar) White-tailed Stone (Bush) Chat, and the attractive Plumbeous Redstart, further down the valley.

Brown-throated Sand Martins, Barn Swallows and red-rumped Swallows swooped about near the river bank, as did the insignificant Little (House) Swift and the svelte Crested Tree Swift, with its elegant slender wiry tail. We motored on, seeing a Black Drongo; the eye-catching large Racquet-tailed Drongo; a Long-tailed (Black-headed) Shrike; a Red-billed Blue Magpie; a Great (Himalayan) Treepie; a Common Kestrel and a Little-ringed Plover; Redshank and Greenshank near yet another stretch of water. An Indian Roller displayed its magnificent two-tone, blue-turquoise wings as it flew upwards to alight on a high branch over the road. Egrets, great and small: the Great White (large) Egret, the Intermediate, Cattle and Little (with its black bill and bright yellow feet) dotted the countryside.

Raptors figured memorably in the day's list. The Black (Dark or Pariah) Kite; the scarce Grey-headed Fishing Eagle, rediscovered twenty years ago in Chitwan National Park; and, with more white on its tail than the plain Himalayan variety, the large brown Steppe Eagle sitting in a tree; the huge weighty-looking Himalayan Griffon; the smaller Osprey showing its smart, checked underwing pattern in flight; and a graceful Hen Harrier.

Doves and Pigeons were represented by the Spotted Dove, the Blue Rock Dove, and the Orange-breasted Green Pigeon, which also had a touch of lilac about it. White-breasted Kingfisher, Pied Kingfisher, came into view and, later, the Common Kingfisher which I consider to be the prettiest and most neatly proportioned of them all. It did bring 'oohs' and 'aahs' from the most seasoned twitchers.

A Greater (Large) Coucal, also known as the Crow Pheasant - which name depicts the right visual image for me - ambled clumsily in tall grass near some cultivation. We stopped nearby to eat our picnic lunch in a peaceful Sal wood, or at least it was very quiet until a host of children, and goats of all colours and sizes, came and studied us with noisy curiosity. Tika spoke to them gently and they strode on, the goats trailing behind them. A Black Francolin flew just above the ground, and a Red Jungle Fowl, for all the world like a Bantam cock we once had, made a noisy entrance and an even noisier exit. Not so quiet after all!

I saw a Wryneck for the first time in my life. I'd always wanted to see this bird since viewing a strange painting which depicted it twisting its head round in a very curious way. This one was, disappointingly, just looking like a rather boring little brown bird sitting on a low branch of a tree. A Grey-capped (Crowned) Pygmy Woodpecker was distinctly more interesting. White-cheeked, Red-vented and Black Bulbuls announced their chattering presence, as did a Common Mynah and an Asian Pied Starling (Pied Mynah).

Tika drew attention to a Common Tailor Bird, high up in one of the trees. How does he do it? Even with everyone's help, I can't say I got a good view as it flitted about in the overhead canopy. A Grey-headed Flycatcher was not much easier, although I did see it flipping its tail quite convincingly. I had fewer problems with the Asian Magpie Robin. The wood was thick, and here and there a great Termite mound rose up amidst the undergrowth, almost like a miniature temple. Powerful vines, with stems like gnarled tree trunks, twisted their way round mature vegetation and crushed the life from well-established trees. Strange fungi of exotic colours and shapes added to the rich, alien mystery of the place.

As usual we were not allowed to linger over lunch, and were soon back on the road. We passed a large Buddhist Temple, a diminutive house called 'Evergreen Cottage' and a 'Marie Stopes Clinic'. As we approached Chitwan Jungle Lodge, we transferred ourselves and our luggage from the minibus to a Landrover, although we were to see the minibus driver again in the morning. We had a welcome introduction and a cup of tea in a covered area, where skulls of local rhinoceroses, poached and otherwise, were on display in a mini natural history area. I was longing for the loo really, but managed to survive the formalities. The tented rooms were very pleasant and airy, and a quick testing of the bed comfort boded well.

Once we'd deposited our belongings, we were rushed out for an Elephant ride. This was very exciting, a first for me, and four of us climbed on to the square seat from a raised platform at the top of the flight of steps. We were required to sit one in each corner with legs astride a corner pole. Poor John, the heaviest by far, was placed in one of the rear seats and, as there seemed a lot of uphill walking for the Elephant, his crotch was under pressure and he was worried about his manhood! We rode for two hours, our driver steering his animal skilfully through the uneven terrain and the tall, tall Elephant Grass. We came across a Rhinoceros quite early on and spent some time just watching the creature, which looked deceptively unconcerned, but we were assured that if anyone disobeyed the rules and, for example, got down to take a photograph, the animal would be anything but welcoming. Our driver had a hook for pulling the Elephant back, a spear for pushing it forward and a hammer for stopping it going in the wrong direction which all sounds very brutal, but he just held them in readiness and we did not see them used. The Elephant's name was Avasculana, which sounded vaguely clinical.

Birds were not mentioned for a while but then John, in spite of his discomfort, (there's dedication for you) spotted an Eagle sitting out in the open, conveniently in our path. It was a Crested Serpent Eagle, a magnificent dark, chunky bird sitting bolt upright as if very alert. Needless to say we all took pictures as we got closer and closer until it made its take-off.

We returned for a wash and change for dinner. The water, it was explained, was heated by solar panels, but as there had been little sun, it was barely luke-warm. Kerosene lamps were lit after dark, but there was electric light in the shower (cold) and the loo until 10 pm. It was my turn to buy the drinks and the barman made no fuss about my Indian rupees. We watched a local dancing display by a group of men from a village 'a few miles away', whence they would be returning by foot afterwards. It was pleasant sitting by open fires, listening and watching, and some of us were persuaded to accept an invitation to join in. The meal by candlelight was tasty and satisfying, a Nepali menu buffet. John had a serious accident with a green chilli which he mistook for a bean, and presented whole to his tastebuds. It was minutes before his throat recovered and I was genuinely worried that he might go into a proper laryngeal spasm. We were all quite tired after such a long full day, and I actually got to bed before the electricity went off.

FAMILIAR ELEPHANT - and other LARGE ANIMALS

and PLANTS : and, of course, - BIRDS!

13.1.98 Tuesday   It was a 6 am call again for an early Elephant ride, same driver, same Elephant. The morning was damp and foggy and we saw very little but somehow it didn't seem to matter. It was balm to the soul just to ride gently above the earth in the misty silence. It seemed that everyone felt the same, for no-one spoke.

Today I had an omelette for breakfast, which was probably just as well for immediately afterwards we took a three-hour walk through the jungle area. The foggy start had turned to a fine misty rain, and the tall trees dripped incessantly, holding off the drizzle from us for a while but eventually it seeped through. I'd left my waterproof, along with other 'surplus' luggage, at the Greenwich Village Hotel. We studied fresh Leopard and Tiger tracks. An extra guide, who had joined us for this walk through such a large, animal-inhabited area, took a piece of long grass, bent it round the circumference of the Leopard prints, and declared the beast would be twice as high. Quite a sizeable animal.

We saw deep evidence of the Sloth Badger's digging and, later, his (or her) scraping tracks up a tree towards a nest of bees to get the honey: I presume such animals are impenetrable to the stings. Twisted vines, strange fungi, something which resembled closely the Japanese Knotweed (was it here as well?), magnificent Mahonias, large colourful Buddleia-like plants, Mugwort, huge Ageratum, and many other plants lined our path. Between these botanical observations, we added to the previous day's bird lists: Eurasian Collared Dove (Indian Ring Dove); Parakeets of the Alexandrine, Ring-necked, Moustached (attractively rose-breasted), and Slaty-headed varieties; a squat little Jungle Owlet; Himalayan (Edible Nest) Swiftlet - added to the Apodidae; Lineated Barbet (more mottled than lineated I thought); and the huge Giant Hornbill.

More Woodpeckers! What a lot there are: The Greater and lesser Yellow-naped; the Grey-headed (Black-naped); Himalayan Golden-backed (Three-toed); and the Large Golden-backed; The Scarlet (more like orange) Minivet and its related Small Minivet were bright and cheerful and contrasted with their cousins such as the Bar-winged Flycatcher, Pied Wood Shrike and the Large Cuckoo Shrike. The Red-whiskered was added to the Bulbul list. The canary-coloured Lora and a glossy black long-tailed White-rumped Shama were viewed convincingly through the scope.

As usual the warblers presented me with identification difficulties. It was stated in the evening, when we studied our tick lists, that 'we' had seen, Aberrant Bush Warbler (with yellowish eyebrow like the Yellow-browed (Plain Leaf) Warbler); Grey-sided (Rufous-capped) Bush Warbler; the dainty Blyth's Crowned Leaf Warbler; Western Large Crowned Leaf Warbler (depressingly similar); Greenish (dull green) Warbler; Plain Prinia; the more interesting Grey-capped Prinia; and Grey-breasted Prinia. White-throated Fantail Flycatcher and Pale-chinned Flycatcher flitted by for their ticks, as did a White-bellied Yuhina and Puff-throated and Jungle Babblers.

The Crimson (Scarlet-breasted) Sunbird cheered me up no end and a Great Tit gave me a comfortable familiar feeling, similarly the Velvet-fronted and White-tailed Nuthatches. A Black-headed Oriole was spotted at the edge of the forest and we were lucky enough to see the Ashy, Bronzed, and Spangled (Hair-crested) - 'Hottentottus' - Drongos. The Rufous Treepie and Grey-backed Shrike completed the list for the morning's walk.

We arrived at the other side of the forest near the bank of the Rapti River, where we took over two dug-out canoes and went steadily downstream. I liked nothing more than being on calm waters and found I was really getting much better at using the binoculars, especially from the sitting position. We saw more 'new' birds in this environment: Little Cormorant; Lesser Adjutant Stork; Goosander; Brown Crake; White-breasted Waterhen; River and Red-wattled Plovers; Temminck's Stint; Green and Common Sandpipers; Brown Fish Owl; Sandlark; Asian House Martin; and, just before we reached the end of the river trip, a stately Peacock picked its way elegantly along the far bank.

After lunch and a very brief rest (we seemed to be cramming a lot in today) we had another long walk in the afternoon and saw many of the birds we'd seen in the morning. A heap of Grey Hornbill feathers below a dropping-spattered perch prompted a lengthy investigation and search for signs of the guilty raptor, but nothing more was found. I pocketed some of the feathers.

Tea was particularly welcome before a wash, change and pack ready for the morrow. The water was cold and the generator wasn't working so there was no light in the loo and the scheduled slide show had to be cancelled, which was a pity. I talked to the bar tender and paid him in Indian rupees for my giant orange and soda. I was very thirsty. The currency prompted questions as to what I'd been doing in India and I told him about Mark and Helen. He responded very warmly, took my hand and said he was a Baptist.

Tika was very talkative over dinner, giving us a blow-by-blow account of an encounter he had had with an Indian guide whom he'd been assisting with a tour there and who had cheated him. Members of the holiday group had bailed him out and Naturetrek had later compensated him and had refunded the money to its clients. He said he would "never go there again", which was sad. The rest of us were all very quiet, tired I suspect, our minds full of new images, not to mention new species. I haven't said that we'd also seen Wild Boar, Sambar Deer, and the Rhesus Monkey: it was a bit of a bird take-over.

We all left the table for bed at 9.15 pm.

PASSING VILLAGES : FATAL ACCIDENT

KOSHI TAPPU NATIONAL PARK

14.1.98 Wednesday   It was a 6 am start again: there was a remote possibility that I might get used to this. My stomach felt turbulant so I breakfasted on coffee and Lomotil. Today we were to travel by road along the east-west highway - (a flattering description and, anyway, we should be travelling from west to east) - to the Koshi Tappu National Park. Once outside the Chitwan National Park, we changed from the jeep back into the minibus. It was a clearer morning and driving through the Tera of lowland Nepal we passed through fascinating villages and towns. I wished we had the time to stop and stare. Alistair took pictures of interesting scenes as they flashed by, from his uncluttered but shaking seat at the back of the vehicle.

It was, Tika explained, some special day in the local religious calendar and as we passed over the Bagmati River, small campfires roasted sacrificial goats, surrounded by extended family groups. We stopped for an early lunch of the usual picnic food.

I ate little: my inside was feeling better but I didn't want to tempt providence. During the early afternoon we came across a road block in the form of piles of worn tyres, and a cartoon drawing of an accident, which included a skull and crossbones. We stopped obediently: there was no option for the only possible escape route, a small side road to the right, was also bridged with tyres. Tika moved down the no-go area to discover that there had indeed been an accident and a four-year old child had been killed by a lorry. It got worse: the lorry driver had been reported by witnesses to have knocked down the child and then reversed over the body 'to make sure she was dead'. A death commanded a one-off fine, but an injured body required financial support during disability, which could mean for life. We Brits were predictably horrified at this information. I thought Steve and John were going to cry.

The negotiations were protracted. A large collection of people of all ages came from nowhere and gathered at the barrier, staring at our Caucasian faces. An enormous goat appeared on the scene (one of the lucky ones not destined for the day's sacrificial fate) and foraged amidst the scant vegetation. Small roadside stalls opened up but such initiatives were quickly closed by someone said to be 'an official' involved in the accident negotiations, although I noticed that one stall, with its little collection of oranges laid out on the ground by a woman with a young baby, seemed to continue with its meagre trade: I took a picture.

We had arrived there at 1.30 pm and two hours later there was no sign of any progress. A second 'official' took off down the side road, from which the tyres had been removed to allow the arrival on the scene of an army vehicle. Tika had explained that these situations can occasionally become violent and the army is often called as a matter of routine. Tika had pleaded on our behalf, and for tourists in general at the actual scene, to be allowed through: this was, after all, Nepal's 'year of the tourist'. Some of the crowd had been sympathetic but the answer was 'no'. Our driver spotted the open side road, summoned us speedily to the minibus and we were on our way again.

It was a hairy journey, over a narrow bridge and a muddy unmade track through agricultural land and, at one point, a car which had also taken the same advantage, got stuck in front of us, but concerted pushing got it (and us) back on course. We rejoined the highway beyond the accident. Further on there was a more light-hearted road block, by some young students who were collecting for the Festival of the Goddess of Education. Small donations were handed over good-naturedly by Tika and the driver, and we were allowed to proceed. "They'll be having a party" said Tika.

Eastern Nepal looked dry and flat as we drove through all kinds of small villages and patches of cultivated well-irrigated land, where people were working until nightfall. One such village near our destination had electricity and I was full of hope that we might have the same at Koshi Tappu Wildlife Park, but was quickly put right by Tika: it was to be kerosene and candles again. The hold-up had delayed us very considerably and the staff had been anxious about our welfare. As it was so late we went straight into dinner and received a warm welcome. The dining room was an impressive, high, round building, and in the daylight the following morning, was seen to be neatly thatched with a raised cupola, also thatched, over the dome.

14 January 1998

Roadside "accident" Stall

The food was good and I found I was now hungry enough to do it justice. We did the tick list ritual and added Purple Heron; Eurasian Griffon Vulture; Northern Sparrow Hawk (shades of home); Barred Cuckoo Dove; Alpine Swift; the diminutive Green Bee-eater; Grey Hornbill (alive!); Ashy-crowned Finchlark; Blue Rock Thrush; and the beautiful, pale green Verditer Flycatcher.

I retired to my No 8 two-bedded walk-in tent accommodation, unpacked and used the washroom, which was situated a short distance to the rear, but with the torch (provided here) there was no problem. A hot-water bottle warmed the bed. I'd forgotten how comforting they can be, and snuggled down, thankful that we had three nights in what promised to be a lovely place.

PEACEFUL RIVER KOSHI and SANDBANKS

15.1.98 Thursday We had the usual 6 am start, and then went for a long walk in the cool mist: no need for the sunhat or sun cream we'd been advised to bring, as yet. On reaching the River Koshi, we boarded a raft. I was very happy for although the visibility was not particularly good to begin with it gradually improved, and it was just lovely to be on the water. We saw families living from the river and the environs gathering wood, fishing, and living on the minimum. Every now and then we stopped and climbed on to one of the river banks, or an island sand-bank.

We saw Little and Great Crested Grebes; Darters; the Cinnamon Bittern (Ixobrychus Cinnamoneus but called Chestnut Bittern in "Birds of Nepal"); Green-backed and Black-crowned Night Herons; also the Grey (Heronslake!) and Purple Herons; the strange-looking Asian Open-billed Stork; and the Black and Blacknecked Storks contrasting sharply with the Oriental White Ibis, and even whiter Eurasian Spoonbill. Oh, I do like big birds! Then there were the ducks and allied species: Lesser Whistling Duck; larger Ruddy Shelduck and the familiar Eurasian Shelduck; Eurasian Wigeon; Gadwall; Northern Pintail; Northern Shoveler, swimming as if it was bill heavy; Common and Baer's Pochard (I can't remember or find the difference); Common Teal; Mallard; Spot-billed Duck (too distant, so I was not convinced); Ferruginous and Tufted Ducks; and Bar-headed Goose and the Goosander.

It was a good day for raptors: White-tailed Eagle; Long-billed Vulture; Eurasian Black Vulture; Short-toed Eagle; Eurasian Marsh Harrier; and a wonderful Pied Harrier which stayed visible for minutes in the sunlight. There was also Bezra (Sparrow Hawk); and the, (to me) almost indistinguishable Shrika; easier were the White-eyed Buzzard; Long-legged Buzzard; Greater Spotted Eagle; Osprey; Common Kestrel; the compact Red-necked Falcon (Red-headed Merlin); and Peregrine Falcon. A Great Black-headed Gull made its presence heard (not many Gulls about) and, at around the same time, we saw a Stone Plover; and Caspian, River and Black-bellied Terns.

We picnicked on one of the sand-banks, hearing the river flow by and always looking and listening. It was a bit hurried, as usual - as if we might be wasting time and missing something. Back at the lodge we saw almost as many birds again. A pool in the garden and the varied vegetation attracted all sorts. The watching was easy here and I was delighted to see a Pond Heron, which became so conspicuous when it took to the air, with its whiter than white wings against the brownish vegetation. It became almost invisible again when it landed and folded them away. Other birds round the pond: Water Rail; Common Moorhen; Purple Gallinule; Eurasian Coot; Bronze-winged Jacana; and, in the more wooded area, the Yellow-footed (Bengal) Green Pigeon - and its feet really are yellow; Stork-billed Kingfisher; Hoopoe; Bengal; Bush and Crested Larks; Siberian Rubythroat - which I missed, but over which everyone else went into raptures, so I felt I must mention it; Black Redstart; Paddyfield; and Thick-billed Warblers; Tickell's Leaf Warbler; and the Chiffchaff; Black-naped Oriole; Brown Shrike; White-bellied and Crow-billed Drongos; Ashy Woodswallow; Chestnut-tailed Starling (Grey-headed Myna); and the Common Starling. Phew!   What a list.

It had been a great day, not just for the birds but for the feeling of the place, and the time spent on the river. I like to think I'll come back here one day, but I've said that before, about other places I've loved, and then the challenge and seduction of a new destination has always won.

We had a satisfying Chinese meal for supper and an early night again: it was becoming the norm with all these early mornings.

INQUISITIVE CHILDREN : KOSHI RIVER BARRAGE

WILD WATER BUFFALO : WOMEN of SUBSTANCE

16.1.98 Friday   We took an early walk in the park; it was warmer and the mist had melted away. We could see a few children playing in the grounds. "They're not supposed to be here," said Tika, pointing to a large gap in the surrounding fence. Four men in army uniform appeared at the end of the footpath, and the young look-out spotted them and warned the others. They came running out of a shrubby area, far more of them than had been visible to us, shouting and laughing, but running hard. Only one of the soldiers appeared to take any notice, but he also came running as if his life depended upon it, in an effort to intercept the children before they made their escape. Two of the younger ones were trailing the rest and were caught but the interrogation looked pretty low key, while the rest looked on light-heartedly from their safe position on the other side.

The guards on the park gates were not so relaxed, and questioned Tika with expressionless, stony faces, as to who we were and where we were going and why. Later we drove to the barrage, one kilometre long, which spans the Koshi River, built in the early 1960s to prevent flooding of the northern plains of India to the south. We picnicked nearby and watched girls and women cutting powerful reeds in a trough of land just below us. Suddenly a large Wild Water Buffalo appeared on the far side and Tika shouted to warn them, for the reeds were so tall they could not have been aware of anything except those that they were cutting. It was rather like the children earlier, in the sense that far more women came stumbling out than we had been able to see, and they all stood on the bank watching the beast, until it took itself off beyond the far shore. The women were mostly slightly built, quite scantily clad, and Tika explained that today was one of fourteen days each year when they were allowed to harvest the reeds for thatching and other essentials. Some of the reeds were already bundled and tied near where we had picnicked. Big John went to pick one up and could barely lift it from the ground.

16 January 1998

Reed women on Koshi River Bridge

Later we saw these women, some of them only children, carrying such ten foot long bundles on their heads, mostly without using their hands, in a long line across the barrage bridge, for all the world like a column of Soldier Ants. This was a very powerful image which I shall never forget. I asked Tika about their lifespan, aware of the wear and tear on their skeletal system. He was proud to tell me that it had "gone up, to fifty-one", having been "only forty-seven, five years ago". I felt almost guilty to be alive. I wondered how far they had to carry their loads as they plodded on inexorably into the distance. Later on, we caught them up (in the minibus) and stopped on the bridge to look at the great expanse of water. The women brushed passed us, somehow keeping their balance on the narrow pavement and out of thc way of the constant passing traffic.

We were lucky enough to see the Gangetic River Dolphins, two of them leaping right out of the water, long-nosed and pale in the afternoon light. We left the vehicle and walked along the river bank. Photographs were forbidden, it said on the bridge, but I took one of a passing fishing boat, with the bridge in the background. Groups of children came and studied us with the usual undisguised curiosity. A school-uniformed collection giggled and lingered around us until their teacher appeared, smiled at us and urged them on.

16 January 1998   Reed Women on Koshi River Bridge

We saw many of the water birds of yesterday but added to the list: the tiny Cotton Pygmy Goose (Teal); the not much bigger Garganey; the Red-crested Pochard; Great White Pelican; and Woolly-necked Stork. We saw a rare raptor, the Imperial Eagle, as well as the Lesser Spotted Eagle (I didn't see any spots), and the Black-shouldered Kite, and then the much larger Oriental White-backed Vulture.

The day's walks had given us sightings of Common Snipe; Grey-headed Plover; Koel Cuckoo (to me, just like a crow); Spotted Little Owl (Owlet); the colourful Blue-throated Barbet; Rufous-bellied Plaintive Cuckoo (bit of a mouthful), Short-legged Lark, Richard's Pipit, Rosy Pipit, Black-winged Cuckoo Shrike, Pied Bushchat, White's Thrush, Smoky and Dusky Leaf Warblers (help!), a comfortingly familiar Goldcrest, and the Black-faced and Yellow-breasted Buntings.

My legs were tired: it had been a long walk. Tika said we were walking as far as the Pink Tower, a look-out building erected when the barrage was being built. It loomed ahead in the distance. John said jokingly that there would be a cup of tea, and Paul's face lit up. We climbed to the top of the tower, which was in a state of disrepair, and sat down thankfully to drink our water. Tika told a creepy tale of a visit by David Mills (of Naturetrek) and some bird men who, years earlier, had slept in the tower. They left their belongings in the locked premises and went off with the binoculars. When they returned they found everything disarranged, nothing stolen, and there was no evidence as to how the perpetrator had entered or left, and the locks were still intact.

I was just wondering whether we had to do the long walk back to the barrage, when I saw that our vehicle had crept silently up to the tower. We sat a little longer, enjoying the wide views of the surrounding countryside and then motored slowly back, making occasional stops, on one of which we saw a Great White Pelican. There were no guards at the gates and the driver got out and lifted the barrier.

Back at the lodge we saw a Swamp Francolin (Partridge); a Pheasant-tailed Jacana; and a Citrine (Yellow-headed) Wagtail near the pond. Nearby was a Dull Slaty-bellied Tesia, (what a name), and a stunning little Bluethroat.

Some army guests were staying at the lodge so we made our way to the showers before they returned, and then did more than justice to the 'Chicken Princess' at dinner. We adjourned to the bar, where we talked and drank the local spirits, half the price of those with recognisable labels: there was no tonic so we made do with soda water. I was really late to bed - around 10 pm!

DOMESTIC SCENES : Flight from BIRATNAGAR

Glimpse of EVEREST : SHOPPING EXPEDITION

17.1.98 Saturday   Breakfast was at a civilised 7.30 am. Tika took us for a walk round two neighbouring villages, one relying on farming and the other on fishing. Some houses were better built than others. One such, which according to Tika belonged to a Gurkha, had a small separate building behind the main house, on the door of which was painted 'TOILET' in large white letters. "Most of them just go naturally - in the countryside" explained Tika, who was very impressed with this modern facility.

Most of the villagers seemed to know Tika and greeted him with smiles. There was apparently no fertility problem here, for there were hoards of children everywhere, who all looked happy and well-fed: but perhaps such fecundity would, in itself, become a problem. I wondered, because of the inevitable increase in their expectations, how content the next generation would remain. The Gurkhas' children were at school in Hong Kong: quite a contrast for them when they came home to the village. As well as children, there were lots of goats and chickens: one man was very proud of his nanny goat which had, unusually, just produced twins, dear little bundles of tan and white, suckling contentedly.

We watched a man ploughing his field with Buffaloes, another making a basket from reeds, another thatching his house, and two women stitching, from large leaves, a plate big enough to take a T-bone steak. The people in the fishing village had come from India several generations back because it was 'malaria free'. Their houses had artistic paintings on the outside walls and fewer unglazed windows. One of the children got an uncontrollable fit of the giggles when a camera flash startled him. I liked having a glimpse of this self-contained village community, which didn't seem to mind our presence.

However, Paul kept calling Tika to order and asking him to look at the birds. We saw Red and Oriental Turtle Doves, and a Blossom-headed Parakeet. Later there was a Jungle Myna, and an Asian Paradise Flycatcher, its long tail trailing like some advertising ribbon behind a plane. It was time to pay the bill and assemble for our departure by the time we got back to the lodge. I bought one of their T-shirts to save the Ibisbill and the Bengal Florican. Actually I liked the little picture of the Racquet-tailed Drongo (the logo for Bird Conservation, Nepal), which was in the top left-hand corner of the T-shirt, better than the larger ones of the threatened birds.

We left our tips in the box provided and climbed into the jeep with our luggage. The route to Biratnagar was through interesting-looking hamlets and villages and, at one point on the highway, we stopped where a dead Buffalo (presumably a road accident) was being eaten by a selection of vultures, including a new one for the day, the Red-headed Vulture, also known as the Black or King Vulture which, with its naked red head, looked something like a Turkey.

We stopped near the airport to view the Flying Foxes, which roost in large numbers in trees in a small clearing between some backstreet houses. They were amazing, every now and then folding their wings more closely round them, like a woman wrapping herself in a cloak, except of course that the foxes were hanging upside down. A female Koel Cuckoo spent some time near us which was a bonus, as did several children who seemed bemused as to why we should be so fascinated.

Biratnagar was a friendly if smelly little airport where, once we had checked in, we were allowed to sit on the grass outside and eat our last packed lunch while we waited. We were entertained by the 'taxi rank' of cycle rickshaws and the bargaining ritual of all the potential customers. The security check of the hand luggage was merely a gesture or, as Alistair said, 'a joke'. We waited again and a couple of friendly, moth-eaten dogs mooned around us and I reminded myself that it was not a good idea to encourage them. I had more of a thing about rabies than malaria.

Once on the plane, no time was wasted and we were off into a clear, clear, blue sky with rare views of Everest. "Some people pay £100 for a flight to see Everest" said Tika, "and don't get a view like this". A lottery was run on the plane, using the seat numbers with a prize of a free flight. An elderly man on the opposite side of the aisle won but seemed to have difficulty in understanding the concept.

Back at the Greenwich Village Hotel I was looking forward to a couple of hours to bath, change, sort the luggage, reassemble with what I'd left behind, and write my diary. I discovered that the place had a fine swimming pool, in a courtyard which was surrounded by a sweet-smelling climbing plant, with exotic yellow blossoms, called 'Golden Shower'.

The hotel employee on the gate saw me looking at some goods in the hotel shop. I fancied a pair of ear-rings really (as I always do). He had "a brother down the road" who sold "better things cheaper." There was no harm in looking I decided, and it ended up with all of us going with him after he finished work at 5 pm. The shop had a variety of attractive, reasonably-priced goods - no ear-rings but then you can't have everything.

I bought T-shirts for grandchildren, and a powerful-looking Water Buffalo carved from Yak bone (it weighed a ton - what was I doing?). The others bought small presents but John wanted a wall-hanging and Paul wanted a carpet no less, and this gentleman did not sell either. Coincidentally (?) two men walking by with a rolled-up carpet were waylaid by Paul, who bargained relentlessly and did a deal for £30. It was not the closest of piles but very attractive for all that and, well, for £30 ... He said he was going to give it to his mother who lived a few streets away in Sheffield but whom he had not seen for several weeks. Steve expressed surprise at the purchase, knowing he had just lost his job and had said he was very short of money: all the more special for his Mum, I thought.

Our friendly gateman saw an opportunity here and said he knew a carpet shop "quite near" where John could buy a wall-hanging. We decided to go with him, John saying he'd like my opinion on any proposed purchase. I'd talked about 'close pile', and so many 'loops to the square inch', which suddenly made me an 'expert'. Anyway, "It wouldn't take very long", avowed our local. We walked for twenty minutes and asked "How much further?" and got the reply "Just beyond that tree" - a tall straggling specimen, which looked a long way ahead in the fading light. At this juncture, John suddenly said "Look at that" and we did: one of those unforgettable mind prints - of a pinkish glow of the setting sun on snow-capped mountains, between two buildings behind us. A Brit-looking couple nearby also responded to John's command, and I recognised them as Richard and Janice Clark, whom I'd met with Helen and Mark in Delhi.

We were feeling a bit fed up by this time, not to mention tired, and our friend summoned a taxi: he climbed into the boot. We arrived at the intended store only to find it closed: "Oh", said our man, "I'd forgotten it was Saturday". Great, I thought, we can take this taxi back and get sorted. No such luck: we were driven to another area of the town where the street seemed to be lined with open carpet shops. We visited three and John tracked down a lovely wall-hanging, at a reasonable price, and was very happy. The rest of us (excluding Steve who'd had the sense to go back to the hotel after the closed 'brother's' shop) all bought cushion covers. Alistair chose particularly carefully I thought, and collected several in subtle, blending tones. My selection was more random but I was pleased with them. The locally bought pads back home cost me more than the very attractive hand-worked covers.

It was pitch black by now, the taxi had got fed up with waiting and disappeared, and there wasn't another in sight. We walked for ages and then got one back to the hotel for the last leg of the trek. We paid the fare of twenty-seven rupees and tipped our 'guide' who collected his bicycle. It had been intended that we should leave the hotel for that great Bjohan Griha restaurant at 6.30 pm, but it was now already 6.25 pm, so departure was postponed until 6.45 pm, which still left little time for the cleaning-up operation. The meal was excellent, as was the entertainment, with some different numbers this time. The next Naturetrek group, which had just arrived, was having its inauguration dinner at the far end of the room: five again, plus their guide and another token woman. She had short grey hair so wouldn't have the hassle of getting it up in time for breakfast each morning. One of the men had very long black hair and a heavy beard, and another was very drunk. A third had a black patch over one eye and it was said, unkindly, that it would be easier to look through the telescope. I thought I preferred 'my' group and counted myself lucky.

We paid the bill in a variety of currencies. It had been our intention to treat Tika but it seemed he ate free there when he took his group. The faithful driver was waiting and had us back at the Greenwich Village Hotel in no time. We tipped him and said goodbye and then had a farewell drink in the bar - where Steve was just about to hand over collected tips to Tika and to make a short speech - when the inebriated member of the next group fell across the room with a great crash, managing to hold his drink upright, and virtually unspilled, in a practised hand. Tika looked sympathetically at his fellow guide.

Tika was well pleased with what we had seen during the week, relieved that no-one had fallen ill or fallen over (a first for me but I'm not home yet). He was looking forward to a week at home with his wife and sons. I promised to write and send photographs, and felt quite sad to see him go. He was an empathetic, well-informed and tireless Nepali gentleman. Now, it had to be bed at 11 pm, ready for that 5.30 am call tomorrow. It seemed to get worse.

HOME SWEET HOME eventually : AFTERTHOUGHTS

18.1.98 Sunday   It was muesli and a cup of tea at 5.30 am. The minibus took us to the airport, where we were pursued by would-be porters and a man with English coins (no use in Nepal). He was hoping to exchange ten £1 coins for a £10 note. One of our party obliged. We managed to commandeer a trolley each, so the luggage (even mine) was no trouble. The queue for booking-in was long and slow but when it was our turn we were all done at once. I wasn't sure whether this was a good idea as the luggage was all lumped together, and there were time-consuming queries about Paul's carpet.

We boarded the plane one hour late and I had an aisle seat which was great, with Alistair on my right and the others just across the gangway. A chatty young fellow from Woodstock had been trekking for five weeks and looked very fit. He'd taken the break between a job in a National Park in Northumberland and starting a new job with the Society for Nature Conservation. His late father, and a local doctor in Woodstock, had set up a museum there. His attention turned to one of the Nepali stewardesses later in the journey. Breakfast was substantial, with very welcome fresh orange juice.

At Dubai the bird-spotting continued, with a flock of too-far-away-to-be-identified gulls taking off from the airport as we landed, and an Arab carrying a hooded Laggar Falcon through the waiting area. The wait at Dubai was shorter than scheduled because of our late arrival, so we were soon airborne again. A lamb lunch with a glass of reasonable red wine helped to pass the time and settle the stomach. We put our watches back three hours, and there would be a further two hours' difference before we completed the trip. I thought I'd sleep but for some reason I couldn't. Alistair read a book about the life of an organ, which I remembered as having been reviewed favourably, and John was immersed in 'Last Chance to See' by Douglas Adams and Mark Cardwardine, which I mean to read. I have always considered taking a good book on holiday but, because I'm such a diary fanatic, I've usually decided I wouldn't have the time. Paul was restless and fidgeted constantly, perhaps anxious at the reality of unemployment now that the break was over, and I was glad I was not sitting next to him. After the stop at Frankfurt it was evident that we were going to be at least an hour late arriving at Gatwick, and I was so glad that I was going to use that extravagant Shuttle Service to get me home.

There was no problem going through Customs. Paul just walked through with his rolled-up carpet (very different from years ago when John and I tried to do the same on the way home from Turkey). John and Steve gave me a hug: they'd been good friends, treating me kindly as one of them, and not going over the top because I was a woman. Alistair shook hands very formally as I expected, and Paul wouldn't have said anything to anyone if we hadn't approached him as he waited for his luggage, which was among the last to appear on the carousel.

I trolleyed my luggage through to the outer entrance hall but couldn't see Mr Ludgate. After a few minutes, a neat little white-haired lady appeared and looked at me questioningly. Her husband had told her what to look for, and we introduced ourselves. She was really pleasant and good company for the drive back, which she accomplished in excellent time on the deserted roads.

It was, as always, a good feeling to turn into the gates of Heronslake when I'd been away, and I asked her to stop at the entrance so that I could put a note through my neighbour's door, asking her not to disturb me when she came down to check the place about 8 am. I fancied a long sleep after a very long day, and all those early mornings. I'd ring her. What I didn't know was that violent storms earlier in the day had taken down some trees and, with them, the telephone wires. Some glass had been blown out of the greenhouse and there were tiles off the roof, but the house was fine, so I was lucky.

I didn't unpack a thing but switched on the heating and the electric blanket and loved my own bed. I couldn't believe it when I awoke at 5.30 am and couldn't get back to sleep. Surely the holiday had not ruined my sleep rhythm? But by the following night, thankfully, all was restored to normal.

COROLLARY

It had been a wonderful three weeks, and a week longer than I normally like to be away. When I read through the diary, I was surprised to discover that there were several powerful images and memories that I had not recorded, and which had passed through my mind many times since my return. One was that of solemn men carrying a swathed corpse into the Mecca Masjid in Hyderabad on that first day of Ramadan: a special day for a funeral, I suppose. Another was a cosy conversation with Mark and Helen - and the aid of a names book - as we discussed what their baby should be called. As the expected day drew near I had felt a sense of excitement tinged with sadness that I should be so far away.

Another vivid recollection was Alistair's very noisy indisposition as he vomited his heart out (not much sound-proofing in tents) the first night at Koshi Tappu. He was bravely uncomplaining on the river trip the following day.

One of the bird mind-pictures is of two Lesser Golden-backed Woodpeckers at the top of a tall tree (I can't remember just where), foraging about in Red Ants' nests with the disturbed incumbents falling all about them. A less happy experience was finding a heap of the most beautiful blue feathers; "from a Bluethroat", said Tika. I kept a few of them.

So that was it. My sixth independent January holiday fix since John died. Tanzania and Kilimanjaro; The Galapagos Islands; Namibia and the white-water-rafting on the Kunene; the Philippines; Zimbabwe with charismatic Lake Kariba; and now the latest India and Nepal trip; all extraordinary in their own way, and comparatively trouble free. I was hooked!

Back to Africa : a visit

January 1999

BOTSWANA and

NAMIBIA - revisited

with **AFRICA TRAVELBAG**

and

WILD DOG SAFARIS

BOTSWANA and NAMIBIA revisited
January 1999

AIRPORT INTRODUCTIONS to KATE, JOHN, and JEFF

15.1.99 Friday   In spite of going away two weeks later than usual, I seemed less prepared, being lulled into a false sense of security at not having to be virtually packed before Christmas. A reliable BT alarm call at 4 am on Friday, 15 January, assured that I was ready when Nick arrived from the Shuttle service at 5 am. He already had a younger business couple on board, bound for a birthday celebration in New York. She was very chatty but he seemed very tired and I suspect he would have preferred to sleep. As always, I was surprised by so much traffic, all busy going somewhere as dawn was breaking.

We dropped off the entrepreneurs at Terminal 4: their flight was scheduled an hour before mine, and Nick took me on to Terminal 1. We arrived in good time in spite of very slow progress on the last leg of the journey. Nick commandeered a trolley for my 12 kg luggage and, as I pushed it through the automatic revolving door, my heart quickened a little with the sense of excitement at having actually got away, and taken the first step at the beginning of solo adventure number seven, anticipating the prospect of joining who knows who in the group of half a dozen or so, I guessed. It was too early to check in so I rearranged my pack to accommodate my fleece.

After check-in later, and having got rid of the luggage - just for the flight I hoped - I treated myself to a croissant and a cappuccino and, while sitting people-watching, a pleasantly plump, cheery young woman, with plenty of hair and a well-used rucksack, introduced herself as Kate, who worked for Africa Travelbag and through whom I had booked my holiday after lengthy discussion. I imagined she must be the tour leader but no, this was a perk, she was an 'ordinary' member of the group, but would be expected to make a detailed report on her return.

She tracked down another group member, a slip of a young man called Jeff who worked as a chef for Barings Bank, had travelled widely, especially in Montana, and had a girlfriend in Seattle to whom he sent old Beatle records and Stilton cheese. We boarded at Gate 25, British Midland flight to Frankfurt, on which I had a row all to myself. There followed a five-hour wait in Frankfurt for the on-going Air Namibia flight to Windhoek. We had decided not to leave the airport, it being necessary to travel some distance to see anything, everything was said to be 'very expensive ' and in any case there was the currency aspect. Frankfurt airport struck me as a pretty sterile place, with miles of long, grey, super-glazed corridors.

Kate and I decided that a lone midddle-aged gentleman in a Fair Isle sweater, could be another member of the group, and Kate approached him. He was indeed, and seemed pleased to find the company. Once aboard, and after the safety ritual had been delivered in German and English, we were told there would be an 'indefinite delay' because of 'a substance on runway 1', which meant that all arrivals and departures had to use runway 2.

Eventually we took off, the drinks trolley surfaced, and a large gin followed by the beef dinner, accompanied by an excellent red wine, gave a comfortable sense of well being. The plane was half empty so I moved from my seat next to Kate to the twin seats in front, and curled up into an embryonic position. We were all alerted at 4.30 am with cabin lights and noisy breakfast trolleys. I exchanged my thick wool skirt for a pair of light trousers, and removed the faithful chunky travel sweater.

The BEGINNING : BIRDS and BEASTS : GABABIS

WELKOM REST CAMP

16.1.99 Saturday   It was, of course, now Saturday: we'd arrived. Everybody's luggage came through complete and we were joined by Rick, an Australian who'd been travelling for six months (not just from Australia to Windhoek of course). We were met by Allan and Liz of Wild Dog Safaris and boarded one of their safari vans (with trailer). It was a ten-seater, so with the five of us, plus our tour leader Ben, and his assistant Stephen, it was not over-crowded. Our luggage was arranged on top of the vehicle, tents were installed behind the back seat, and all other equipment put in the trailer.

We drove east, through flat scrubland, on a good road. This was cattle country and there were many healthy-looking beasts about. We had fleeting glimpses of wild flowers: one in particular profusion was yellow to apricot in colour, and was in glorious wedge-shaped spikes that rose from clumps of leaves similar to those of an iris: I think it may have been Broad-leaved Bulbine.

A small group of Helmeted Guinea Fowl scuttled noisily away at our approach, as did a solitary Northern Black Korhaan. A Pale Chanting Goshawk was identified: I thought it looked a bit too brown but Ben said it was immature. The next large bird we saw was easier to read - a Brown Snake Eagle.

A charming family of Warthogs, mum and three young, charged across an adjacent field. We saw Greater Kudu with their geometric vertical body stripes and spiral horns, handsome Oryx with their spectacular rapier horns and distinguished black and white faces, and the less elegant Red Hartebeest. We stopped for fuel and water behind an enormous cattle truck, the incumbent cattle looking fit and well-nourished. Large African Monarch butterflies flitted about all around us as we journeyed on, passing horses and mules in several of the adjacent fields.

Gobabis, the administrative centre of the Tswana Bush People, is a very attractive town with pleasing architecture, especially of the churches. 'Too many churches' declared a pleasant young assistant in one of the many shops. She showed an interest in us tourists, asking where we came from, where we were going etc. We bought some cards (not that I ever send any, they're for the holiday diary later) as she talked about the Herero people. One of the Herero women passed in her voluminous cotton full-skirted dress and ostentatious matching hat. For comfort I imagined I preferred the neat linen dress worn by the shop assistant: I was beginning to feel very warm.

A little later we parked for lunch, which was produced from the trailer: 'fresh' meat (frozen!), tomatoes cut up by me, and cucumber peeled by Rick. The Cape Granny Smith apples had not had that far to come but Jeff peeled his because he said the skins were 'too waxy'. We arrived early evening at the Welkom Rest Farm Camp which was in pleasant, open countryside, and where I was more than grateful for Kate's expertise in tent erection. The Etosha tents were splendid when erected, like small conservatories, but the assembling of the flexible jointed poles, and the manoeuvering of them into such a position that the canvas could be hooked on to them, was not as easy as it had looked when Ben and Stephen had given us the demonstration.

I did the necessary luggage sort, and then went and sat by the swmming pool, not a luxury we would have at every stop. A very noisy, and I suspect inebriated, bunch of white South African men were indulging in boisterous horseplay in the water, so Kate and I decided to bide our time. In the interim we admired the butterflies, a black and white variety which may have been the False Monarch. We watched a White-browed Sparrow Weaver and a brilliant Yellow Lesser Masked Weaver. On the way in to the farm we'd seen a collection of Abdim's Storks, sitting hunched up, stock still and silent in a dead tree, all facing in the same direction: spookey!

Once the noisy party had departed to a nearby table with their bottles of beer, Kate and I enjoyed the small pool: it wasn't particularly clean but it was refreshing and we showered afterwards. Towel, costume, and hair dried in no time and it seemed a long time since yesterday. Ben took us on a walk to see the contained Leopard: very handsome but somehow sad in such limited space: as it turned out, it was the only one we would see. We moved on to a Lion similarly confined, and then viewed a group of Giraffes, lolloping free.

An excellent supper was cooked over an open fire: beefsteak, Cumberland sausage, squash, baked potatoes, with red wine from a carton which was difficult to open so that Ben got drenched in the process. We chatted for a while, then washed up and cleared away (this is a 'participation safari'). Soon we were horizontal, me in my beloved sleeping bag on my lovely Thermorest, by 9.30 pm. I died immediately.

I should mention that during the day we had recognized a Grey-backed Lark; Swainson's Red-billed Francolins; Laughing Dove; and a sharp-faced little Titbabbler nestling in the Camel Thorn tree above the camp.

BORDERS : BUTTERFLIES : BLISTER BEETLES

SAN BUSHMEN

17.1.99 Sunday   I felt I'd slept like a log and it was reported that I had done more than my fair share of snoring. I told Kate she must wake me if it happened again. It was a 6.30 am call and I staggered out to the shower, then packed and struck the 'Etosha' tent, into which an amazing amount of Kalahari sand had crept from the day before. I made a mental note not to pitch so close to overhanging Thorn trees in the future: progress kept being halted by vicious thorns catching in my bun net - my preferred old-fashioned variety of which it is difficult to track down in today's stores.

Over breakfast two Yellow-billed Hornbills perched nearby and we had a really good view for several minutes. Jeff gave me a run-down of his family's medical history: no doubt he'd heard the 'Dr' bit, as our passports were studied at check points etc. One of his sisters had died of muscular dystrophy, and Jeff is reckoned to have some odd metabolic disorder, which possibly accounts for his light weight and cachectic appearance: certainly not related to his appetite, for he ate like a horse.

We bade farewell to the noisy Titbabbler overhead and loaded up the van: the sturdy waterproofs were secured over the roofrack and the supplies organised in the trailer. Red-billed Buffalo Weavers were constructing a dishevelled nest near the gate and a little further on a Common Duiker ran across the road, followed by a Secretary Bird with its crown and long tail feathers streaming out behind as it hurried purposefully on some vital mission. A section of new road led us to the Namibian and Botswana borders where the ritual was similar, with forms to complete and passports to be stamped. A wealth of colourful butterflies fluttered around these offices of officialdom, and the strange little strip of no-man's land in between. It was comparatively green following heavy rain, and difficult to believe that we were in the Kalahari.

We stopped for fuel at a small town en route, where Ben spotted his aunt, a teacher, who came over to talk to him. She had a wonderful smile and said proudly "Ben is my elder sister's second son". Lunch was set out and eaten by the roadside, where a whole host of heavily black-veined white butterflies congregated around a damp patch of earth, and a pink flower, Naaldbossie, bloomed in profusion.

During the remainder of the journey to Ghanzi, more Duiker and a single Steenbok came into view. A vehicle in front of us blew a tyre noisily, and dismembered bits floated across the road, but it drew into the side without mishap. Judging by the number of tyre remains we saw over the subsequent days, this was not an uncommon occurrence.

At Ghanzi we had a coffee at a pleasant hotel where we were able to change currency at the rate of 50 Namibian Dollars for 30 Botswana Pula. We bought small cans of coke and water elsewhere - much cheaper. Ben had temporarily to forfeit his can of drink before re-entering the hotel grounds to pick up the van. We drove on to the nearby campsite at D'Kar, which had been overtaken by an outsize insect that looked like a cross between a Locust and a Grasshopper: it was rumoured to be something called a 'Blister Beetle', so-named because it exuded a fluid that was very irritating to human skin. I'm not sure about its identity because, from what I remembered, it didn't particularly resemble the Blister Beetle illustration in the book which I subsequently bought.

We visited the Kuru community development project run by San Bushmen, which included a small museum and art gallery, a tannery, a cochineal plant where the relevant beetles feed on giant cactus leaves, and a craft shop where I bought a necklace-collar made from Ostrich eggs, spines and seeds. I'd forgotten it was Sunday, when normally they are closed, but they opened up especially for us. We pitched our tents and eventually, when the water came on, had a lukewarm shower: the water is never cold, and it doesn't seem to matter if it isn't hot.

Supper started with hot, juicy corn-on-the-cob, followed by rice with some kind of delicious fish. Local storytellers came and spoke in the local Bushman's language, but one of the threesome did the translating. The first 'teller' was an older man who was very lame. "He is not old but he had a hit on the leg," explained the young interpreter. A vivacious young woman had expressive and fascinating facial movements, which were compelling to watch even though we didn't understand what she was saying. The tales were a weird amalgam of Aesop-like fables, and stories where the characters had gruesome cannibalistic tendencies, eating each other's daughters - or the eggs which would have become daughters. It was memorably atmospheric sitting there round the fire in the dark.

We were late going to bed - 10.45 pm!

Some time during the day we had seen a Shaft-tailed Whydah: its chest was a rich buff colour, almost orange, which contrasted smartly with the black crown, back, and elegant, elongated tail feathers.

OSTRICHES : OKAVANGO : WOODED CAMPSITE

18.1.99 Monday　　　　　　　　　It was a 6 am start. I packed and struck tent. I was still not very good at this and got reprimanded for standing on bits of tent. I can't help being only 5'4" - but I suspected Kate was even shorter and she managed. I put my boots on, in the hope that they would give my feet less chance to swell in the humid heat. There was to be a long, sedentary, van-bound journey ahead. We continued across the vast plains of the Kalahari and were stopped at the Ghanzi District border, where a large 'Foot and Mouth' sign indicated the reason. It took me back to the UK epidemic and my days as a veterinary wife. Another check point announced 'Lung Disease' and I wondered whether this indicated tuberculosis but nobody seemed to know.

The terrain became less flat and more interesting. A family of Ostriches, parents and four chicks, came out from the side of the road in front of us. While the female scurried quietly away with her brood, the flamboyant male displayed ostentatiously, flapping his white wings and chestnut tail and successfully distracting us from the rest of the family. We saw two magnificent Tawny Eagles, coloured just as their name suggests, and a Kori Bustard with festinating gait, and self-important beak in the air. Pale-winged Starlings opened up like exotic fans when they took flight, suddenly revealing the red and white of their primary feathers.

It was very hot and we stopped for a drink in the middle of nowhere. Later we took a left turn for Sehethwa and almost immediately saw Bradfield's Hornbill, which I thought was a Redbilled Hornbill: well, it did have a red beak! We stopped for a lunch of salad, white bread and bologna, which was just right. I experienced a touch of colonic disturbance and scratched my legs on yet another Thorn tree when returning from relieving same. We drove through Shakawa and then to Sepupa where we waited for the shop to open so that Ben could buy bread. Storm clouds gathered overhead and lots of men were just sitting about. I suppose it was siesta time. Two Herero women sat talking to two men and a younger woman: I took a quick picture from the minibus when they weren't looking.

We drove to the Okavango River where it makes its way along the northwest spur of the Okavango Delta. Lots of white Cattle Egrets flew back and forth. Spots of rain fell as we transferred all the luggage and equipment from the van and the trailer into a motor boat. We were to be accommodated in another boat. Two other waiting craft had covers but ours were exposed and open to the elements. It looked very 'Empire' when the folding camp chairs had been erected on board. The luggage boat disappeared at the rate of knots and, as we followed, the wind blew and the rain got heavier: there was a chill in the air and it suddenly felt like Devon.

I think the trip was probably about two hours. The river was lovely and we saw Goliath Herons; Cormorants; Darters; the heavy-crested Hammerkop; Southern White-crowned Shrike; Little, European and Swallowtailed Bee-eaters; Pied, Striped and Malachite Kingfishers; and plaintive Blacksmith Plovers. Observation was rather hampered by horizontal sheets of cold rain blowing into the eyes. Kate and Stephen (Ben's assistant) were drier than the rest of us as they were sheltering under Kate's shared, voluminous poncho. At one point a crocodile slid silently into the water.

At the end of this journey we awaited the arrival of our luggage - something I found incomprehensible as it had set off ahead of us at such speed. The rain stopped and, once off the river, the air felt warm and comforting. We transferred to an amazing vehicle which resembled some amphibian army truck. We should have been taking an hour's ride but because the Delta was so dry, the schedule had been changed. There was less scope for messing about in boats, so we'd be camping nearby on a site which was normally under water, and staying there for four nights. I quite liked the thought of this comparatively long-term residence.

There was a mosquito warning and we all located our insect repellant. This campsite was well hidden under a large clump of tall, broad trees, which looked just like all the other neighbouring clumps of trees from the outside, thus giving much scope for getting lost! The central feature was an enormous grey Termite mound: I must say I much preferred the red variety round Lake Kariba and in Namibia's Waterberg Plateau district. A family of resident Vervet Monkeys peered at us restlessly from overhead.

The 'floor' was a thick, grey, heavy dust, the leaves and other natural debris having been swept away for us by Sefa (an expert naturalist) and his helpers, the Polermen, who were to pole us along the still-flowing creeks and channels of the Delta in mokoros (dug-out canoes). We pitched our tents and unpacked. There was no water to speak of for washing so we just wet our hands and faces. It was time to get used to being slightly less than clean. We were directed to the loo, which was in another, smaller, clump of trees where the toilet roll hung on a branch outside: the absence of same indicated occupation.

We ate a good supper of chicken and a tasty pasta. There was the most wonderful sunset, which I should have photographed: there wasn't another like it, but I still have its clear image in my head - possibly the best kind. We talked till 9.30 pm and then went contentedly to bed. Rick snored loudly in the next tent.

SNORING (mine) : NIGHT and DAY LILIES : LILY TROTTERS

A 'short walk'

19.1.99 Tuesday   It was a 6.30 am start. I was told that I'd been snoring again: I had had a very good night! We left at 7.00 am and walked for fifteen minutes or so to a collection of mokoros on the water's edge. It was two to a canoe, plus the Tswana Polerman. Kate and I got into the first one and we glided off in the tranquil waters. It was like something out of a dream, as the blue, mauve and purple of the closing night-lilies and opening day-lilies caught the early morning light. We were poled along narrow channels, some of them very shallow because of the dearth of rain, from one wide stretch of water to another. The sun came up and it got steadily warmer as the morning progressed. I should have had my shoulders covered.

We saw the aptly named Goliath Heron, as well as Great White, Squacco, and Rufousbellied Herons. African Jacanas (Lily Trotters) picked their way lightly over the lily pads: (one of those special memories). Redbilled Buffalo Weaver, Red-shouldered Widow (something like myself!), and the eye-catching Red Bishop were not difficult to spot. Spurwinged Geese made asthmatic noises as they flew overhead. Kingfishers and Bee-eaters (including the startling Carmine) hovered and flitted about, and a watchful Whitebreasted Cormorant sat waiting its chance on a nearby bank. LBJs ('Little Brown Jobs'), including the Greybacked and Blackbacked Cisticola, moved about, most of them (for me) anonymously in the beds of reed and papyrus.

We saw a Grey Hornbill; Yellowbilled Kite (very common here); African Marsh Harrier; Whitebacked and Cape Vultures - both wearing 'French knickers'; a resplendent African Fish Eagle sitting high in a tree; and three long-legged Plovers catching the ear with their high-pitched call, and the eye with their striking white wings. Another Crocodile performed its sliding-noiselessly-into-the-water feat.

We stopped for a while, got out of the mokoros and took a short walk over another area which should have been covered with water. Ben talked to me about his elder brother who had died of AIDS at 35. He was very bitter about the lady from whom it was deemed he had caught the disease: she was still "alive and well". If this was the case, I wondered how many other men she might be infecting. Ben had high standards and at 34 would like to find a wife, but was desperately anxious to make the right choice. Having been asked my opinion, I ventured to suggest that he might do worse than go and visit his mother who lived further north in Botswana, and perhaps find a girl there whose background and family he knew. He frowned disapprovingly and said that that was what his mother had said. His father had left life in the Bush to go and work in the tin mines, and had died of cancer of the stomach at 57: "He drank a lot", said Ben. He asked about my family and said how lucky I was that they were all married: I agreed.

We ate fruit from the Wild Date Palm Tree and then returned by mokoro to camp for a cup of tea. We'd been out on the water for five hours and my legs and shoulders were red. We lunched on pasta, sweetcorn, asparagus, tuna, beetroot, and bean salad, all very welcome. The noisy Vervet Monkeys were not too happy about our presence and kept bombarding us with half-eaten fruit and occasionally something less pleasant. The men all slept the afternoon away. Rick did go off, with some transport which was going to the nearby store, to buy some beer but, being still half asleep, he couldn't find his money so borrowed mine. There was a familiar mooing sound and I went outside the site to see a herd of really good-looking cattle, black, brown, white, and some which were Jersey-like. One tolerated a Redbilled Oxpecker living up to its name as it poked busily about for insects in its neck. I wrote up the diary.

Later, I opted to go on the 'short walk' with Sefa, John, Ben, Kate, and one of the Polermen. It was 4.30 pm but still very hot. I felt like a grease spot. I commented on a lovely greenish white flower, with a small apple-like fruit. "Milkweed", said Sefa and showed me an illustration in the local flora book. We saw another Redshouldered Widow and his paler female, and then the graceful Pin-tailed and Shaft-tailed Whydahs. A vocal Grey Lowrie kept telling us to "Go away". There were Cape Sparrows; Bluecheeked Bee-eaters; Sombre and Redeyed Bulbuls; a speckly Hartlaub's Babbler; Ground Hornbill (they do remind me of turkeys); Forktailed Drongo; Lilacbreasted Roller; a pair of smart little Meyer's Parrots; and a Redbilled Hoopoe: quite a colourful collection. This 'short' excursion around the environs of the camp lasted over two hours and at 6.30 pm it was still surprisingly hot.

By the time we got back, a bush shower had been erected. This took the form of a large container of water hung upside down, with a stiff knob which opened a rose from the water. It was contained in a three-sided standing area with a carpet of leaves. The knob was only just within my reach, but I managed, and enjoyed the experience, being careful not to use too much water: it was rumoured that the one who emptied the 'tank' was responsible for re-filling and replacing. Bats swooped around us continually while we had supper: Cape Serotine I think.

OKAVANGO RIVER : Beautiful shallow-water flowers

SELF-CATERING!

20.1.99 Wednesday　　　　　　Jeff said he was celebrating the one-month anniversary of his nipple piercing, which he attended to every morning, moving on the silver ring a few centimetres after he'd put in his contact lenses!

We started out on a similar venture to yesterday morning, but began with a long walk through tall grass, on very uneven ground, where Hippos had been. It was cooler, thank goodness, but even so I managed to get a bit behind. There was a lot of scrambling over tree trunks and through very muddy areas to the Okavango River. Dear Sefa recognized I was struggling and took my daypack. We saw a couple of Greater Striped Swallows and the striking Senegal Coucal en route. Large yellow-green Hibiscus caught my eye. We sat by the river for a while and some of the party climbed an overhanging tree. I settled for the grass and watched a Golden Weaver busy on the far bank.

We took a more direct route back to the mokoros, passing what Sefa described as a 'Nomad Camp' on the way. I think they were mostly Germans in the group: not very communicative, anyway. Their tents were mostly right out in the open without any shading trees. The long ride through the creeks and open waters was in a different direction. I wondered how these men knew the complicated maze. Ben said the men dug out many of the channels themselves. Kate helped by using the paddle in the very shallow areas. We saw masses of beautiful Water Lilies again, the night-lilies already closed to chunky spikes, and the day-lilies opened wide to the sun, some as blue as the sky from which all the clouds had now cleared. Splashes of colour were provided by Water Gentian, Water Chestnut, pink Watershield, and a starry little white flower, said by Sefa to be called Floating Heart.

There was a mokoro race over the last stretch of open water and Ben got the gold medal. We swam before the walk back to camp, where we had a cup of tea and I changed out of my wet clothes (just top and shorts) into the day before's dry ones. There was a discussion as to who should do the scrambled eggs for lunch (participation safari). Jeff was elected: he was a chef, after all. Ben put out twenty-four eggs for seven people, which Kate and I thought was rather excessive so we participated with our tongues and said so! Jeff broke just twelve, one at a time in his right hand like the true professional he was, and we enjoyed these with bacon, beans and bread; (there was hardly enough egg for Ben!).

I was on washing up, which I preferred to the drying - achieved mostly by flapping a plate backwards and forwards in each hand - "More hygienic than using a cloth", declared Ben. The sky was very grey now and it seemed certain that we would soon have rain. I sat in the tent to write up my diary, and heard the crescendo song of a Heuglin's Robin (identified by Sefa). The rain came, sure enough, and cut short the afternoon's walk which just John, Kate, and I had gone on with Sefa. We had a convincing view of a Long-crested Snake Eagle, along with repeat sightings of birds already seen. A huge Hamerkop nest sat among an abundance of sweet-smelling honeysuckle.

Lightning flashed all around us as we ate a superb dinner of pit-roast lamb, butternuts and mashed potato. We went to bed early and put down the flaps because of the rain, which made it hot and stuffy. I steeled myself to go out for a wee some time during the night and got soaking wet. The tent zippers were going up and down all night as flaps were released or fastened down depending on the weather. No-one slept very well.

WESTERN CAPRIVI : BABOONS : HIPPOS : Mud

21.1.99 Thursday   At 7 am we started to board the army truck in search of Hippos. We bumped through lots of wet grassland, normally covered in water. The truck was open which made for good viewing, but it was necessary to keep arms and heads in from the sides to avoid being mutilated by the notorious Thorn Trees. Olive Baboons observed us closely. We saw a small flock of Longtailed Starlings, their blue-green iridescence catching the morning light and contrasting dramatically with that of two Carmine Bee-eaters. I saw my first 'ordinary' Hoopoe of the tour, and an impressive Marabou Stork.

The flowers presented an occasional multi-coloured carpet and the grasses were in all shapes and sizes: spikes, spirals, wedges, clusters, and candelabras, and one strangely attractive species had a flattened head made of five delicate prongs. It was hard to imagine this entire area under water.

We travelled for about an hour and a half with no particular landmark and one of the Polermen shouted the direction every now and then: I wondered how he knew. Eventually we came to some open water and there between twenty and thirty Hippos wallowed about, grunting and snorting and opening their vast mouths in everlasting yawns. Sefa got out of the truck and advanced on the Hippos in an effort to make them get up and be more photogenic. They obliged to a limited extent and Sefa came running back, very wet. We watched and recorded their clumsy entertaining antics for some time and then started the rough drive back.

We stopped at Sefa's village so that he could see his family. One of his sons had been very sick, he told us, but he came back to the truck with a broad happy grin on his face to report that he was "much better". The driver was very impatient and kept sounding his horn while Sefa was on this brief mission.

The last call was at the 'Overseas Liquor Restaurant' a somewhat flattering description of the basic facility, but they did sell all kinds of liquid refreshment, alcoholic and otherwise, and there was somewhere to sit and drink if you were so minded. A couple of us got out the maps of the Delta, and Sefa showed us our exact whereabouts in the Western Caprivi. After a tasty pasta lunch, I felt quite sleepy and joined the siesta brigade, much to Kate's disgust I suspect. I slept solidly for an hour and a half and then lay working out a birthday poem for her birthday, to which we had been alerted by Jeff, who had been sent a birthday card by her company, to be given to her on the 29th.

No-one suggested a walk this afternoon: it was grey, and rained every now and then. During a dry spell I went for a walk alone and watched a little Bee-eater at close quarters for ages. I noted my direction carefully so that I would be able to identify the nondescript clump of trees round the site and distinguish it from all the others on my return.

We had a well-seasoned mushroom and tomato dish with rice for supper and I indulged myself and had two helpings.

The rain got heavier and steadier and everything was taking on a wet, muddy hue. I was going off the dusty, dark (now muddy) floor of this wooded campsite and I longed for some green grass.

I couldn't face another bush shower and went to bed at 9.30 pm.

175

RAIN : TRANSPORT DELAYS : GREAT ANIMALS : GRASS!

22.1.99 Friday The day started with a 6 am call. I managed to be ready, packed, tent struck etc, in preparation for the scheduled truck-arrival time, 7 am. (I got my hair up rather better this morning: always a hurdle when camping). The truck arrived at 9.30 am, after prompting from Ben who walked to the village in the pouring rain.

We drove to the river where the luggage was all piled into one boat and we piled into the only uncovered boat and sat on the camp chairs. Other boats unloaded and boarded 'our' truck. The rain remained heavy and persistent and I donned my waterproof for the first time; even so, I was soaked through, as were we all. It was too wet and cold to be bird-spotting and we sat with our heads down. At the other end we waited for our luggage and then loaded up the familiar red van and trailer again. They were like old friends and their return was somehow comforting. Sadly the comfort was short-lived for, as we approached Sepupa, Ben suddenly stopped, saying that there was "something very serious". I wondered how he knew: I hadn't noticed anything. He was right. The bearings had gone on the offside trailer wheel. There followed a long session of removal and examination. He carried spares but said they were the wrong size. This was not his usual trailer and he seemed quietly angry about the whole situation.

22 January 1999   Oryx and Termite mound

While discussions continued, John, Jeff and I walked the short distance to the shop to buy bread and fruit. It was hot and sultry again now. I couldn't believe we'd all been so wet and cold only a short time earlier – remembering, especially, sitting under the dripping trees in the bush campsite, waiting for the belated truck. It was just after 1 pm as we reached the shop door, which was being most definitely locked by the proprietor. We explained our mission. "Open at 2" he said, unsmilingly.

By the time we got back it had been decided that the trailer would be abandoned temporarily at the police station, where it was deposited across the entrance to the prison cell. All the gear was loaded on the top of, and inside, the van: not much room for manoeuvre. Shortly afterwards we went through the crossing-the-borders routine again, and back into Namibia at the Western end of the Caprivi Strip. We were behind schedule with all the delays the day had brought, so we drove fairly smartly through the Mahango Game reserve, which was a pity but couldn't be helped.

The skies were threatening and overcast again and the van was chock-a-block. Nevertheless we saw Red Hartebeest; Blue Wildebeest (Gnu); two beautiful Oryx standing like bookends to a huge Termite mound; lots of Zebra; scurrying Warthogs; roaming Giraffe; Roan Antelope with their checker-board faces; great African Elephants flapping their outsize ears; and many graceful Impala. Ostriches danced for us and a weird Knob-billed Duck waddled into view on our offside.

We arrived at the Popa Falls campsite: with grass … hurrah … and with the sound of the teeming waters in the background. It was lovely. Maybe I won't opt for a SAGA cruise next year after all.

We erected the tent. The bedding was still wet from the day's experiences but it just didn't matter. I enjoyed the luxury of a shower and electric light, but I was looking so dishevelled that I could have done without the long mirror. Kate and I went for a short walk by the water and then had a cosy chat over a bottle of wine in the tent. She talked about her daughter Sythey, a long-term legacy from her life as a tour leader in India. She was with one of Kate's sisters during this African adventure. She showed me a photograph: at three and a half she looked a really beautiful child.

We didn't light a fire but ate a goulash supper cooked in the site kitchen, which seemed very civilised except for the fact that all the chairs were in the abandoned trailer, so that we had to eat standing up!

This was the end of a not-so-perfect day but then this was Africa and it was the rainy season. And so to bed at 9.30 pm, ready for a 5.30 am start.

A STEADYING HAND at the POPA FALLS

SARASUNGU RIVER LODGE

23.1.99 Saturday   I was awakened by Ben after a good night's sleep. We packed all our damp belongings and had that essential cup of tea. Then I went to clean up, and do my hair, in the luxury of the washroom: but, no lights! By the time I got back it was getting light and Kate had almost struck the tent single-handed. We all helped to fit the luggage and camping gear in, and on, the van, and when it was properly light we went for a walk to the Popa Falls, over rocks and water. I was glad of

Stephen's steadying hand every now and then. At other times I did my usual method of locomotion under such circumstances - on all fours. There was interesting and attractive vegetation all around us, including copious spreads of Dodderwort, giving a pinky rust shroud to many of the bushes.

The Popa Falls consist of a long stretch of rapids cascading over a series of rocks as the Okavango descends sixty-five feet over a distance of nine miles, cutting across the Caprivi Panhandle to drain into the Delta. It reminded me of those rapids along the course of the Kunene where I had white-water rafted and I felt a certain surge of adrenaline. We sat about for a while and took photographs and then returned to the faithful waiting Toyota van and set off in the rain. We stopped at the little shop for Ben to check the tyre pressures: we must be over-loaded. A slow-moving, lugubrious attendant lady eventually agreed to wash the windscreen: very reluctantly and without any change of facial expression, let alone a smile.

Once on the road someone decided to open the cool box to see whether there was any coke left: the smell was positively foul so it was closed again with all speed. We were bound for Rundu. A sign read '184 kms'. I found myself dozing but came to life when "Rundu" was announced. It was a scattered, new-looking township, all of which Ben referred to as "the centre". It had "picked up" since the end of the Angolan war he said, being virtually on the border. Some of us went to the bank: I decided to change some US Dollars for South African Rand. The queues were incredible and we learned that most wages are paid into the bank on a Friday night. We were attended to relatively quickly and then directed to a queueless window, where we presented the forms we'd been given and the usual documents.

We had passed a market en route so I made for that and John joined me. John was the chap in the Fair Isle sweater whom we'd identified at the airport. A retired civil servant, he'd travelled widely and was a perfect gentleman, not overgiven to the participation element of the safari, but very pleasant company. The market was not full of genuine local goods as we had imagined it might be, but we had a mooch around and I bought a colourful scarf in genuine polyester.

The rain got heavier and heavier again so that, on the return walk, we stopped under a noisy, corrugated awning and fished the waterproofs out of our daypacks. My cagoule had a loose net lining, all very good for the sweating and the hygiene, but it created difficulties when trying to put it on in a hurry. It proved to be good entertainment for three young girls standing nearby.

We reached the Hotel rendezvous, where we had an excellent pot of coffee (two decent-sized cups each for nine Namibian Dollars, less than £1) sitting on a covered terrace overlooking open country towards the border, with the river in between. The rest joined us and suddenly the rain started to splash down into the terrace area while I wasn't looking and in no time my daypack was sitting in a puddle of water. We went inside and the tolerant proprietor didn't seem to mind our general state of wetness.

We were the only patrons at the Omarashara Hotel, which undoubtedly catered for many in season, judging from the extensive semicircular terrace of tables and chairs surrounding a sizeable swimming pool. We bought some cards when we paid for our coffee, and then Ben arrived, saying that it would be pointless setting up camp in the heavy rain: the site was only a short distance away. Jeff made a big decision and got his one clean, dry shirt out of the van and we all cheered.

The rain stopped at last and we proceeded to Sarasunga River Lodge where the campsite was, not surprisingly, very wet, but at least it was wet grass and not mud. We erected the wet tents before the next downpour and ate a very late sandwich lunch. Our spirits rose as the sun came out and Kate and I went for a swim in the very clean, pleasant pool. The resident dog, Tessa, ran round the pool constantly, often chasing a Dragonfly unsuccessfully but she never put so much as a paw into the water. We showered and sat in the sun and talked. Rick and Jeff played cards in the bar all afternoon. We walked down to the river, everything fresh after the rain and a few frogs sounded appreciative croaks. Back at the campsite our sleeping bags were dry after just a couple of hours in the sun.

We watched a Senegal Coucal, a Woodland Kingfisher (Kate's only claim to ornithological fame) and a Longtailed Shrike. We ate dinner in the site restaurant, which was excellent: I revelled in a generous smoked salmon and prawn starter. The smoked salmon was sliced more thickly than the traditional UK portion, was not as deeply coloured, and was positively delicious. I followed this with a Portuguese chicken dish, and washed it all down with a shared bottle of Chardonnay.

Above the restaurant there was a display of locally made goods for sale: I went and had a look, and finished up buying an attractive African drum - (was this wise?) - which was housed under the front seat of the van for the rest of the trip and then carried as hand luggage.

Ben talked about finding a wife again. He and Stephen did justice to large portions of beefsteak. The other three men had pizzas: how could they?

It had been a day of contrasts. So, finally to bed - late - at 10 pm!

A MAGIC DAWN : THREE LIONS

THANKS for the THERMOREST

24.1.99 Sunday   It rained heavily again in the night. For some unknown reason not one of us had put the fly sheets on our tents so we had drip, drip seeping through the seams, in spite of all the flaps being zipped down. I kept moving in an attempt to avoid the worst of them. It stopped about 4 am. Around 6 am, just as dawn was breaking, there was the most wonderful dawn chorus I had ever heard anywhere. Maybe the birds were happy with the results of all the longed-for rain. There were rhythms of all kinds, regular at different speeds, repeated irregular songs, tones of different intensities, and pitches high, medium, and low, with one very low. It was quite glorious and I found myself moved to tears. Surely this kind of cacophony must be the very essence of the inspiration for the African Sanctus.

Lots of Longtailed Shrikes were breakfasting on an explosion of all kinds of insects on the wet ground. The day was grey. We had our breakfast, packed all the re-wetted luggage, and struck the very wet tents. I began to wonder whether I would ever again be really dry: it wasn't cold. The overloaded van was smelling dank and musty. A bulldozer seemed to be re-making the rough road to the campsite as we came up to the main road. We waited while they levelled an area for us to drive through the red mud. We stopped at a roadside wood-carving stall, where Jeff bought a walking stick and Kate a mask. I tucked my drum under the seat and decided that that would do.

It was about now that Ben realized he had not left the all-important trailer documents at the Sarasungu campsite, where it had been arranged for the chap to bring the replacement trailer and to collect the unusable one to which the papers related. Hence we retraced our steps, but Ben used the back entrance to the campsite to avoid disturbing the bulldozer operations again. Jeff and Rick played a very vocal game of cards on my right. Rick addressed Jeff as Dirk Diggler and seemed to win most hands.

We splashed through puddles and areas of more serious flooding, one of which surrounded - and had presumably moved - a huge Termite mound in the middle of the road. We had a brief but clear sighting of a Caracal making its way acoss the road in front of us. It was like a big brown cat with long ears. We arrived at Namutoni - at the Eastern end of the Etosha Pan - just after 2 pm and erected the wet tents in the rain, which stopped when the job was completed.

25 January 1999

Etosha Waterhole

Kate and I rushed off to the waterhole but there was little to see. It was rumoured that now that the game had plenty of water everywhere, it had no need to travel: that's what you get for going in the rainy season, I supposed. This was so different from my one previous experience of this part of the world, when the drought had driven all kinds of thirsty animals to the waterhole, and it had been halfway through the night before we could drag ourselves away.

We retraced our steps part of the way and had a coffee at the little bar-café where we saw a couple of Blue Waxbills pottering about under the table, like Sparrows. A whole crowd of Red-billed Buffalo Weavers were adding untidily to well-established nests in a great Palm tree of some kind. We went on a drive in the Park in the early evening and were fortunate enough to see three Lions, amongst other large game. We saw a Hadeda Ibis (so named because of its characteristic call), and an elegant Blue Crane.

Back at the campsite the rain was pouring again, and one part of the area had become a lake. Our tent was not in the wettest patch but it seemed to be leaking more than the rest. There was a protracted, inconclusive discussion going on, so Kate and I opted for a hot shower. When we emerged from the shower block, the flood water had extended and we had to wade our way back. Our tent, luggage, and bedding were all thoroughly soaked and there was no way I was sleeping in there.

We put our luggage into the van, and then supper was cooked on the calor gas unit in the laundry room, which was dry and waterproof. We ate spaghetti bolognaise and a fair slurp of gin (purchased at less than half UK prices in Rundu - and it was all right!).

Kate and I decided to sleep in the laundry room, which was big enough for everyone but (thankfully) no-one opted to join us. Jeff couldn't face the heavy presence of stunningly beautiful moths, and the others moved their less-wet tents on to higher ground. My sleeping pad (provided by Travelbag) was soaking but, having been advised over the phone by one of the company's employees that it might be a good idea to take my Thermorest, I had done just that and blessed this 'unnecessary' piece of luggage which, up until then, had seen the light of day only once. By some miracle it was only mildly damp, and I had an unexpectedly good night with it between me and the concrete floor, in the secure knowledge that I wouldn't be dripped upon. The laundry had a pleasant, spacious, airy feel after the claustrophobia of the flaps-down tent. The Thermorest was a bit narrow, and in the morning I vaguely remembered rolling on to the concrete floor a couple of times.

EARLY START : LARGE ANIMALS - Old and Young

Real and Imaginery

25.1.99 Monday   We were up at 5.30 am, clearing away all evidence of a bedroom, then had a cup of tea and were out of the gates by 6.30 am. It was grey and forbidding, with little bird song, but we had a really good game drive. There were groups of young Zebras and Blue Wildebeest, with enchanting young of various ages; Greater Kudu; White Rhinoceros; Elephant; a splendid close-up of a handsome young male Lion; Giraffes; Oryx (Gemsbok); Black-faced Impala (seen only in Northern Namibia), with dainty young; Springbok (my favourite), one with a new-born lamb; and steady Black-backed Jackals - just standing looking at us, as we looked at them: they mate for life.

The birds had to take second place while we searched for game but we couldn't help but notice some of the larger ones, such as the Whitebacked Vulture; Tawny Eagle; Marabou Stork; African Spoonbill; distant Flamingoes; Kori Bustard; Ostrich; Helmeted Guinea Fowl; the leggy Black-winged Stilt; the neat Little Stint; Common Piper; and the Laughing Dove, which seemed to find us entertaining as it entertained us with its rising and falling 'oos' and 'coos'. So this was a pretty good list considering that we weren't really looking. We took a break at a legitimate stopping-and-getting-out point, where there was a loo and, praise be, the sun came out. We returned to camp just after 12 noon and I was amazed to find I'd taken a whole 36-picture film.

We were all ready for the bacon, egg, and beans brunch. (We didn't question the number of eggs this time.)

I still had pictures of big game in my mind. The searching and anxiety to see as much as possible can lead to all sorts of mis-spottings. I was convinced once that I was looking at a distant African Fish Eagle but, when I got it in the zoom lens, it was the back end of a Springbok! Another time I was certain I could see a sitting Lion and couldn't make out why no-one else had seen it: it was a Termite mound. There was no end of dead and dormant trees, which successfully mimicked many of the long-necked birds, or even a Giraffe.

We cleared away and then visited the shop before it closed. I bought Fanta drinks and an Etosha T-shirt. We spent the afternoon writing diaries and looking things up in various guide books, and at 5 pm we went for a drive. We were lucky enough to see the diminutive Damara Dik-dik, the sort of vulnerable-looking animal which brings out my maternal instincts.

25 January 1999   Springbok, Etosha

A whole nursery group of young Springbok lived up to its name, and leapt repeatedly, high into the air from the same spot, with an occasional short run and another leaping session. This was very special and joined the collection of indelible, joyous memories.

Red Hartebeest looked richly brown in the strange evening light, which shafted through and between heavy, threatening clouds - again. A pair of Black Jackals gave us the once-over: maybe the same faithful pair as this morning. Very dramatic lightning flashed from heaven to earth and back again.

A large Zebra lay very dead at the side of the drive - not struck by lightning but killed by other trauma, with wounds on its thick neck and blood spattered nearby; it had been a great strong beast and we felt quite sad.

The exchanged trailer had arrived when we got back and Ben was over the moon. "My friend!" he said. This was his original vehicle, which he much preferred. There was the odd drop of rain and the clouds were ominous but though the lightning flashed continuously overhead it wasn't followed by the threatened storm. We were able to cook, and eat a good supper of steak, squash, and butternuts outside, and sit and chat about the day, afterwards. And it was bed by 9.30 pm.

HALALI : HYENAS : HATS : HELMETS

26.1.99 Tuesday It was a dry night, with a good sleep. But a lovely rainbow suggested that all the precipitation was not yet over. Noisy Swainson's Francolins went about their business on the edge of the campsite. The dustbins had been upturned by Hyenas during the night.

Kate and I were ready first, packed, and tent rolled into its bag. Rick was last as usual but to be fair he didn't keep us waiting, he just wasn't available to help us with the general camp chores. We set off just after 8 am. We spotted Spotted Hyenas, a Red Hartebeest standing like a statue in the morning sun, and then came across another dead Zebra, which made us wonder whether there was some fell disease lurking in the herd.

Our destination was Halali, to the south of the Etosha Pan. We drove past carpets of bright yellow flowers, fresh and newly-opened after the rain. There were wide vistas, stretching as far as the eye could see, which gave the impression that there must be an ocean somewhere beyond: this was all the Etosha Pan, of course. It was like an everlasting seaside. We stopped to observe very distant Flamingoes - again.

The most exciting moment of the morning was a quick but vivid and identifiable flash of a Cheetah, ambling, then picking up speed, and moving powerfully between the vegetation. As we approached Halali a Yellow Mongoose stopped, studied us, and then ran on a little and stood on its hind legs in characteristic pose. Cameras clicked all round. This personable animal is another which brings out my maternal instinct. We prepared and ate a savoury rice and salad lunch, and then had a swim in the large pool. Jeff and Rick continued their card game at the side.

We left about 2 pm and drove on towards Okaukuejo, where we were to camp. The journey took us through sweeping areas of near desert, which had remained so in spite of the recent rains. We saw another Mongoose, Rednecked Francolins, large Black Crows, and Steenbock, amongst other birds and game which we'd seen before. We were greeted by the sight of the fort, (now the administrative headquarters of the park), and blissful, warm sun.

We put up the tents in the hope that they might actually have the chance to dry off properly, and then went in search of life-restoring Fanta and Sprite, and now water, in the shop. In most areas we had been assured the water, usually from boreholes, was safe and fit to drink. I had filled my flexible water bottle each day, and had been carrying the full bottle in my daypack when I discovered serious soaking on a rare day when it wasn't raining. I had also carried an extraordinary, squashable sunhat, (made in the Philippines) and pierced with a substantial hatpin, which served to secure it to my bun. Unfortunately on this occasion it had pierced the water bottle and thereafter I was obliged to buy bottled water. Incidentally, Rick said it was the ugliest sunhat he had ever seen. I was very attached to this much-travelled piece of holiday apparel and retaliated by suggesting that his drooping, multi-stringed, mucky example was hardly anything to write home about!

Industrious, sparrow-like Sociable Weavers and Southern Masked Weavers were a joy to watch near the tent. At 5.30 pm, as the light was fading, we went down to the waterhole, where the surface of the water was studded with the helmet projections of the Helmeted Terrapins. Multitudes of beautiful Dragonflies flew around and a Barn Owl swooped low, followed by several Bats. Black-faced Impala and a few Blacksmiths Plovers hung about on the far bank. I recalled again my earlier waterhole experience during a drought, when so much large game had taken advantage of the rare refreshment. We gave up hoping for something exciting about 10 pm and went to bed. At least it wasn't raining.

FRONT SEAT : NAMIBIAN FILLET : PETRIFIED FOREST

The FRAME

27.1.99 Wednesday It was a 6.30 am start and my turn for the front seat. We drove along good roads (almost boringly so at times, they were so straight), through farmland and into Damaraland. We stopped first at Outjo for petrol and a short break, and then at Khorixas, Damaraland's capital. Here we went shopping for the ingredients for supper, for which Kate, Jeff, and I were responsible. We were amazed to find, in the local butcher's, fillet of 'Scottish' beef for 28 Namibian Dollars a kilogram, that is, for less than £3.00. We decided that one kilogram would be plenty for seven of us but Ben advised us to go for one and a half. The lady assistant, who looked very clean and smart, brought out a whole delicious-looking fillet and our mouths watered as we watched her cut into it. For the moment we made do with a coffee and a Danish pastry in the next door café.

We followed a long, long road through the desert and it became hotter and drier as the morning wore on. In the Aba-Huab River Valley we stopped off at the Petrified Forest, where the recumbent trees are reckoned to be somewhere between two and three million years old - figures I cannot conjure with. For some reason I had expected to see them standing up, but it was explained by the local guide that they had been carried there by flood waters, a theory supported by the fact that there are no roots or branches. There are said to be fifty-three in all, the largest ninety-eight feet long (high) and with a circumference of nineteen feet. The growing rings and texture of the bark are clearly visible, and have enabled positive identification of the trees as Gymnospermae. These were cone-bearing plants which are known to have flourished during the afore-mentioned two to three hundred million years ago.

The whole area, with its leafless, upright trees which will spring to life with the first decent rainfall, and the flourishing male and female Welwitschia Mirabilis, sometimes called a 'fossil plant', suggested the ambience of an alien planet. The Welwitschia plant is really a tree, turned dwarf by the rigors of the desert, which produces only two large leaves in its entire lifetime, which may be up to 2000 years. The leaves are torn into long, thorn-like threads by weathering. We took pictures of these weird reminders of nature's incredible ability to adapt. It was searingly hot and I wasn't sorry when we finished the circular walk.

It was not far to the Twyfelfontein campsite, very sandy, very hot, where we pitched our tents under a clump of trees. Healthy-looking cattle and, for the first time, a flock of sheep roamed about: I wondered what they lived on. The scene had an Old Testament feel.

27 January 1999   Welwitschia in Petrified Forest

We had lunch and then it was most definitely siesta time. I opted for an A frame, an airy Bamboo construction, shaped as its name implies, open at both ends and raised about three feet from the ground: it was bliss and I dozed happily. Wonderful butterflies hovered around and sometimes settled inside the A frame but I was too idle to get the camera.

There was a brief sandstorm and then at 4.30 pm, when it was still surprisingly hot, (oh, for a shower of rain) we went off to see the Bushman site of ancient rock engravings carved into petrified dunes. I had imagined we would be moving from one cool cave to another and foolishly left behind my 'ugly' hat. As it was, the paintings were exposed to the sun on vertical and horizontal surfaces and I could feel my shoulders sizzling. I made for every suggestion of shade but there was little. Occasional small clouds dulled the sun's blaze for a few seconds. A diminutive local lady called Juliana, a dwarf in fact, was our guide and she talked to us with knowledgeable enthusiasm. When we got back to the entrance for proper shade and a drink, she introduced us to her sturdy toddler son, Jeno, who gave us a series of big smiles. As we sat there talking and sipping, a pair of Pririt Batis poked about in some seed on the floor of the remains of a derelict farmhouse. One of them did its descending "teu teu teu" as it flew off.

I went into recovery in the A frame when we got back and then had a shower, open to all the world, but not many of the world were thereabout, and anyway I really didn't care. The sunset was breathtaking and this time I took a picture. Kate, Jeff, and I cooked the evening meal, as planned, and the fillet lived up to expectations - and there wasn't too much: every last morsel disappeared.

We sat and talked in the cooler night air. I decided to sleep in the A frame: I'd become quite attached to it. Kate opted for the tent. And that should have been the end of the day - and so it would have been if a large male Elephant hadn't come and stood outside the door of Kate's tent. She saw and heard it, lay terrified until it moved on, and then got up and woke us all to tell us about it. She moved into the A frame next to mine.

CAPE FUR SEALS : SWAKOPMUND : SHOPPING

FRESH OYSTERS

28.1.99 Thursday We struck tent in the gentle light of a lovely sunrise. I washed and had two cups of tea. The hair ritual was interrupted by the return of the Elephant, not actually in the campsite but near enough.

We took a rocky road round, and with good views of, the Brandberg Mountain (8500 feet). I spotted a Korhaan which was probably a female Northern Black Korhaan, but I like to think it might just have been Ruppell's Korhaan, seen occasionally in this area. We stopped at Uis, a sad-looking old tin-mining town, and bought Fanta and crisps.

We continued south west to Cape Cross, where we could smell the hundreds of Cape Fur Seals before we actually saw them. It was a short walk over sandy ground to the limiting wall above the shore. Cape Fur Seals of all sizes and ages flopped about on the flat rocks, sometimes fighting for a favourite perch. The pups are born towards the end of the year: there were too many little young black ones to count. The occasional small corpse was visible: evidently parents sometimes go off fishing for days on end, and their abandoned young may not survive their absence. I watched one hopeful orphan (I presumed) getting a physical rejection from a cow it tried to suckle. She gathered up her own youngster and surrounded it with a protective flipper as it fed.

A couple of huge bulls dwarfed the crowd around them. The adjacent waves were full of shiny bodies of Cape Fur Seals moving in and over the water. Kelp Gulls, Caspian Terns, and Cape Cormorants added their seaside noises to the Seals' comforting grunts. We took lots of pictures and then just sat and watched in silence. When we had had our fill, we walked back to the van and went to look at the cross (and explanatory stone) erected by Kaiser Wilhelm II in replication of the original, erected by Diego Cão on the headland at Cape Cross.

We moved on to another spot on the coast for lunch: it was a warm, sunny day and I'd almost forgotten the rain as I paddled on the edge of the powerful breakers, aware of a strong undercurrent. Kate and I picked up a few shells. Less distant Flamingoes were visible, along with graceful Avocets, Blackwinged Stilts, and African Black Oystercatchers - with a call indistinguishable (to me) from that of the European Oystercatcher.

Swakopmund was today's destination and we found it to be a very pleasant, spacious modern city, with attractive architecture: it is Namibia's second city. Here we were to have the luxury of two-bedroomed flats. In ours, Kate and I had one bedroom, and Jeff and John the other. It was more like a small house with a good kitchen and a decent-sized bathroom. We dumped our things, had a quick wash, and went shopping. We bought books, including a well-illustrated 'Wildlife of Southern Africa' field guide (which had a comforting general air about it and was not too specialised), a photographic Mammals Guide (of which I already had a copy but wanted one for Kate's birthday), and a Bird Field (tick) List - I've got to impress the boys!

I also fell for a striped blouse, a 750 ml bottle of Gordon's Gin (£3), a poster of Halali (Etosha), some local greetings cards, a small tin of Nivea Cream (I'd lost mine), and some shampoo (I'd finished my sachets). Thus pleased with our purchases, we walked back to the flat and had a glorious shower and hairwash. I then did a bit of washing and sorting of dusty luggage, in what seemed a confined space - which it wasn't really: I'd just got too used to the wild outdoors.

We went to Kucki's Pub for supper, that is, we all did except Rick, who opted to drink in another nearby pub with some folk he'd met there earlier in the evening. The meal and the general atmosphere were excellent: fresh oysters, large and fleshy, followed by a generous Wiener schnitzel on an appropriately large plate. The vegetables and side salad were really fresh and crisp. The waiter agreed to take a couple of pictures of the happy party: some of us were masked by a clowning guest from another group (on his way to the loo, I suspect) and a powerful shaft of rogue light getting into the camera. Ben and Stephen went in search of Rick, while the rest of us walked back to base.

I slept soundly and didn't hear their return from 'O'Fagan's', during what was reported as 'the early hours'.

KATE'S BIRTHDAY and TREATS FOR ALL

29.1.99 Friday   I awoke at 7 am. It was Kate's birthday. Breakfast was in Ben's flat, where he and Rick were slow to rise: Stephen had done the preparation. When everyone was eventually assembled we sang the ritual "Happy Birthday" and presented the card, the doggerel and the Mammals book.

Rick decided he'd go sand-boarding (he always has to do something different). John, Kate and I took the flight over the dunes, scheduled to last two and a half hours and, in spite of the cramped conditions, it was worth every penny. The plane was a six-seater so, with us and the pilot, the half dozen was made up to the full number by a middle-aged German couple, who fought energetically over their camera and shared a small can of drink!

It was very noisy in the plane so conversation was impossible. The pilot pointed out landmarks and then indicated them on the illustrated map with which we had been provided. My big camera refused to oblige - something to do with the very bright light it was suggested, so I fished out the little one and it performed to order. The vistas were amazing. Some transitory rivers ran brief and occasional courses according to the pilot - who said things such as "I've never seen water there before." The great dunes were bathed in light on one side and varying shade on the other. They were like mountain ranges, almost denuded of vegetation except for the occasional lonely tree. The pilot flew low to show us one such. What was its secret? How did it survive? And why was it the only one? There was something very special about it.

There were some disused diamond mines in a dry desert of sand: I wondered how anyone had ever known that there were diamonds there in the first place, in such inhospitable terrain. Shipwrecks told their own tragic story. There were heaps of Fur Seals, looking like large collections of black beetles from the air, and, over Sandwich Bay, flocks of Flamingoes which resembled clouds of fluttering pink butterflies. The way the dunes came down to the sea presented a dramatic coastline, and the pilot tilted the plane skilfully at one stage so that it looked as if a mountainous sea was running down to the dunes. Somewhere in the middle of nowhere there was an abandoned cart. What stories all these relics could tell. As we flew back over Walvis Bay, and into Swakopmund, it was hard to believe that we had been airborne for over two hours. A young lady connection of the German couple took a picture of us all standing under the wing of the plane, so I asked her if she would use my camera as well. (The German lady insisted on combing her hair first!)

We were driven back into the town, where we went into the Flights Office and I paid for Kate and me with some US dollar Travellers' cheques which I'd had for ever. Kate took the receipt so that Travelbag could reimburse her (and me). We waited some time for Rick to return from his sandboarding expedition and I sensed that Ben was not too happy. It seemed there had been some misunderstanding about the pick-up point, but we eventually ran him down (not literally of course) outside the flats.

We had provided ourselves with a light lunch purchased in Swakopmund, as we had a long drive ahead. Rick was excessively sandy and sweaty (he'd had a "wonderful" time) and I was glad I was not sitting next to him. The subsequent drive was spectacular, taking us by the Kuiseb River and through the Kuiseb Pass, and then the Gaub Pass, with grand views of the Rantberge. The intermittent rain, the shadows, and the sun all added to the drama of the scenery. A Pale Chanting Goshawk sat surveying the world, and a Booted Eagle presented an effortless resemblance to a Buzzard. We approached Solitaire to read the place name written in white stones on the hillside, the first three letters depicted fully and the rest just in outline: there were very few stones about. The place was aptly named. It was very hot and I bought more water after I'd drunk a cup of good coffee.

We drove on to Sesriem, spotting among other birds a Crimson-breasted Shrike and Red-billed Buffalo Weavers. The Sesriem campsite was sheltered by a magnificent Camelthorn Tree. Kate and I swam in the pool, and nearby a Whitebacked Mousebird nosed about in a side patch of grass. We ate succulent pork chops for supper and gloried in another colourful sunset.

A bright moon gave us a clear night light and we celebrated Kate's birthday with a couple of bottles of sparkling wine. It was a very hot night and I had indigestion, possibly a combination of the wine and the weekly Avoclor

SOSUSSVLEI : DUNE 45 : Last AFRICAN SUNSET

30.1.99 Saturday   We were called at 4 am and drove for forty-five minutes to the Dune 45 (a very unromantic name), reputedly the longest and highest dune in the Namib Desert and possibly in the world. The plan was to climb to the top in time for the sunrise.

It was like walking in snow, each step taking more effort as the foot sank into the sand, only to be pulled out ready for the next step. Before we started the ascent there was not a single footstep or any disturbance of the golden surface. It had a transient perfection so that it seemed like vandalism to sully it.

John led to begin with: he was very fit, and did a lot of fell and other walking. Stephen strode on to take the lead and Rick put up an impressive performance. I was content to take it at a steady (my own) pace and brought up the rear, taking twelve steps and then stopping for the count of twelve while my pulse slowed a little. Jeff didn't hurry either, and there was a moment when I thought we might not make the top in time for the sunrise, but we did - and it was wonderful.

We all sat on the top of the ridge and revelled in the experience. As the sun climbed quietly over the horizon, long shadows were accentuated by the new light on the higher mountains of sand in between. The shadows got shorter and shorter until the whole area was bathed in shadowless, shining sand-scape, as far as the eye could see.

Coming down was a bit like screeing, but not nearly as physically demanding. A French family arrived and I envied the boundless energy of their young twin boys, who raced up the dune. Their mother said she was hoping to tire them out. Rick decided to photograph them and asked them to say "fromage" which, not surprisingly, they didn't seem to find relevant.

We had breakfast and recovered, and then drove on to a parking place from which we walked the 5 kms to Sosussvlei. I had planned to take the taxi service, thinking I might have had enough exercise after the dune climb, and I had already removed my walking boots with this in mind. However, I changed my mind (a woman's privilege after all) and walked in open sandals and got my feet burned. It was an amazing walk, like going across some kind of sea, with towering golden waves all around.

We rested and looked around the clay pan for a while, then the legitimate transport drove us back to our van. (It is forbidden for any but authorised vehicles to take this drive). It was worth the twenty Namibian Dollars. Pied Crows flocked all around the vehicle which took us the hour's drive back to camp. It was only mid-morning and we seemed to have lived a whole day already. I showered and washed my hair, and later we had bacon, eggs, and beans for lunch.

We went to ground afterwards and battened down the flaps when a sandstorm suddenly blew up out of a sky which had been clear blue only moments earlier. It lasted about half an hour by which time nothing had escaped penetration. Some tents on an adjacent site, belonging to a German group who had gone out for the day, had been rolled several yards.

When everything had calmed down, we drove to Sesriem Canyon, where we climbed down to look at all kinds of conglomerate rocks. There were collections of twigs and debris high up in branches of trees, indicating how deep the water had been in the comparatively recent past. Today however the water was low, although there was a deeper area downstream where a few people sat about in bathing costumes. A couple of bats zoomed about under the overhanging rocks, Red-eyed Doves cooed from above, and Swifts flew against the sky as we looked up from between the towering rocks on either side.

We drove a little way to see the sunset; (Rick opted to join his Swakopmund friends in the camp bar). The sky was grey and threatening, and the wind was blowing sand from the top of nearby dunes, like smoke from a chimney. Many weirdly-shaped Camelthorn Trees stretched out their ancient, twisted branches against the red of the sunset dunes and a dramatic sky.

Back at camp it rained for a while but cleared to give us a second chance for our last African sunset of the tour. We had a tasty supper of goulash and mealypop, which is a bit like savoury semolina. This was the last night and everyone was very quiet. Rick was anxious to escape to his friends and actually started the washing up. It was bed by 10 pm.

For me, the dawn on Dune 45 had been one of those especially memorable travel highlights.

30 January 1999
Dune 45 - Sosussvlei

LAST DAY : REMHOODGE PASS : WINDHOEK TOUR

Flight 287

31.1.99 Sunday   Last Day! I can't believe it! I had had quite a good night in spite of noise from the bar and Rick's snoring. A rowdy group left before 5 am to go for the dune walk. We were up at 6 am, packing away the tents for the final time. There was intense interest and some alarm when Jeff and John came across a large Scorpion which had spent the night underneath their tent. It came into view as they were on their knees rolling it up. It appeared very disorientated and didn't seem able to find its way out of the compound.

We set off at 7.30 am and retraced some of the route (the only time), going through the Remhoodge Pass where the mountain scenery on either side was spectacular, and the occasional Ostrich, Kestrel, and Booted Eagle were to be seen. Some areas had produced a thin film of green after the recent rain and, in others, dead-looking 'sticks' sported delicate flowers, often white. There were Scented Thorn Trees with generous yellow blooms and low bushes with fulsome pink spikes, to mention just two of the carpet's colours.

There was a sense of urgency about the drive, as one of our group was booked on a flight to Johannesburg in the early afternoon. The driving was very difficult for Ben, with rocky roads and, every so often, the hazard of a river of earth across the road, where the rains had produced a temporary flood that had brought all the silt with it. I didn't envy him his job.

Back on the main road to Windhoek, when we were enjoying an easier ride, there was a sudden 'pop' and, not surprisingly after the morning's excursion, a tyre had gone. Ben changed it with very little fuss, and all the men took it in turns to pump it up until Ben considered it to be 'all right'. The French family stopped to offer help, which was very kind of them. We had a brief stop for a salad and cold meat lunch by the roadside, where ants of different sizes had a field day with the crumbs. A huge African Monarch butterfly fluttered back and forth over the picnic table.

We motored on towards Windhoek, passing herds of fine cattle and even a flock of variegated sheep on the way. We went straight to the home (office) of Liz and Alan (who had met us on our arrival) - the Wild Dog Safaris representatives under whose auspices we had been travelling. They were a very pleasant couple with two Boxer dogs.

We chatted for a while, said goodbye to Rick who was flying on, eventually, to Mauritius, and then, after ditching the trailer and all the equipment there, we put our luggage inside the van and Ben took the four of us on a tour of Windhoek. He pointed out buildings of interest and then drove to the suburbs of the town, where estates of small houses (which he called 'flats') had been built. The mortgages were organised by the government and a housing association. He had bought such a dwelling fairly recently and was justly proud of his property. His younger sister stayed there while he was away because it would almost certainly have been burgled if left empty, he explained. We called but he spoke to his sister only briefly, and seemed angry that she had not kept the place in good order.

He showed us older, small houses, including one where he and his brothers and sisters had lived with his mother. "Not a lot of room!" he said. "Fortunately my father was away working in the fishing industry in Walvis Bay and then in the tin mines most of the time". His mother had gone back to her village in Botswana but we met some of his relations who were still in the neighbourhood: all very neat and clean in their appearance, and their houses had the same orderly look about them.

Further out was the shanty town, hill upon hill of extraordinary little shelters made from all kinds of materials, some looking more permanent than others. Since Independence in 1990 people had been able to come and look for work. Prior to then, it had been necessary to have a permit to come to Windhoek. Ben admitted that few of them had any work. Yet they looked well nourished, particularly the children - "and very smartly dressed", I commented. "Their extended families help them," he replied, "and food is cheap at local markets. It's too far to go into the town to shop. As for their clothes," he continued, "well, the English have forgotten how to dress. They are more interested in property. Clothes are one of Africa's priorities ".

"We are on holiday," said Kate defensively - and it was Sunday. A shanty town is anything but ideal, I know, but this one looked infinitely preferable to the one I'd seen in Manila. Here there was space, air, and wonderful views, and most of the incumbents looked happy. Efforts were being made to get all the children to school so that they wouldn't be illiterate, as most of their parents were. It was good for us to see this reality, which I suspect eludes most tourists.

Ben dropped us off in the town, all except for Kate, who went back with him for a business session with Liz and Alan. We gazed into closed clothes and other shop windows and then enjoyed a Cappuccino, and an enormous slice of Black Forest Gateau, for £1 a head. The restaurant was doing Sunday family meals but they treated us very courteously, and had charming waitresses. We sat and discussed the tip for Ben and then walked to a small park near the pre-arranged pick-up point. It was overcast and a few drops of rain fell every now and then: preparation for our return to the UK.

Ben took us back to the office, where we collected Kate. She seemed pleased with my choice of a Hippopotamus from a roadside spread of wood carvings: I'd been commissioned to buy one for her to give to her sister.

There was serious rain as we drove the 28 km to the airport. We gave Ben his envelope, and a last-minute £10 to Steven, prompted by hearing of his family responsibilities. I took Ben's address and said goodbye. He'd been exceptional, for he did everything: the responsibility was entirely his. Steven was new to the assistant's role and had been learning on this, his first trip - and this was the first time that Ben had had an assistant. Ben had been the organiser, provisions planner, cook, driver, car mechanic, and had to listen to all his group asking questions, with different accents, when English wasn't even his first language. He had a puckish sense of humour and was altogether very tolerant and patient. I hoped he would find a good wife who would appreciate him!

I changed out of my shorts into light trousers. I had felt distinctly underdressed in civilised Sunday Windhoek, walking about with bare legs. The others executed various changes in their apparel after we'd checked in. I bought a cup of tea with the very last of my Namibian currency.

Flight 287 was called: Kate and I were somewhere in the middle, with a useful empty seat between us. We indulged in the mandatory gin, and had red wine with the meal. We'd enjoyed each other's company and I reckoned we would meet again: I'd like to see Sythey. I slept on and off and longed to be home.

FRANKFURT : SHUTTLE : HERONSLAKE MALLARDS

1.2.99 Monday   The stop at Frankfurt was something of a shock when we saw the thick covering of snow. I visited the washroom and added my wool skirt and thick jumper to my light clothing, having put them in the hand luggage in readiness.

Breakfast came and went and, in no time it seemed, we were landing at Heathrow, on a thankfully mild dawning of the first of February. The adventure was nearly over and I felt a sense of relief that I was back in the UK and that, up to the present, had not fallen over, as I usually did, at some juncture.

The luggage came through on the conveyer belt, in close proximity to that belonging to John, Jeff, and Kate. We walked through the 'nothing to declare' for we had nothing to declare - but I was glad that no-one had wanted to search my untidy, sandy pack. Several 'nothing to declare' passengers were having their bags emptied and inspected: I wondered how they decided whom to stop.

I was expecting Nick of the Shuttle Service to meet me but having had nothing but a sideways-on, dim vision of him in the dawning day of my departure, I wasn't that sure I'd recognize him. But I thought I did, and this was confirmed by the 'Dr Tyler' on his placard. I bade farewell to John, Jeff, and Kate, and we promised each other photos, etc. I suddenly felt Nick was like an old friend, probably because he was my route to home. I was now wide awake and we chatted all the way back to Devon. I related the highlights of the holiday and hoped that I hadn't bored him to death. I was the only passenger on this occasion but I had the happy surprise of some reimbursement for the outward journey, which had been shared.

Heronslake looked wonderful under a pale blue sky: snowdrops, crocuses and a few wild daffodils were blooming, and two Mallard drakes fought over their rights to a long-suffering mate. It all hinted of spring and made me very happy.

I unpacked, deposited quite a sample of the Namib Desert outside the back door, watered the houseplants, telephoned Ann and Veronica - who had been keeping an eye on the house, had some lunch from the freezer, went through the mountain of post, had a bath and washed my hair, and, finally, retired to bed for a scheduled two hours, with the intention of going to Barnstaple Amateur Operatic Society's 'Merry Widow' rehearsal at 7 pm. In fact I was awakened by my elder daughter Wendy, who informed me it was 9.30 pm!

It had been a good adventure with, as always, a few very special memories which I reckon will stay with me for ever: the 'African Sanctus' dawn chorus, the leaping young Springbok, the close view of the seated young male Lion, the explosion of desert blooms after the rain, and the mokoro journeys through the Water Lilies with the Tswana Polermen, to mention but a few.

It was possibly more demanding than my two previous January holidays, with the pitching and striking of tents, and the domestic participation, but I felt well and had had little trouble from my arthritic feet, apart from during the heaviest of the rains.

As I finish writing this up from the scrawled daily diary, it is only ten days since I returned. I've been a bit obsessive because I am aware that, in a week's time, other aspects of my 'ordinary' everyday life, such as the Community Development Trust, the garden, and music, and drama, will swing back into action. The photographs seem pretty good and I am looking forward to putting together the whole illustrated story.

The anticipation and the recapitulation are half the fun!